Brooke Elliston is a lawyer-turned-breath-educator who trains yoga and Pilates teachers, health and fitness coaches, and therapists to integrate breath into their work with precision and depth. She is the founder of the Advanced Breath Instructor Training course, a highly regarded program for wellness professionals.

Brooke is known for her ability to distil complex science into simple, memorable insights that spark curiosity and excitement. Personalisation and embodiment are at the heart of her approach, and her highly engaged audience values the way she brings detail and nuance to life in practice. Frequently referenced by other wellness leaders and educators, Brooke has become a trusted authority in her field.

The Breath Reset Plan

Brooke Elliston

affirm
press

First published in Australia in 2026 by Affirm Press,
a Simon and Schuster (Australia) Pty Limited company
Wurundjeri Woiwurrung Country
Level 3, 162 Collins Street, Melbourne VIC 3000

Affirm Press is located on the unceded land of the Wurundjeri Woiwurrung peoples
of the Kulin Nation. Affirm Press pays respect to their Elders past and present.

New York Amsterdam/Antwerp London Toronto Sydney/Melbourne New Delhi
Visit our website at www.simonandschuster.com.au

AFFIRM PRESS and design are trademarks of Affirm Press Pty
Ltd, Inc., used under licence by Simon and Schuster, LLC.

10 9 8 7 6 5 4 3 2 1

© Brooke Elliston 2026

The moral rights of the author have been asserted.

 A catalogue record for this
book is available from the
National Library of Australia

9781923293496 (paperback)
9781761639760 (ebook)

Cover design by Andy Warren
Cover image by iStock.com/Tori Art
Author photograph by Jake Holly
Typeset by Post Pre-press Group in 12/17 pt Garamond Premier Pro
Printed and bound in Australia by the Opus Group

For Lhotse Blue, sunflower and the little starseed in my belly.

Contents

Introduction   1

Part I   Understanding Breath
Chapter 1   The First Breath Reset   15
Chapter 2   Small Steps   33
Chapter 3   Breath and the Biology of Stress   43
Chapter 4   The Four Dimensions of Breath   56
Chapter 5   The Past Is in Your Breath   71

Part II   Breath Resets
Chapter 6   Crossing the Threshold   85
Chapter 7   Awareness   90
Chapter 8   Connection to Safety   97
Chapter 9   Connection to Context   112
Chapter 10   Connection to Real Life   128
Chapter 11   Sleep   141
Interlude   Sleep and the Limits of Breathwork   156
Chapter 12   Sleep and Stillness   163
Chapter 13   The Gut   181
Chapter 14   The Gut and Breaking the Bias of Survival   203
Chapter 15   Movement   220

Part III	State Shifts	
Chapter 16	The Reset Breath	249
Chapter 17	State Shift or State Escape?	258
Chapter 18	Integration	266
Acknowledgements		291
References		295

Introduction

I was one of those people who got things done. Less talk, all action. Boxes ticked. I was always 'on'. From the outside I looked calm under pressure, moving with poise and patience, while everything inside me was rushing.

I built a career that made perfect sense on paper, just as my grandmother had said I should. I had a corner office with floor-to-ceiling glass and I stood in court, where the stakes were high but the repercussions blew back on lives far more seasoned than mine. The markers of success were all there, with competence and control and a polished exterior. From the outside it *looked* like success, but inside something was quietly unravelling.

Then, one day, my legs gave out.

The symptoms had been gathering for months. There was tightness in my throat and tingling in my fingers. Strange rashes came and went across my skin. The day I ended up in hospital, I could not walk in a straight line and I could not answer the simplest questions about myself. It was clear that a threshold had finally been crossed.

The emergency ward was crowded and I waited for hours before the MRI machine was free. I half-heard doctors murmuring about the possibility of multiple sclerosis – or perhaps it was only the echo of my hypervigilant mind.

The next morning, the neurologist flung open the curtains and broke into my tenth hour of staring at the stark white ceiling in a frozen panic. He held up my scans and said the problem was my breathing.

I could not comprehend it. I was healthy. I woke up at 5am each morning buzzing with energy. I was always moving, always. Breathing was automatic. And I was smart, so how could I be so wrong about something so simple?

It was not multiple sclerosis, thank the stars. I was chronically over-breathing. I had been living in a stress state for so long that my body had normalised it. I felt fine only because I hardly felt anything at all. I was impatient and always rushing, yet perpetually fine. I had been breathing as if I was jogging, twenty-four hours a day, for years.

My body had been sending up smoke signals through a fog I could not see and I kept trying to evacuate the emergency with my mind. But you cannot out-think a body that has trained itself to stay on guard, especially when the mind and body no longer speak the same language. The disconnect had become so complete that I could not interpret my body's warnings until they broke through in ways I could no longer ignore.

That day in the hospital was the moment when my mind finally caught up with what my body had been trying to say all along. I had ignored its call to stop until it spoke in the only language left, collapsing my legs beneath me and leaving me, quite literally, with nowhere to run.

What followed was a slow pilgrimage into another way of inhabiting myself. Yes, I did the cliché thing and left law to become a yoga teacher, but that was only the point of passage. The reorganisation of my life was gradual, and it continues to unfold more than 15 years later. This book begins there, with breath as a compass. At first breath served as a diagnostic tool, and later – with nuance and personalisation – it became a therapeutic ally and guide into the nervous system states that had been shaping my thoughts, feelings and actions.

Perhaps you, too, have woken up and thought, 'How did I get here? And why do I feel so flat even when life looks full? Why do I keep doing the work and still feel stuck, as if something is off?'

This book is about answering those questions by moving from inside physiology outwards. It begins not with the mind's explanations and not with the kind of breath you may call 'deep' – because if you are anything like I was, that breath may not reach deep at all. It may lift at the collarbones, big in volume yet shallow in function, rising high without the support of the diaphragm, and you may not even notice.

We will start with the simple act of noticing breath as it is. Whether the inhale opens the body, whether the exhale draws it back in, and whether a pause lingers before the next breath arrives. It may appear simple, but breath has a way of being both disarmingly simple and profoundly complex.

Why Breath?

Breath is the only system in the body that runs continuously and is still available for you to guide. It is the built-in interface between consciousness and nervous system. You cannot consciously slow digestion or adjust blood pressure, but you can change your breath, and when you do everything downstream begins to shift, including your heart rate, emotional regulation, memory access and mood.

Breath offers access to the physiological state beneath the story. It helps you move beyond managing symptoms from the top down and shift towards working with the nervous system from the bottom up.

The nervous system can pivot in a heartbeat, but it is through repetition that deeper patterns are written, because the brain thrives on prediction. Each return to a state strengthens its imprint, the way footsteps press a trail more firmly into the ground. Over time, those trails become the paths the body follows without thought. What you practise in the small moments of daily life – from how you breathe to how you meet stress – settles in to become the baseline your system learns to expect.

Physiological fluency is the foundation for lasting energy, resilience and genuine wellbeing. It is not only about feeling better, though that is often the first change you notice. It is about staying connected when you would normally disconnect; about coming back to yourself when your system wants to accelerate or shut down. Physiological fluency starts with safety, moves through regulation and grows into something deeper: a capacity to choose how you respond and to hold agency, whatever life places in front of you.

State Shift: From Tight Spaces to Expansive Ground

Most people think change is hard because it is unfamiliar. The truth is that change is hard because it *feels* unfamiliar. Your body not only resists new habits, mindsets or goals, it resists new states. A 'state' – as I will use the term in this book – is not simply a mood or a feeling. It is the body's current physiological configuration, including breath, posture, heart rate, blood pH, muscle tone and emotional tone – the ground from which moods, feelings, thoughts and behaviours arise.

If the body is a home, then the state range is how many rooms you can access. Some people are confined to a single room: tight and repetitive with no real space to move. Others can walk through an entire house, or even a mansion, with room to stretch, shift and settle where they need to be. They can move between focus and rest, urgency and ease, protection and openness.

The greater your state range, the more fully you can show up in different moments without being trapped in one mode of being. What you experience as mood, vibe, energy or even personality is, beneath it all, state. It is less about who you are and more about the physiological state you are in.

When we become stuck in a single state, it is often because the body has come to recognise that state as comfortable and familiar. Many people live in stress the way a goldfish lives in water; so immersed in it that they no longer see it. The nervous system gravitates towards what it already knows and calls that safety, even when the 'safe' pattern is breaking the body down more than it is holding it together.

Sitting still, for example, may not feel safe. The nervous system speaks through sensation, and in the mind those sensations are translated into thoughts like, 'Slowing down is a waste of time. I'd rather not.'

Quick Test

If I asked you to lie down in the middle of your day, with no phone, and no agenda, just stillness, what comes up? Perhaps restlessness, irritation or fear? Perhaps a voice that says, 'You could be doing something better with your time right now'?

Deep down, your nervous system wants to be like a crocodile, conserving energy until it matters, then surging with explosive force when the moment calls, before settling again. That is the economy of a healthy nervous system.

If your nervous system has learned to associate urgency, tension or stress with thoughts like 'I am okay here' or 'This is what success feels like', it will keep drawing you back. The pull is not in logic but in physiology, and the body equates that state of distress and pressure with survival.

Humans are built to belong. When movement, output and overfunctioning have helped secure a sense of safety, they become your baseline. That is why someone experiencing burnout does not look in the mirror and see flames. They see momentum, productivity and drive. To the nervous system, that overdrive can feel like reprieve, and the mind follows the story the body tells, just as a child wiggles when they're asked to sit still. At a fancy restaurant, you may plead with them to stay in their chair, reminding them of the cost of the holiday or the meal, but their tiny bodies have only one signal rising through them: move. Inside your adult body, the same restlessness can live on. In a child, it is biology still learning its rhythms. In an adult, this is overdrive – the nervous system repeating what it has practised until the body no longer negotiates and simply shuts down. We confuse what is familiar with what is right. We call it normal, when in truth these states are only what we have rehearsed the most.

Even if a new state is beneficial, your system may not trust it if it has rarely been felt before. This is where breath becomes pivotal. Breath is the most direct way to shift a state; interrupting the nervous system's patterns and the brain's predictions. Breath teaches the body how to feel different on purpose, even before anything in the external world has changed.

Breath training is not simply about breathing. It is about understanding how physiological states shape perception, behaviour and the ways you encode and recall emotional experience. Breath can be used to retrain states from the inside out. To work with the breath is to work with the state itself.

Who I Am

Yes, I used to be a lawyer, and now I am a dedicated student of breath, bodywork and yoga. I completed my first yoga training in Australia and soon after travelled to Thailand to practise, study and eventually teach at an esoteric tantric yoga university. Since then, I have lost count of how many yoga trainings I have undertaken. Each one has deepened my embodiment, widened my perspective and, most importantly, re-patterned my relationship with breath and the nervous system.

For five years, I travelled regularly between Australia and Thailand, practising for hours each day while lectures and rituals stretched late into the night. Month after month I lived within this rhythm – immersive, intense and transformational – and it laid the foundation for my yoga and pranayama (yogic breathing) practice.

Embodiment and the mystical, often magical experiences I encountered in Thailand were my starting point. The science came later. A profound shift occurred when a dear friend introduced me to Robin Rothenberg's *Restoring Prana*. Her integration of Buteyko breathing, traditional yogic philosophy and functional respiratory science completely altered my understanding of breathing. It revealed the difference between what is healthy and what we often mistake as normal, and this forever changed the way I taught.

Further studies deepened this understanding. Training with Patrick McKeown through the Oxygen Advantage gave me a structured exploration of breath's biochemical, biomechanical and psychophysiological dimensions. Martin McPhilimey, a respiratory and sleep scientist, introduced me to affective neuroscience, state- and context-dependent memory, predictive processing and influential insights from researchers such as Jaak Panksepp and Lisa Feldman Barrett – concepts that now underpin the nervous system frameworks in this book.

For years I travelled internationally, leading workshops and retreats, mentoring teachers and sharing breath and movement on stages and at festivals. From Britain to the French Alps and Indonesia, I collaborated with acclaimed musicians and artists, dedicating myself fully to a life rooted in embodied learning.

About seven years ago, I began running retreats for people living with spinal cord injuries in collaboration with the disability accommodation provider Sargood on Collaroy. Because adaptive yoga training is so rare, nearly everything I offer at these retreats has emerged in real time through conversation, experimentation and collaboration with participants. I will never forget our first retreat. Most participants remained in their wheelchairs for the entire time. Now they arrive and move straight to the ground. We breathe, we explore new edges of possibility, and we tend to the inner world with curiosity. To some, it might seem paradoxical to explore the felt sense and mind–body connection with people whose sensory experience is altered, reduced or even absent in parts of their body. However, what I have witnessed is that breath and awareness still open doorways into the nervous system, and inner connection remains profoundly possible.

My path has been enriched by dedicated mentorship, countless hours on the mat and ongoing exploration within the laboratory of my own body. Through breath, I was not merely retraining respiration. I was retraining my nervous system to inhabit a state that not only felt better but that I could sustainably hold better. That is the essence of what I am here to share with you.

The Breath Reset Plan

At the heart of this book is a three-part plan for nervous system transformation: understanding breath, breath resets and state shifts. This plan covers the five core areas where your breath, nervous system and daily life meet:

- **Awareness:** The ability to recognise your baseline, to see the breathing patterns and nervous system responses you default to, and to step in when they no longer serve you.

- **Connection:** The capacity to stay in relationship with your body's internal signals, other people and the world around you, even in moments of discomfort or intense activation.
- **Sleep:** The foundation of repair. Often disrupted by disordered breathing, and essential for long-term nervous system resilience.
- **Gut:** Where breath, digestion and chemistry meet, shaping the nervous system state through gut–brain signalling and internal feedback loops.
- **Movement:** Where breath meets posture, rhythm and expression. Movement becomes a visible echo of internal change, the body's way of saying, 'The conditions have changed, and freedom is possible.'

I'll walk you through the science behind nervous system state shifts, real-world applications, breath-based tools to interrupt old patterns and the lasting change that becomes possible when your system learns to orient to a new baseline.

Understanding Breath

Your life is not shaped only by what happens to you. It is shaped by the state you are in when it happens, and that state is shaped by your breath. Learning to understand your breath – what I call 'becoming a breath detective' – is the first window into your nervous system, and a mirror back to yourself.

Breath Resets

Breath resets work by interrupting habitual patterns and creating conditions for the nervous system to build new predictions. You will encounter them throughout this book, woven into the chapters as practices that let you embody what you are learning as you go.

In the final chapter, the resets come together in three distinct Reset Plans. Each one is built around a nervous system profile, offering a clear map towards self-understanding, breath retraining and lasting change. You begin with the profile that most closely reflects your current experience, and you can experiment from there.

Breath resets form the practical spine of this work, turning ideas into experience and giving your system a way to practise change from the inside out.

State Shifts

State shifts happen when breath resets begin to take hold; when the breath retrains the nervous system to become more flexible, responsive and resilient. You build the capacity to shift from chronic arousal into steadier regulation and out of reflexive reaction into deliberate response.

As internal states reorganise, perception reorganises with it. Signals that were once encoded as threats are reclassified as manageable. Choice points widen, and the capacity for deliberate change emerges.

Who Is This Book For?

This book is for you if:

- you have done the work through talk therapy, mindfulness, ice baths or self-help, but still do not feel fully yourself
- you have already tried breathwork but it felt overwhelming or disconnected, or it simply did not last
- you want to stop outsourcing your regulation and begin cultivating it from within
- you want to feel alive and grounded without escaping your life, bypassing what is difficult or numbing your pain.

Introduction

Think of this book as a newly revealed map of the house you live in. Breath is the key in the door and the lantern in the hallway. With this map, you can move beyond the single room you know too well into the many rooms of your nervous system, each with its own light, its own shadows and its own way of being.

Part I
Understanding Breath

Chapter 1

The First Breath Reset

Why Breathing Less Could Mean Living More

The therapist leaned forward, her voice gentle but clear. 'Try taking a deep breath, one that expands your lower ribs and leaves your chest relaxed. That is a healthy breath.'

I nodded politely, though inside I was blank. Healthy breath, of course. Yet the moment I tried, my shoulders lifted, my neck tensed and my belly cinched into something like a mini crunch. Exactly the opposite of what my mind had instructed. My breath arrived as a startled gasp, sharp and sudden, like a possum sniffing from inside my lungs.

In that instant, I caught my reflection in the glass of her framed honours certificate on the neutral-toned wall. I looked composed: pencil skirt, heels, hair pulled tight in a bun. Yet beneath my ribs something fluttered. Was it confusion or fear?

The therapist sat steady, quietly writing notes, her handwriting looping upside-down across the page: *Sits stiffly at edge of chair, legs tightly crossed.* Had I always sat like that?

She kept repeating the same phrase, 'What I am hearing you say is ...' – reflecting my words back to me, which only fuelled irritation. Then she said something that pierced the room. 'Your breath is telling me a story. Your body's been holding itself together for a long time.'

I nodded again, outwardly composed, but inside my mind scrambled. Many would expect tears at such a moment, but none came. If you are someone who does not cry easily, you may understand. Like me, you may have assumed that it is simply who you are – I now know that it is often an echo of your conditioning.

In that warmly lit room, my usual strategy failed me. My intellect, always dependable, was suddenly useless. Emotions were speaking in a language that my brain could not translate. I did not know it then, but that was my first real clue. I had stumbled onto what I now call a breath reset, a moment where something old is interrupted. It does not yield to force or determination, only to the quiet intervention of awareness.

For three persistent weeks, I sat cross-legged on my bedroom floor, hands resting on my lower ribs, patiently coaxing each breath downwards, as though luring a stray cat. Most days it darted away. In time, a relaxed breath arrived – still uneven, but softer. My body and mind had begun to communicate with one another. A tentative greeting; a little wink, for now.

We trust breathing because it happens on its own, but automatic does not mean efficient. Patterns laid down by stress can become the body's baseline, altering how air moves, how posture holds and how easily the nervous system adapts. Relearning to breathe with depth and ease was more accretion than event. My nervous system recalibrated itself in increments too small to notice until the pattern had changed.

Yoga came next, gently suggested by my therapist as 'perhaps just a hobby'. I remembered a disastrous class I'd attended at 15, stiff and out of place beside my mother, watching white-haired bodies moving with ease, draped over chairs or suspended from wall straps, while I grimaced in silent pain and I dismissed the practice at once, certain my body did not belong in that room.

Yet something in me nudged again, and this time I found a style that fitted. Within weeks, shifts appeared as the unexplained rashes, the tingling limbs and the choking grip in my throat all eased, dissolving almost imperceptibly from within.

It was not only the postures that made a difference, but also the offhand things the teachers said. Their remarks were delivered as if they had a window into my private life – I would register these words in passing and only later find them resurfacing in the shower, while driving or in the middle of a conversation.

'The way you do one thing is the way you do everything. What if this was the best day of your life? Because you only ever have this moment.' These seeds of reflection travelled further than expected and made me pay attention.

This movement medicine returned me to sensations I had long ignored. Breath was entering the foreground of my awareness and becoming a teacher in how I met life. In small and almost hidden ways, I was sensing what I now call a state shift – the transformation that emerges when the nervous system starts learning something new; when safety meets novelty and curiosity is allowed, then adaptation follows.

And still, there were times when my body tensed, uncertain it was ready to release. Many studios encouraged loud breathing, emphatic exhales, Darth Vader tributes and the push to breathe bigger, deeper and louder.

My body recoiled from all that. My intuition knew what my mind could not yet explain: force is not power. Driving breath into a hypervigilant system does not produce calm, it magnifies disturbance. Only later did I understand why. Over the years I met thousands of others like me – successful, polished and outwardly thriving, yet inwardly suffocating beneath their own perfection: yoga teachers who could fold with elegance but could not breathe with ease, executives in tailored suits, gasping sharp inhales and sighing habitually, and athletes masking panic beneath performance.

We had all mastered the art of appearing fine. We mistook the mechanics of survival for the marrow of life. I did not fully grasp it that day in the therapist's office – a space I only visited once or twice – but noticing my breath was the first piece of the puzzle. It was a thread, a quiet truth-teller, revealing how far I had drifted from myself.

I did not have the language then, but later I would name it the 'breath reset' – the moment awareness splits the husk so the tender shoot inside can emerge.

What If the Way You Breathe Is Holding Everything Back?

Breath is not only a life-sustaining reflex – it is a real-time indicator of internal load, neurochemical demand and system-wide efficiency. It reflects how your body has adapted to your environment, posture, pace and physiology. In most modern bodies, those adaptations carry a cost. Your breath calibrates perception, influencing how life feels from the inside, and sets the predictions that drive how you respond to the world around you. In this way, breath moulds the experience of inhabiting a body, shaping not only your interactions with the outside world, but creating the very texture of being alive in the present.

When signals from the breath are distorted by habit, tension or unresolved physiological noise, the system begins to treat them as truth, and over time that interpretation settles in as the baseline.

Most people do not breathe in response to their immediate oxygen needs alone. They breathe in patterns that have been laid down by past experiences and reinforced by the nervous system. Breath functions as a messenger and a regulator, organising energy, attention and the capacity to adapt. However, many of us breathe in ways that deplete us, and in patterns sustained by muscle tension, postural strain and a reduced tolerance for the sensation of air hunger.

As these adaptations take hold and become habitual, our sensitivity to internal cues increases, and signals that should feel ordinary begin to feel unsettling. These adaptations are long-practised responses, repeated until they feel familiar, even while they cost us efficiency and ease. Breath becomes the body's ongoing prediction of what each moment requires – whether that prediction is accurate or not – and repeated often enough, this prediction embeds as an internal script. That script touches everything from how blood pressure and pulse are maintained to how breathing mechanics support spinal stability and trunk control, and how oxygen is released to the cells.[1]

Even when oxygen is plentiful in the blood, inefficient breathing can mean that less of it reaches the tissues, and with that inefficiency, capacity declines.[2] What once registered as a minor input – such as a glance, a certain tone of voice, a kitchen bench cluttered with dishes – can begin to trigger a disproportionate cascade of reactivity. The buffer shrinks, the threshold reaction lowers, and signals that were once filtered out are now flagged as threats. What should be background noise starts to feel like interference. And yet, we rarely question the role of our breath in all this.

We assume that because we are doing it, we must be doing it well. However, that is like assuming you understand nutrition because you eat, or relationships because you have been in one. We have absorbed many well-meaning but incomplete ideas about breathing, and these ideas can keep us looping in physiological patterns we scarcely recognise as our own. Nowhere is that more evident than in the advice repeatedly offered about how to breathe.

When Advice Misses the Body

When I was 16, I came down with appendicitis. The pain felt like my insides were being whipped with a wet tea towel every time I moved.

Naturally, my ever-caring mum (an avid Iyengar yoga enthusiast and part-time 'teach-a-class-at-work' type) decided the solution was a DIY sequence of therapeutic yoga. Brimming with the confidence that only 'Guruji Jane' (as she liked to call herself) could, she led me through a full routine of twists, folds and even an inversion or two, always reminding me to breathe and to 'try to relax into it, darling'.

I am not religious, yet in that hour, I came close to calling on a higher power to save me. That is not what yoga teachers mean when they talk about connecting to the Divine. As the pain morphed from searing to unbearable, my mother finally conceded that perhaps the hospital was a better idea. We sat in emergency – me doubled over, her flushed with guilt – and she surprised me with a Mars bar from the vending machine. The gesture was sweet, wildly out of character and, best of all, had nothing to do with a yoga pose.

All I could manage to say was, 'I'd rather put a fork in my eye.' Even caramel could not fix my purple, soon-to-explode appendix. Surgery it was.

Just as my mother's well-meaning but misplaced attempt to relax away a medical emergency demonstrated, we are often given advice that sounds wise but does not translate into anything the body actually *needs*. Nowhere is this more common than in breathing. The familiar cues are everywhere:

- 'Take a deep breath.'
- 'Find your natural breath.'
- 'Breathe into your belly.'
- 'Take a big breath in and a big breath out.'

These prompts sound soothing, carrying with them the scent of calm. However, without attunement to the person in front of you, the essence – the state the person is in – is missed. Without awareness of someone's baseline, their physiology or the condition of their nervous system, even the most familiar cues can land sideways.

The difficulty with such cues is not that they are entirely wrong but that they are vague. Lacking specificity, they offer no clarity about what is being asked of the body. When they are practised in this unclear way, these cues can reinforce the very patterns they were intended to change.

So let us look more closely at what these breath cues are really doing, not just to your lungs but to the deeper patterns that shape physiology and steer state.

'Take a Deep Breath'

When I begin a workshop, I often ask people to take a deep breath. Each time, the room becomes a display of different versions. Some people lift their shoulders and puff their chests. Others perform the so-called three-part breath, filling the belly, then ribs, then chest in sequence. A few push their abdomen forward so far it looks as if the top button of their jeans might give way.

Each person believes they are doing it right, and for most the act feels satisfying, as though they have done something good for their body. Yet if every response looks different, what does 'taking a deep breath' really mean?

Most people interpret 'deep' as 'big', and 'big' often shows up as upper-chest breathing. This is the pattern your body defaults to under stress, and it is how confusion becomes conditioning. Thoracic-dominant breathing is linked with breathlessness, reduced diaphragm efficiency and increased respiratory effort.[3] It can feel expansive, but at rest this is a low-efficiency pattern designed for short bursts of activity rather than sustained metabolic support.[4] In physiological terms, the upper-chest breath bypasses effective abdominal-diaphragmatic recruitment, limits vagal stimulation, decreases gas exchange efficiency and over-activates smaller accessory muscles.

The sigh that often follows may feel like a release, but in effect it is a quick escape. In that moment, the body blows out carbon dioxide, which creates a brief sense of relief, but does nothing to shift the underlying pattern.[5]

Now imagine instead a breath that is nasal, quiet, light and low, spreading in all directions around the lower ribs. This kind of breath sends a very different signal and gives your body something more stable to move with. When breath begins to work with the system, you breathe less but provide more accurate information about your internal state to the nervous system.

'Find Your Natural Breath'

This cue sounds beautiful, but what feels 'natural' is not always functional. Clinical studies show that altered breathing patterns are common in adults with postural imbalance, anxiety, trauma histories or chronic stress.[6] For some, breathing becomes shallow or rapid, and for others it can be uneven or strained. These patterns often arise through a mix of emotional suppression, postural compensation and long-term nervous system dysregulation. So, when you return to your 'natural' breath, you may in fact be returning to a pattern that your body learned under stress.

Dysfunctional breathing comes from many sources. In athletes, dysfunctional breathing can be concealed by the exertion of performance, but often reveals itself in the overuse of accessory breathing muscles in the neck, chest and shoulders and the underuse of the diaphragm. In women, the picture is further shaped by hormonal rhythms, particularly in the luteal phase of the menstrual cycle when rising progesterone naturally increases breathing rate.[7]

....

The **diaphragm** is your body's primary breathing muscle. It is thin and dome-shaped, sitting just beneath your lungs and separating the chest from the belly. When you inhale, the diaphragm contracts and moves downwards, spreading pressure evenly through the abdominal cavity to draw air in. That pressure only builds support if it is met from below by your pelvic floor. Together, they create a stable pressure system that supports your spine and core from the inside out. This is the foundation of functional breathing and real core stability.

....

Instead of aiming for 'natural', we want something else. We want your evolutionary breath. The breath your system was designed to use before modern stress reshaped its patterns. A breath that supports your physiology in motion, at rest and under demand, not one that merely gets you by.

Once dysfunctional breathing becomes your baseline, your body adapts around it. The nervous system begins to predict the world through that pattern, shaping perception and physiology alike. What emerges is a closed loop: breath reinforces state, and state reinforces breath.

The cycle of dysfunctional breathing reminds me of when I was 17 and totalled my father's car, 'Strabo', his red-leather-seated pride and joy. Strabo was a Greek geographer whose name means 'squinter' – a fitting detail given what unfolded. I was turning a corner near the refurbished Oaks Hotel in Sydney when an elderly woman drove into me. Neither of us were going fast, but the impact was enough to write the car off.

Later I learned she had rigged a homemade steering aid after her vision began to blur – a piece of string tied from the wheel to the car roof near the ceiling light. It did nothing, but it gave her the feeling of control. That is a good metaphor for what dysfunctional breathing does – you think you are steering, but the wheel is tethered to a string.

'Breathe Into Your Belly'

Another familiar cue is 'Breathe into your belly and you will feel more relaxed'. To be clear, air never enters the belly; it always moves into the lungs. What changes is how the lungs expand. That expansion can create movement in the abdomen and beyond.[8]

When the diaphragm contracts and moves downwards, it displaces the abdominal contents and the belly shifts outwards. This is why it can look as if you are breathing into your belly, when really, the pressure is adjusting from above. It is a reassuring sign that the diaphragm is engaged.

The nuance is that belly movement can occur without any breath at all, or during breathing without true diaphragmatic engagement. You can consciously push the belly outwards, or the body can use it as a compensation strategy, even when the diaphragm remains underused. Belly breathing may feel calming at rest, but it does not provide the integrated support the body needs when it is upright, in motion or carrying a load.

I have encountered this confusion many times. A client once told me with pride that she had mastered belly breathing after working with a physiotherapist who had prescribed breathing exercises. However, when we looked more closely, it became clear that the intention had been to cultivate lateral rib expansion rather than abdominal inflation. Somewhere between instruction and practice, the message had been lost.

At its core, belly breathing is not the same as abdominal-diaphragmatic breathing. The difference reminds me of a moment when I was ten years old, trying to thread the strap of my overalls before stepping on stage for a dance performance. With no one around to help, I rigged something that looked secure, but the instant I started dancing, the overalls collapsed around my ankles.

That is belly breathing. It is genuinely relaxing in stillness because the gentle abdominal excursion lowers the perceived effort and helps settle arousal. However, once the body begins to move, the support this breathing offers often becomes less coordinated and insufficient for dynamic tasks. The belly pushes forwards while the lower ribs stay narrow and the diaphragm descends without a matched response from the pelvic floor, so pressure remains low and poorly distributed and load transfer through the trunk becomes unreliable.

Abdominal-diaphragmatic breathing behaves differently. The ribs widen in all directions, and the diaphragm works in concert with the pelvic floor, transverse abdominis and obliques to generate responsive intra-abdominal pressure, which stabilises the spine and gives the brain continuous evidence of support. As a result, movement can organise itself around a steady centre.

Understanding Breath

Breath Detective Check-In: Your First Clue

Place one hand on your chest and the other around the base of your rib cage. Without changing a thing, simply notice:

- Which hand moves first when you inhale?
- Is your breath smooth or choppy? Fast or slow?
- Do you feel your ribs expand outwards subtly as you inhale, and recoil on the exhale?
- Can you sense movement in your back body – the ribs widening and relaxing behind you?
- Can you feel your pelvic floor respond to breath, lengthening downwards on the inhale and contracting back up on the exhale?

You are not trying to correct anything here, nor aiming for a specific pattern. You are simply gathering information by observing your current breathing with magnified curiosity.

'Take a Big Breath'

This one might be the most pervasive. 'Take a big breath' does not mean more oxygen. In fact, the opposite is often true. Breathing in more than your body needs lowers carbon dioxide too quickly, and carbon dioxide is essential for oxygen release.[9] Without enough of it, your red blood cells cling too tightly to their payload, becoming travellers who never unpack.[10] Oxygen circulates, but it does not arrive to the tissues and cells where it is needed the most.

The relationship between carbon dioxide and the release of oxygen is known as the Bohr effect. This is a fundamental law of respiratory physiology, and one that functional breathing relies on. It shows us that carbon dioxide is not just a waste gas. A sufficient level of carbon dioxide is required to ensure oxygen is released from the blood and delivered to the tissues that need it most, including the heart, brain and working muscles.[11]

This balance between oxygen and carbon dioxide is also one of the body's most fundamental chemical regulators. Through the bicarbonate buffer system, carbon dioxide helps govern blood pH, setting the conditions for how every other system in the body functions. Immune responses, hormonal signalling, vascular tone and even brain activity all take their cues from this chemistry. Shift the balance, and you shift the set point your entire body uses to regulate itself.

....

A Little History of the Big Breath

I used to teach using 'big breath' cues in yoga. Like most people, I believed they were helpful, even healing. But that changed when I began studying respiratory physiology, starting with the work of breathing coach Patrick McKeown. That is when I realised that many of our most trusted breath cues are not based in biology. They are inherited from history.

Yoga scholar Magdalena Kraler traced the roots of 'big breathing' back to the Hygienic Movement of Europe and the United States in the 19th century, a time marked by widespread disease, poverty and rapid urbanisation. Pulmonary illnesses like tuberculosis were rife, and the image of the sunken chest became a visual shorthand for weakness and death. Reformers promoted deep, high-volume breathing as a way to 'cleanse' the lungs and to expand the chest – a visible sign of health and vitality in an era of wasting bodies.[12] In that context, the belief that bigger was better made sense, especially for those battling respiratory disease.

Through colonisation, these beliefs spread across continents and into yoga. William Walker Atkinson, writing under the pseudonym Yogi Ramacharaka, published *The Hindu-Yogi Science of Breath* in 1903. His 'yogic complete breath' advocated for bottom-to-top lung filling. It wore the language of tradition, yet it was not traditional pranayama; it drew on Western breathing theories, reframed in Eastern language.

And here we are, generations later, still carrying forward the same message in the form of 'big breathing' and the 'full yogic breath'.

....

Taking a big breath is not harmful, but the promise it carries is mostly symbolic – a gesture we inherited from history more than a cue grounded in physiology.

We're often urged to breathe *more*, as though bigger must be better. But big breaths do not equal better oxygenation. At rest, your body thrives on intelligent breathing that is subtle, nasal, rhythmic and finely attuned to your metabolic and emotional state.

Large, amplified inhalations can set up an even bigger exhale, and it is that sudden offload of carbon dioxide that brings the fleeting sensation of letting go. Blood oxygen levels do not change, yet paradoxically, taking in more air than the body metabolically needs means less oxygen is delivered where it matters. The breath might feel big, but the true benefit never reaches the body's tissues. It is like filling a grocery bag, tying the top shut and then wondering why you are still hungry. In other words, the oxygen is present, but without sufficient carbon dioxide it cannot be released from the blood to the tissues that need it.

That persistent feeling of needing more air, even when oxygen levels are adequate, is called 'air hunger'. It arises when the brain interprets rising carbon dioxide as urgent.[13] Through repeated conditioning, air hunger can become a behavioural response rather than a reflection of a biochemical imbalance.

We see similar processes outside of the breath, too. With people who have spinal cord injury, I have noticed on my retreats that during sound journeys, vibration can bring a rise of sensation, sometimes so intense that it registers as pain. However, the moment the sound stops, the pain dissipates. The same body position without sound creates no pain at all. In this context, the pain does not arise from tissue or position but from the nervous system's state-dependent memory learning, which interprets rising sensation as overwhelm and codes it as pain. Cognitively, participants may say they 'liked the sound', but their body responds through meanings carried forward from past experience.

Imagine learning to ride a horse. At first, the saddle feels natural and comforting and your body learns to trust it. Then one day you fall and the impact leaves you feeling fearful. From that moment, the saddle no longer feels neutral – it stirs anxiety each time you climb back on.

Pain works in a similar way. It is a protective signal designed to keep the body safe. However, when the nervous system becomes sensitised, the signal can grow louder than the situation demands. Air hunger belongs in this same category. Rising carbon dioxide is meant to guide breathing, but when the system begins to misread the normal rise as suffocation, the sensation is amplified into panic and the fear it provokes reinforces patterns of over-breathing. The problem is rarely oxygen, even if that is how it feels in the moment. Rather, the problem is the accuracy of how the signal is interpreted. With practice, the brain can learn to trust the sensation again and the body can return to balance.

The Foundation of Healthy Breathing

Healthy, functional breathing might appear simple, but for many of us it is not instinctive – especially if shallow, vertical or context-driven mouth breathing has become the norm. Functional breathing is a skill that develops with consistent and patient practice, and its essence is revealed in several interwoven qualities.

The breath begins with the nose, with the lips softly sealed so the air is filtered, warmed and moistened before it reaches the lungs. The tongue rests high against the roof of the mouth, its tip sitting just behind the front teeth, shaping the oral cavity and supporting an open airway. This intended pathway is how the body was designed to breathe; a mechanism that maintains efficiency and coherence in most states of daily life.

The breath arrives softly enough to be almost inaudible, its quiet flow signalling to brain stem centres that demand is being met with ease, while interoceptive pathways translate that subtlety into gentle sensations the body can trust.

The breath continues at a pace that is unforced and evenly measured, carrying steadiness without the weight of control. Each inhalation draws the diaphragm downwards and opens the lower ribs in a supple circumference – front, sides and back, widening together before recoiling inwards on the exhalation. In this continuous dance of expansion and return, the diaphragm moves in natural partnership with the pelvic floor and the deeper abdominal muscles, creating a foundation of inner support and stability that allows the whole system to organise itself around balance.

These are the qualities of functional breathing at rest, though they are not always easy to access. Chronic nasal obstruction, asthma, chronic obstructive pulmonary disease (COPD) and sleep apnoea are common conditions that can alter the way breath is expressed and make some of these markers difficult to achieve. In such cases, breath retraining can support the recovery of efficiency, though medical assessment or professional guidance may also be part of the process.

Functional breathing carries universal physiological signatures, yet their expression shifts with each person's health, anatomy, conditioning, emotions and context. When breathing is healthy, it expresses itself as a wave through the torso. The cycle begins as the diaphragm descends and pressure shifts within the abdominal and thoracic cavities. The lower ribs widen, the abdominal wall yields while containing the shift in pressure, and the movement then travels upwards as the upper ribs lift and the chest cavity opens. Exhalation follows as these structures recoil, the chest settling, the ribs drawing inwards and the abdomen returning, with the entire sequence unfolding as one continuous motion.

This wave reduces the workload of breathing and distributes pressure evenly through the body's cavities. Intra-abdominal and intrathoracic forces balance one another, circulation is supported, and the nervous system receives a steady signal of coherence that supports stability across changing demands.

To bring awareness to this pattern into daily life, you can let simple cues act as reminders. A doorway can invite three breaths before you cross, with thresholds becoming places to notice the body's own threshold of stillness. A mark or small symbol in your space can call you back to attention without words. A glance in the mirror can be an invitation to reset, allowing the breath to flow soft, slow, low and even.

Understanding Breath

A Gentle Wave from the Bottom Up

Place your hands gently on the sides of your lower ribs. Close your eyes if you like, and breathe softly through your nose, feeling your ribs expand into your hands. Exhale effortlessly through your nose, noticing the natural recoil of your ribs, and gently press in with your hands to give yourself biofeedback.

Repeat this for a few breaths and feel how quickly your state shifts towards ease and calm.

Remember, healthy breathing is a skill your body already knows. The more you practise, the more naturally you will return to this easeful state.

Important notes

At first, you might notice little or no movement in your lower ribs or abdomen, especially if your breathing is habitually shallow or primarily vertical (rising mostly up through your chest and shoulders). This sense of being 'stuck' or restricted is common and completely normal. With regular practice using the exercises provided throughout this book, your breathing will become more relaxed, expansive and effective. Be patient and gentle with yourself – functional breathing is a skill that develops gradually over time.

If you continue to feel restricted, or if breathing remains uncomfortable despite practice, consider seeking support from a breathing specialist, physiotherapist or ear, nose and throat (ENT) professional. Healthy breathing is adaptable and individual – it is about finding what best supports your unique body and nervous system.

Ground Truths

- Habitual big breaths can reduce oxygen delivery. Taking larger breaths may feel satisfying, but when repeated often, they lower carbon dioxide.

- Carbon dioxide is not simply 'waste'. It regulates acid-base balance, fine-tunes blood flow and creates the conditions for oxygen to be released from haemoglobin and used in energy production. When carbon dioxide levels fall too low (as often occurs in chronic over-breathing), the nervous system becomes more excitable.

- Just because your belly moves does not mean your diaphragm is recruited effectively. True abdominal-diaphragmatic breathing expands the ribs in all directions, creates intra-abdominal pressure, and coordinates with the pelvic floor and deep abdominals to provide internal support and spinal stability.

- Air hunger is a learned perception. Air hunger is the specific feeling of wanting a little bit more air. This feeling is usually triggered not by low oxygen but by rising carbon dioxide, which the brain may interpret as a signal of threat. With practice, the response shifts. The brain learns to experience the sensation without alarm and behaviour adapts to remain calm even in the presence of this sensation.

- Each breath sends information to the nervous system, reinforcing patterns of regulation or dysregulation. As breathing patterns repeat, they condition the set-point of the nervous system, altering what the body expects to return to at rest.

Chapter 2

Small Steps

How Real Change Happens in Everyday Moments

As I was stepping away from law and trying to figure out who I was, my friend Adam, a human magnet for the bizarre and the brilliant, returned from a yoga school in Thailand. It was, he said, 'full of magic'.

I had thought I was breaking free from my Type A life, but I was still looking for the top. I'd just shifted the goalposts from winning in courtrooms to conquering consciousness. I'd turned my lawyer brain towards the pursuit of ecstasy and bliss.

I did not know it yet, but I was craving space – physiological space, the kind that quiets noise, softens the spin cycle and makes room for clarity. Adam had this maddening knack for finding gold in the most unlikely places, while the rest of us were still learning how to slow down long enough to notice anything at all.

He said the school had changed everything.

'There is no going back once you go,' he told me. Not as a warning, exactly, but there was something in the way he said it, a kind of quiet caution, as if whatever shifted there stayed shifted.

We were swimming in the sea and sun-gazing; a ritual that involves staring directly at the sun to 'build a relationship' with it, because what is a little retinal damage between friends? Between salt water and half-blindness, Adam casually mentioned something called 'yogic amaroli' – drinking your own pee.

'Even Madonna is into it,' he added, as if that somehow made it normal.

By that point, he'd dropped enough weird, fascinating hints that I was half-convinced. Not about the amaroli, but about the possibility that this strange place in Thailand might have something I did not even know I was missing. Perhaps this was something that could help me feel well – not just okay, but truly well. So I enrolled, put my belongings in storage, packed my bags and travelled to Agama Yoga.

Adam's warning – that there is no going back – turned out to be right. Agama was not just a yoga school. It was an initiation into breath, into body and into the strange, disorienting process of waking up from a life I did not realise I had been asleep in. Agama was a collision of the profound and the absurd.

Atmospheric drone music created a long, continuous river of sound. Sustained tones with faint hints of flutes and strings stretched into endless melodies. The smell of incense and sandalwood was thick enough to pull you into a trance by your senses alone. Massive yantras – intricate black-and-white geometric symbols – covered the walls, making the place feel like a portal to another world. Everyone was dressed in white. And at the top of the pyramid sat Swami, the orange-clad overlord of the whole operation.

When I went to the school's cafe, the talk was so arcane it felt like I'd stumbled into a tantric version of a law library. Everyone cited their own esoteric case law with conviction: 'It is pronounced CH-akra, not shakra. Okay?'

Swami once claimed that a medieval knight had mastered nauli kriya, an intense abdominal cleansing practice said to build god-like strength, then rode to a castle and did chin-ups on the drawbridge, with a horse between his legs.

Naturally, we were encouraged to practise nauli, too. To be fair, I still do. The foundation of nauli is uddiyana bandha; a practice that has become one of my favourites (and I'll walk you through it properly in chapter 13). Swami also warned us about listening to 'low-frequency' music. According to him, songs like 'Un-Break My Heart' by Toni Braxton would make you 'a cockroach of humanity'. I was not sure whether to laugh or leave.

It was ridiculous at times – but the practices had power. They created a charge in my system, providing a kind of nervous system disruption that felt like a full-body reset even when my mind couldn't make any sense of it.

The daily schedule at Agama was no joke. We began with three-hour asana classes and continued through pranayama, an hour of seated meditation, and lectures that stretched late into the night. Sometimes we were stark naked around a fire under the open sky. Other times, we stood through hour-long Yang Spiral meditations on the full moon, holding hands in a 50-person snake coil, moving energy to the chaotic pulse of trance music, like a music festival had been swallowed by a tantra manual.

There were many paradoxes to process in this place. One long-running joke was that if you were in a bad mood, 50 rounds of uddiyana bandha, the yogic belly vacuum, would 'sublimate' your energy, taking what is dense and turning it into light. At any given moment, someone would be at the back of the room, furiously pumping out uddiyanas like they were exorcising demons or alchemising dark clouds into butterflies.

And, strangely enough, it worked – because breath was updating the system faster than the brain could reframe the signal. There is something about vacuuming the belly into the rib cage that interrupts reactivity in a way the mind cannot. It is the body's way of saying, 'Reset received'.[1]

What the Practices Were Really Teaching

These wild rituals were unforgettable, but the real alchemy was not in the spectacle. It was in what we were teaching the body to do, without even realising. At Agama Yoga, they were giving us a language we did not know we needed – a way to speak to the nervous system through rhythm, pressure, presence and breath.

Beneath the ritual of uddiyana bandha, the intensity carried a purpose. Within its tantric framing, this breathing was described as the sublimation of energy. Through the lens of modern physiology, it was retraining my body's response to air hunger and rising carbon dioxide levels long before I had language for it. As I held my breath, my body learned to override panic and recondition my relationship to fear.[2]

What felt like a struggle revealed something deeper – years of faulty breathing patterns I had not even known were shaping my reactions, my energy, my state.[3]

Agama's methods were eccentric, yes, but they forced me to confront something I'd never paused to meet: my breath. And later, the science helped me understand exactly why that mattered.

Leaving the Bubble

So, how is this all relevant to you? It is not. Which brings me to the point of this story. It is easy to feel amazing when you are living on an island and your biggest worry is trying to feel the cosmic energy descend down your spine. Living in a bubble is pure bliss – doing yoga all day, having your meals cooked for you, lounging in Beverly Hills (the highest hill with the best bungalow overlooking Haad Yao beach) and having your undies washed and folded, all while being surrounded by people who mostly talked about how to have orgasms in their fingertips.

My spiritual ego was in overdrive, and my siddhi superpowers (the extraordinary capacities yoga teaches can arise from deep practice) weren't far behind. But then ... I left. The glow of paradise faded fast. One minute, I was Queen of the Coconuts, flaunting a ten-outta-ten tan. The next, I was drowning in overflowing inboxes, looming deadlines and the monotony of tuna-and-peas dinners. The honey-gold warmth of beachside living gave way to the harsh buzz of fluorescent lights. The symphony of jungle insects and crashing waves was replaced by the dull hum of my washing machine.

It was easy to feel blissed out in paradise, but staying even mildly regulated through traffic jams, office politics and my own dirty laundry proved a different test. I tried to hold on to the halo of island initiation with everything I could gather, from long home practices to joining high-ticket pseudo-spiritual coaching to classes themed around increasingly abstract esoteric concepts. Each offered something for a time, and then the effects slipped away. What I needed was for practice to permeate the ordinary and anchor itself in the way I met myself within the fabric of daily life.

Discovering the Real Magic

The recognition was gradual. Consistency of practice became the throughline that left its trace, and over time those traces accumulated until the old baseline of arousal I once assumed was normal felt far behind me. Breathing well revealed its benefits in my capacity to register sensation without being swept away, to let arousal crest and subside, and to allow enough space so that pressure could shift and release its hold.

When I first arrived at Agama, holding my breath in uddiyana bandha felt like drowning on dry land and confusion rose through every cell. Stillness was unbearable and my body grew restless and intent on escape. Over time, something shifted. I stopped wriggling and I stopped wanting to move when stillness pressed in.

Gradually, my breathing grew more spacious, coordinated and easeful, like a pattern I had once known but forgotten how to tap into. As my breath began to organise itself, thought slowed and urgency receded. I could not live the ashram life forever, but I could carry its imprint – a way of breathing that steadied attention and a way of attending to the present moment that steadied me.

I had already mastered intensity. The long, sweaty, almost transcendent practices were never the destination – they were training my system to recognise that the essence of yoga is a practice of less, of loosening grasp, of needing and holding less, and of becoming at home in your own skin.

I will say it again, because some truths bear repeating: how we breathe shapes the way we live. When breath loses its rush and finds a quieter cadence, perception opens and life begins to feel different.[4] I know 'breathe less' sounds like concerning advice, as if I am about to tell you to stop inhaling altogether. It is not as extreme as it may sound.

Think of it like overeating. You don't need to starve yourself, you simply stop going back for more than the body needs. Breath works the same way. It is not about deprivation; it is about recalibration. Gentle, quiet and light.

Even a few minutes of low, light and expansive breathing can calm your system in the moment, reducing stress and sharpening focus.[5] But to really retrain your baseline, the patterns need to be rehearsed across different internal and external conditions. This means practising when physiology is subtly different: after movement, at different times of the day, in warmth or cool, in states of calm and in states of activation. Because breathing links chemistry, mechanics, rhythm and state, each variation helps the nervous system stabilise healthy patterns under shifting conditions so that they become the default when it matters most.[6] Without that retraining, dysfunctional patterns tend to persist, shaped as much by protective strategies as by mechanical faults.[7]

Understanding Breath

Fantasy Breathing: A Playful Check-In

If noticing your breath feels tricky or awkward at first, you are not alone. To start gently, let's get playful.

Step 1

Grab a notebook (or open a note on your phone) and list 3–5 imaginary places, scenarios or moments where you imagine yourself breathing easily. Be as silly, idealistic or dreamy as you like. For instance:

- Floating off the edge of the earth, moving among the stars and into space.
- At the summit of a mountain, with all your worries tiny and distant below.
- Sitting at a cafe in Paris, people-watching, dressed your best and completely at ease.
- In a cosy library with nothing but a beanbag, time and your favourite music.
- On a comfy cloud, effortlessly drifting along.

Step 2

Pick your favourite of these scenarios. Visualise stepping into that place right now. Close your eyes for a moment, zoom into the details and activate your senses from within. Notice your breath there. Does it slow down? Deepen? Does your body melt a little, especially in the space behind your eyes and the tissues behind your back teeth?

An Important Distinction

Some practices – such as Peter Levine's dissociation exercises in *Waking the Tiger* – deliberately invite you to imagine leaving your body, floating above, or looking back at yourself. I sometimes teach his practices to help spark awareness.[8] Many people say they love that exercise (especially the feeling of leaving chronic pain down below), but the realisation is what matters: 'Oh, I dissociate all the time without realising it.'

That is why I want to be clear that this exercise is not about dissociation. Dissociation is a survival response where awareness pulls away from sensation, leaving you feeling spacey, numb, or not fully present. If jackhammering is happening next door, you put on headphones to block out the noise, and that is useful in the moment. However, if you leave the headphones on forever, you miss the whole music of life.

Here, we're aiming for the opposite: embodiment. Using imagination as a bridge *into* your body, not away from it.

A Sweet Reminder

You are allowed to smile at yourself here. Self-awareness works better when we lighten up about it. This simple exercise establishes something important: your breath responds quickly to your imagination, and your imagination responds just as quickly to your breath.[9] But don't just stop at 'seeing it'. Pair visualisation with sensuality, literally 'sensing yourself fully'. Notice the feeling of your skin against the chair, the ground under your feet, the play of light across the room, the air moving at your nostrils. Being sensual means bringing all of you online, so imagination becomes a bridge back into embodiment.

Progressive Variation

Once you have played with enjoyable and pleasant visualisations, you can weave this new skill into situations with negative valence – everyday moments that carry mild tension, pressure, or discomfort. The aim here is not to apply this exercise to situations of deep overwhelm. Rather, just notice how imagination, awareness and breath interact when the load is higher. Stay with it only as far you have capacity.

It Was with Me All Along

Adam was right, everything did change – but it was not the island that changed me. The shift came when I realised breath was not just something I practised. It was stitched into my very sense of self – what I had once mistaken for a fixed personality. It was there to reflect where I was untethered or fearful, showing me the ground I had not yet found. This is the kind of work that takes a lifetime.

What stayed with me from Agama was the capacity to notice what is alive in the most unremarkable moments, to let life feel romantic through presence and connection with breath: something profoundly simple and yet oh so layered.

Ground Truths

- It is not the ritual that matters, it is what it teaches your system to expect.

41

- Peak states are easy in paradise. Regulation is tested in real life.
- Healthy breathing is an everyday rhythm.
- True change happens when you return to yourself, over and over, gently.

Chapter 3

....

Breath and the Biology of Stress

How Your Nervous System Encodes, Holds and Heals Stress

People often come to me because they are stressed, but stress rarely announces itself overtly. It does not always show up as shaky hands or a racing heart. In my experience, stress frequently walks through the door looking calm, capable and completely in control. It arrives right on schedule, speaks fluently in the language of ambition and politely yet persistently overrides every internal warning signal in the pursuit of achievement.

One particular yoga student embodied this exact form of stress. She'd stride into class with quick, purposeful strides, slapping her yoga mat open, as if laying down a challenge rather than a welcoming to herself. Everything about her was exacting and her practice mirrored that intensity. If a pose did not demand enough of her, she'd invent her own, contorting aggressively to the dismay of those nearby. Watching her was like witnessing a mediation between mind and body – a negotiation in which compromise never made it to the table.

She wore composure like a costume, yet in class, another symptom of her deep disconnect surfaced: sudden, explosive bursts of flatulence, jarring in their abruptness. Passing gas in a yoga class is not unusual (it is practically a rite of passage), but it her case it was not occasional. It was constant and unacknowledged. She casually revealed one day that she was taking laxatives, part of the eating disorder she was living with, which explained the ongoing gastrointestinal dialogue. What struck me was not embarrassment or lack thereof, but the absence of awareness altogether. Even this undeniable signal from her body seemed unable to pierce the armour she'd built against sensation.

This disconnect was both psychological and physiological. Her nervous system was so blunted to sensation that even the obvious provoked only a nonchalant response at best.

I observed that for this student, the deepest struggle was not in ambitious movement but in stillness. When it was time for savasana, the final resting pose of class, she would keep stretching or abruptly leave the room, water bottles clattering in her wake. For her, stillness was not rest – it was confrontation, exposing the very sensation she had worked so hard to dissociate from.

Here's the critical piece of the puzzle: stillness is not automatically safe for every nervous system. At the heart of many eating disorders, like the one this student lived with, sits a difficult relationship with food and a profound disconnect from the felt experience of inhabiting one's body.[1] In stillness, distraction is stripped and raw sensations bubble up to the surface: hunger, shame, anxiety, the uncomfortable awareness of one's own heartbeat. Without trust or the capacity to tolerate these sensations, stillness shifts quickly from refuge to rupture in an instant.

Every yoga teacher recognises this. Some students stare restlessly at the ceiling, fidget through savasana or slip out the moment stillness arrives. It is easy to mistake this for rudeness or disengagement, but in reality, it is self-preservation.

The solution is never forcing anyone into stillness. Rather, it is about inviting the nervous system into a different narrative, breath by careful breath. To build, patiently, a new internal reality, where rest becomes not only possible but profoundly safe.

Over the years, most of my students who once bolted from savasana eventually learned to pause, at first briefly, and meet themselves in stillness without panic.

Stress once put me in the hospital, staring at scans of my own brain, searching for answers. But stress also set me on this path to yoga, to breathwork and to noticing the small electrical storms of my body: the urges, the pauses, the resets. What felt like betrayal was only my body's instinctive attempt at keeping me alive.

This chapter is about recognising stress for what it is: a surge of signals, electrical and chemical, firing through the body. Stress is not inherently good or bad – it is simply information. What matters is how we meet it, and the first lever is breath.

Rethinking Stress

We're constantly told stress is the enemy. 'Stress is the number one killer!' proclaims every wellness article. Doctors nod solemnly.

We chase relief by avoiding overwhelm and managing triggers, desperately trying to erase stress from our lives. But what if we've misunderstood entirely? What if stress itself is not the real issue? What if the problem is our body's inability to recalibrate once the stressor has passed?

Stress is not fundamentally harmful. It is brilliantly adaptive – our evolutionary superpower for survival. The trouble begins when the challenge fades and physiology does not reset, instead holding the pattern long after it is needed. When breathing remains locked in emergency patterns – shallow, rapid, sometimes mouth-based, pulled up by the muscles of the neck and shoulders – the blood gases, hormones and neurochemistry begin to reorganise around unresolved stress.[2]

Breath mirrors and reshapes the nervous system, and in stress, the coupling between them becomes even stickier. Patterns designed for sprints can turn into marathons. With repetition, the body does not just hold stress in the breath, it remodels itself around it: chemistry, posture and even perception bend to that imprint. This is how stress stops being an event and becomes a climate you live in.

What Is Stress?

We think of stress as emotional or mental. Biologically, it is a chemical symphony – a rapid cascade involving hormones like cortisol and adrenaline, shifting the delicate balance of oxygen delivery, carbon dioxide responsiveness and blood chemistry.

Stress evolved to prepare us instantly for action; to face predators, rivals or sudden threats. When stressed, your body automatically floods your bloodstream with hormones that sharpen focus, boost energy and tighten muscles ready for movement. When those chemicals remain chronically elevated, your physiology stays primed, unable to return to balance, this is the sympathetic nervous system at work.

In wild mammals, sympathetic nervous system activation is followed by discharge: fleeing, fighting or shaking it off. Modern humans, by contrast, often hold it in. We suppress, override and carry stress in stillness, masking it with discipline or productivity.

If the body does not resolve the stress response by discharging the mobilised energy (through movement, exertion, trembling or similar), the acute chemistry may ebb, but the underlying biochemistry remains dysregulated. Muscles stay tight, breathing stays shallow and the nervous system continues to behave as if a threat is still present. Recovery can be supported by parasympathetic rebound through rest, the right breathing practices or social connection, but without discharge, the body often remains on low-level alert. Over time, those unresolved survival responses accumulate and set the stage for chronic stress.

Breathing patterns can change quickly under stress, usually tending towards hyperventilation. If they persist, blood gases shift, stress hormones remain elevated and the body drifts away from balance. This breakdown in physiological homeostasis is the true cost of unresolved stress.

Homeostasis is your body's masterful ability to sustain balance – temperature, blood pressure, chemistry – at every moment. The mind-blowing truth? Homeostasis is not just biological housekeeping; it is cellular consciousness. Right now, billions of your cells are actively sensing and communicating with each other, making subtle adjustments well before your conscious mind notices.

Chronic stress keeps hormones like cortisol and catecholamines elevated. That prolonged exposure creates what neuroscientists call 'allostatic load' – a term that describes the wear and tear that occurs when the body's normal balance is repeatedly disrupted. Over time, this increases the risks of hypertension, insulin resistance, chronic inflammation and arterial disease.[3] Chronic stress is also associated with lower heart rate variability, which is a marker of autonomic flexibility whose reduction has been linked with diabetes, cardiovascular disease and other health problems.[4]

The Nuance of Heart Rate Variability, Carbon Dioxide and Individual Differences

'**Heart rate variability**' describes the body's continual moment-to-moment adjustments to your heart rate in response to your internal state and external environment. Low heart rate variability can indicate stress and a reduced ability to adapt to situations.

Every breath subtly interacts with your nervous system. When you inhale, your heart rate slightly accelerates (this is known as 'sympathetic activation'). When you exhale, your heart rate subtly slows (known as 'parasympathetic activation'). This natural rhythm is called respiratory sinus arrhythmia, and it influences your heart rate variability, a nuanced indicator of your nervous system's adaptability.

Research shows breathing slowly at around six breaths per minute (a 5-second inhale and 5-second exhale) typically maximises heart rate variability. However, this can also lower carbon dioxide levels in some people, triggering uncomfortable sensations like anxiety, dizziness or heightened air hunger.[5]

In contrast, alternative breathing techniques such as 4-7-8 breathing (inhale for 4, hold for 7, exhale for 8) or box breathing (inhale for 4, hold for 4, exhale for 4, and hold again for 4) generally maintain carbon dioxide levels more effectively. While these methods may create smaller immediate shifts in heart rate variability, they can offer greater overall comfort, stability and physiological balance for many individuals.[6]

This highlights the need to strike a delicate balance: maximising heart rate variability is just one possible outcome of breathing practice, not the sole measure of whether a technique is the right match for your physiology and psychology at this time.

Biologists now know that repeated stress alters gene activity within immune cells, shifting the body's baseline long after the stressor has passed.[7] Under chronic strain, immune cells increase inflammatory signalling while reducing antiviral defences – a trade-off that helps explain why chronic stress is linked with so many diseases.[8] These molecular imprints can bias the body towards vigilance even in the absence of danger.[9] This anticipatory stress response forms part of allostatic load: the hidden burden that builds when the body adapts to threats again and again.[10]

The Preconscious Breath

Modern neuroscience reveals something remarkable: your breath responds to your emotional state before your conscious mind even recognises it.

In work by neuroscientists Ikuo Homma and Yuri Masaoka, participants exposed to various scents showed changes in their breathing roughly 400 milliseconds before they consciously identified whether an odour was pleasant or unpleasant.[11] Their physiology had registered the emotional significance before their conscious awareness could even catch up.[12]

Why is this so profound? Because olfactory signals bypass the usual sensory relay in the thalamus. Air drawn in directly through the nose travels to the olfactory bulbs and from there to limbic areas like the amygdala.[13] With each nose breath, rhythmic activity sweeps through the brain's emotion and memory centres, but this rhythm weakens when people breathe through their mouths.[14] Breathing thus acts as an early emotional indicator, shaping perception before conscious thought emerges.[15] Breathing can also activate defensive circuits that prepare the body for fight-or-flight, even when the 'threat' is nothing more than a subtle perception.

Breath is both reactive and predictive. Patterns anchored in past stress can keep perception tuned to danger, even in safe environments.

The **olfactory system** is the system of sensors behind your nose that provides your sense of smell. It also contributes to your sense of taste.

Coherence vs Relaxation

Research in neurocardiology shows that the heart is more than a passive pump: it contains an intrinsic cardiac nervous system that communicates directly with the brain.[16] Cardiac activity influences perception and emotion. For example, in one study, fear-provoking images shown during systole (the heartbeat's contracting phase) were rated as more intense than the same images shown during diastole, when the heart was relaxed.[17] This indicates that the rhythm and timing of the heart tune emotional circuitry in the brain.

Relaxation practices typically slow the heart and quiet the mind, shifting the body towards rest. 'Coherence', however, describes a different state. When breathing produces a smooth, sine wave-like pattern in heart rate variability, the heart and brain become synchronised.[18] This coherent rhythm has been associated with emotional stability, positive affect and clearer cognition, supporting a balanced readiness to meet challenges without tipping into stress reactivity.[19]

Coherence and Downregulation

Not all breathing practices are created equal. Each has an optimal use depending on your goals, current physiological state and your nervous system's needs. Understanding the difference between coherence breathing (balanced alertness) and downregulation breathing (rest) helps you choose the practice that best fits where you are right now. Here's how to tell whether your chosen breath practice is doing what it is meant to.

Coherence breathing cultivates balanced, alert calm – like the feeling of being in the zone mid-exam or engaged in your favourite activity. You are in flow, comfortably absorbed yet clear-headed.

Downregulation breathing guides your body into deeper relaxation, rest and safety – like sinking into restful sleep or fully relaxing after intense activity.

It's important to learn to clearly sense which state your nervous system needs, and choose your practice accordingly. This skill is central to creating lasting, personalised state shifts. Remember, breathwork is not about achieving a textbook-perfect breath pattern. It is about attentive listening, and allowing your breath practice to respond to what your nervous system truly needs, moment by moment.

Signs You have Entered Coherence (Balanced Alertness)

- Heart rate feels steady, rhythmic and comfortably paced (as in the clear steadiness of a good conversation or creative flow).
- Mental state is calm, clear and alert, without agitation.
- Emotions feel balanced: gently energised yet relaxed (like the ease of a leisurely stroll in nature).
- Breathing begins to feel effortless.

Signs You are Downregulating (Deep Rest)

- Breathing is softer, quieter and without strain (like how your breath feels right before you drift into sleep).
- Gentle sensations of warmth, heaviness or softening spread throughout your muscles and body.
- Increased salivation, which is a reliable signal of parasympathetic activation.[20]
- A calm, grounded emotional state (like the comfort of settling into a cosy chair after a long day).
- Possibly a gentle decrease in heart rate and relaxed expansion through your chest and belly.

Signs of Over-Breathing (Pushing Too Hard)

- Light-headedness, dizziness or tingling in the hands or face.
- Increased anxiety, restlessness or agitation.
- Feeling 'air hunger' (breathlessness) or struggling to comfortably maintain the breath's rhythm.[21]

The Quiet Power of Breath

Trauma researcher Peter Levine describes the nervous system as a kind of library where shelves stacked with books hold the body's memories: each one indexed by arousal, affect and context.[22] When reaching for a response, the system does not scan the whole collection – it goes to the shelves that match our current state. In an adaptive system, this works with remarkable precision, producing the right rhythm for exertion, another for rest and another still for focused engagement.

Breathing belongs to this library, too. Each book contains rhythms stamped by the conditions in which they were learned: some calm and expansive, others hurried and uneven, each marked by the emotional tone of its origin. Under chronic stress, the search through the shelves can grow narrow. The same volumes are pulled down again and again, rolled out even in benign conditions, while the wider range remains out of reach. This is how protective patterns, once brilliant, can become limiting.

Through practice, breathing expands the nervous system's capacity to search the library more broadly, rather than defaulting to the same familiar shelves, and even allows new entries to be written into its catalogue. This is the quiet power of the breath: to restore choice where it was once narrowed, and to return the body to homeostasis so its natural range is more attuned to the present moment.

Understanding Breath

Heart Coherence Breathing

Visualising breath moving gently in and out of your heart space, combined with actively cultivating heartfelt positive emotions, deepens heart–brain coherence. This harmonises your nervous system, enhancing emotional stability, cognitive clarity and overall resilience.

Your practice should always feel comfortable and sustainable. If the rhythm feels too long or if emotions become overwhelming, ease off. Shorten the cadence, pause or simply return to your natural breathing. This prevents over-breathing and helps the practice stay responsive to your body's feedback.

Step 1: Choose a safe, calming scent

Select a pure, natural essential oil (such as lavender, cedarwood or chamomile). Avoid synthetic scents, incense sticks or fragrances containing toxins or endocrine-disrupting chemicals. Use sparingly – a subtle scent is best.

Step 2: Gentle heart-focused breathing

Inhale softly through your nose for about 5.5–6 seconds, imagining or sensing the breath entering through your heart space (at the level of your physical heart but centred in your chest). Exhale gently through your nose for about 5.5–6 seconds, visualising or sensing the breath flowing outwards from your heart area, maintaining a balanced, even rhythm.

Step 3: Activate and expand heartfelt positive emotions

Bring all of your attention to the centre of your chest, at the level of your physical heart. Recall a genuine positive memory or feeling such as gratitude, love, compassion or joy. Let that feeling gather and grow in your heart, and begin to expand, as if a subtle field were radiating outwards with each breath. Allow this feeling to amplify the coherence between your heart and brain, cultivating calmness and clarity. You do not need to summon the same memory or feeling each time. Any positive experience can serve as the anchor.

Step 4: Anchor your coherent state with scent

Occasionally inhale your chosen natural scent throughout the practice, allowing the aroma to pair with the coherent state and make it easier access again in the future.

Step 5: Relax into coherence

Keep your shoulders, face, neck and jaw relaxed throughout your practice and attend to the felt sense of coherence as it emerges through your whole body, strengthening its imprint.

Ground Truths

- Stress is physiological as well as psychological.
- Chronic stress disrupts normal physiological regulation, and over time, this cumulative strain can raise the risk of disease.
- Breath both reflects and shapes stress states.
- Breathing and scent have direct pathways into emotional processing.

Chapter 4

The Four Dimensions of Breath

Integrating Biochemistry, Biomechanics, Cadence and Behaviour

For years, functional breathing has been explained through a three-pillar model:

- **Biochemistry:** How carbon dioxide, oxygen delivery and blood pH are regulated.
- **Biomechanics:** The role of the diaphragm, intercostals, rib cage and accessory muscles in breathing, movement and posture.
- **Psychophysiology:** How the rate, ratios, variability and continuity of breathing cycles impact the nervous system.

This framing, popularised by breathing coaches such as Patrick McKeown, has been extremely useful for teaching and training practical breathwork, specifically breath retraining.[1] Each pillar is grounded in established physiology and gives us clear ways to observe what is happening both in the visible pattern and in the processes driving it.

However, this framing does not account for the whole picture.

Patterns are shaped not only by chemistry, mechanics or cadence but also by the neurobehavioural dimension (which is sometimes described as 'state-dependent'): the way internal and external conditions are stitched together with arousal, memory and emotion. Internal conditions are your physiology in motion – blood gases, pH, autonomic tone and the breathing pattern itself. External conditions are the environment and relational field – light, noise, temperature, posture, social cues, ritual and even the nervous system of the person guiding you.

This layering is why the same rise in acidity can register as manageable expansion for a freediver or as suffocating panic for someone with a history of anxiety. When arousal and affect rise, the nervous system searches the 'library' of prior responses, pulling out not only old breathing patterns but also the emotional tones and images stored with them.[2]

This fourth dimension (the neurobehavioural state) explains why the same person can breathe functionally in one context and dysfunctionally in another. Breathing patterns are often both mechanical faults and protective strategies – not just dysfunctions to be 'solved' in isolation but adaptations to be understood across different states and contexts.

This is why in this book I use a four-dimensional model of breathing: biochemistry, biomechanics, psychophysiology and neurobehavioural state, each shaping and being shaped by the others:

Biochemistry: Rethinking Carbon Dioxide Tolerance

A surf-apnoea coach – someone who trains surfers to extend breath-hold capacity and stay calm during wipe-outs – once reached out to me about a talented surfer named Trace. Trace had trained extensively, building impressive carbon dioxide tolerance through structured breath-hold training: dry static exercises that pushed carbon dioxide levels higher, and high-heart-rate apnoea drills such as underwater rock running and simulated wipe-outs that combined both low oxygen (hypoxia) and elevated carbon dioxide (hypercapnia). Biochemically, he was highly adapted, able to sustain long holds and tolerate dynamic drills, as long as they were structured and predictable.

But in the ocean, unpredictability led to entirely different results. When a real hold-down caught Trace by surprise, rising air hunger and his body's survival response pushed him into distress. His biochemical training was solid, but less attention had been given to how his nervous system perceived and reacted to sudden, uncontrolled immersion.

In performance and functional breath training, carbon dioxide tolerance is often treated as the central measure of capacity. This is for good reason: rising carbon dioxide is the body's primary chemical signal to adjust ventilation. It also shapes oxygen delivery through the Bohr effect (as outlined in chapter 1), which is why lighter, more efficient breathing can improve oxygen availability to the brain, muscle and tissue. When carbon dioxide levels in your blood climb, sensors in your brain stem pick up the resulting change in pH and adjust your breathing pattern. Instead of breathing faster, you take slower, deeper breaths, moving more air with each breath to clear the carbon dioxide.[3] By contrast, when oxygen levels actually fall to a low threshold, the carotid bodies signal for faster, shallower breathing.[4] Importantly, breathing rate can also increase when the brain interprets stress or threat, even if oxygen levels are normal. Thus, carbon dioxide mainly drives ventilation, while hypoxia drives its rate, and stress perception can overlay rate changes from the top down. This distinction becomes significant in the discussion below (see Breath Intelligence Brief).

In states of air hunger or perceived threat (as in the hold-downs that caught Trace off guard), the shift is often towards faster breathing.[5]

While chemistry can drive ventilation when blood gases change, sudden accelerations often come from top-down circuits in the brain: the amygdala tagging threat,[6] the insula turning the rise of carbon dioxide into a felt sense of breathlessness,[7] the anterior cingulate amplifying arousal when events do not match expectation[8] and the prefrontal cortex anticipating what might happen next.[9] These neural inputs can trigger rapid breathing even before blood gases shift.[10]

A rise in breath rate, as Trace experienced, is not always about blood chemistry – it often reflects what the brain perceives. Surf-apnoea coaching, whether explicitly stated or not, works on both fronts: conditioning carbon dioxide tolerance and retraining the nervous system's response to sudden threat. Over time, Trace's system relearned to read hold-downs as challenges he could manage, and his breathing shifted into steadier rhythms even in unpredictable surf. His story illustrates that resilient breathing depends not only on biochemical adaptation but also on retraining the brain's perception of and behavioural responses to carbon dioxide.

Understanding Breath

Breath Intelligence Brief: Calming Your Inner Stage Mum

Think of your breathing as being guided by two characters:

- **Carbon dioxide – the calm mentor (biochemistry):** Like a patient teacher, rising carbon dioxide encourages your body to breathe a little deeper and fuller (increasing 'tidal volume'). It improves oxygen delivery into your cells by triggering the brain stem to adjust your diaphragm and breathing muscles for depth rather than speed. This process (the Bohr effect) supports balanced, restorative breathing.

- **Your brain – the anxious stage mum (neurology):** When breathing becomes rapid and shallow in stress or panic, the calm biochemical signal of carbon dioxide is drowned out by threat perception. Circuits for fear and emotion drive you to over-direct, rushing the rhythm and losing depth. The result is anxious, shallow breathing that does not necessarily match what your body needs.

Retraining the breath means allowing the calm mentor to guide the performance again, while the stage mum quietly steps to the side.

The 'False Alarm' of Air Hunger

Air hunger is one of the most unsettling sensations the body can produce. Many people assume it means they are running out of oxygen, but in healthy people, oxygen levels usually stay high. The sensation is a perceived threat, not a genuine shortage.[11]

Here's how the loop unfolds: a trigger (stress, a thought, or even a small internal sensation) increases activity in the sympathetic nervous system. Breathing rate speeds up before chemistry requires it. Faster breaths lower carbon dioxide levels in the blood, shifting blood pH towards alkaline. The brain interprets this change as danger, the sense of threat grows louder and the nervous system stays on high alert. The cycle reinforces itself.[12]

I explain it to my clients as being like a smoke alarm that goes off every time you are making toast. The alarm is real, the sound is loud, but not every alarm means fire. Sometimes it is just burnt toast.

This is why carbon dioxide tolerance training alone often falls short. The work is not just chemical, it is also perceptual.[13] To break the loop, the body needs to practise building chemical tolerance at the chemoreceptor level *and* learning to reinterpret the signal. It is a bit like learning to handstand: you fight, work and put effort into finding your way upside down, and then suddenly you balance – you are weightless. That is when your brain panics and shouts, 'You are going to die!' But that moment is actually the sweet spot. The same goes with your breath – on the other side of that false alarm is that place where you fly.

A Metabolic Perspective

You have seen how chronic stress hormones build allostatic load: the cumulative wear that reshapes physiology over time.[14] Breathing is one of the ways that load is channelled into metabolism. When carbon dioxide remains chronically low through over-breathing, the chemistry of energy production is altered.[15] The Krebs cycle (the cell's central energy system) continues to generate adenosine triphosphate (ATP; the molecule every cell uses for energy), but it does so less efficiently and at a greater cost.[16]

Those inefficiencies scale upwards. They amplify inflammatory signalling, blunt insulin sensitivity, destabilise sleep and contribute to disorders such as insulin resistance and sleep apnoea.[17] These disruptions accumulate as part of the body's allostatic load, tilting the system away from vitality and towards protection.[18]

If you were to ask me what breathing is really about, the answer might surprise you. It is ultimately about producing energy. Every thought, every movement, every repair in your body runs on ATP; the molecule of energy. Breathing is the process that fuels it.

Breathing is one way that stress gets written directly into metabolism. Later, in chapter 13, we'll see how this same chemistry reshapes the gut, altering not only human cells but the microbial ones that live alongside them.

Biomechanics: The Way Breath Moves Through You

Where breath moves in the body determines how every other system organises around it. Under stress, breath tends to climb upwards, rising into the chest and shoulders, tightening the neck, the cadence quickening as accessory breathing muscles are recruited to lift the ribs. The diaphragm is still active, but its excursion is reduced; the ribs lose their supple swing, the pelvic floor can slip out of timing, intra-abdominal pressure becomes harder to regulate and coordination across the trunk begins to unravel.

This vertical, thoracic-dominant pattern is an adaptation, and it reflects the body's attempt to reorganise when neurobiology leans towards vigilance.

At the centre of breathing sits the diaphragm – a parachute-shaped sheet of muscle that never lands. Made mostly of slow-twitch muscle fibres, it is an endurance engine designed to contract and release without rest. The diaphragm is both conscious and reflexive. When it has space to move, it becomes the hub of a wheel whose spokes reach into the spine, the ribs, the pelvic floor and even the organs of digestion. With every breath cycle, the diaphragm balances pressure, couples with the pelvic floor, supports digestion and sends steady signals through the vagus nerve, keeping the body's gyroscope aligned.

....

The **vagus nerve** is a key player in your parasympathetic nervous system, often called the body's 'rest and digest' system. Among its crucial functions, it regulates recovery from stress, promotes digestive function, maintains homeostasis and facilitates emotional balance.

The activity level of the vagus nerve is known as 'vagal tone'. Higher vagal tone means your nervous system can efficiently shift into states of calm and recovery, while lower vagal tone often reflects chronic stress or heightened anxiety.

Crucially, around 80 per cent of vagus nerve signalling moves from your body to your brain, not the other way around. Why does this matter so much? It means that your brain's sense of safety and wellbeing is largely determined by bodily signals. Your internal state – how you breathe, digest, your heart rate, even subtle visceral sensations – shapes your emotional experience and perception of stress.

Cultivating bodily awareness through breathwork directly improves the clarity and accuracy of the messages your body sends your brain, helping your nervous system find balance from the bottom up.

For that to happen, the surrounding structures must also remain mobile. Rib expansion, thoracic extension and elasticity of soft tissue all create the space the diaphragm needs to descend. When those become restricted, breath migrates upwards. The body works harder to move less air, holding tension the way a dam holds back water; steady on the surface but full of tension beneath.

Rebuilding breath mechanics through exercise means restoring mobility, space and timing so the structure can stabilise from within, without compensation. And when that coordination returns, the structure moves away from burning energy and towards integrity.

How Biomechanics Connects to Movement (and Where to Go Deeper)

Every shape your body takes – whether upright, slouched or somewhere twisted in between – dictates how easily the breath can move. Posture, muscle engagement and alignment are not only about appearance, despite what you may have been told in a yoga class; they set the frame through which your breath passes. Chapter 15 will explore practices such as Core Breathing and Balloon Breathing to Rebalance the Spiral.

Behaviour is the other essential factor here. Habits, emotions and unconscious responses continuously shape posture and mechanics. Biomechanics and behaviour reinforce one another, which is why effective breathwork must work on both at once.

Consider some everyday examples. Mouth breathing while scrolling on a phone keeps the nervous system alert and reinforces a chest-driven breathing pattern. With repetition, the upper body tightens and the diaphragm loses flexibility.

Hunching forward with the chin jutted while sitting at a desk, driving or scrolling folds the front of the rib cage like an accordion pressed shut, forcing the diaphragm into a smaller range while the neck, chest and shoulders take over. Breath becomes trapped high in the chest, and the stress response sharpens.

In another common pattern, the rib cage flares and the lower back arches while the belly spills forward. This extension-compression posture fixes the rib cage in place and limits its natural expansion. The diaphragm still contracts, but less efficiently, reducing lung capacity and encouraging persistent tension. Core muscles and the pelvic floor lose coordination, disrupting internal stability.

Just as unconscious behaviours shape the way you hold yourself, deliberate shifts in posture and breath can reshape the way you respond to the world. Mechanics rediscover their fluidity through slow, nasal, low (abdominal-diaphragmatic) breathing that draws the diaphragm wide while the ribs find their natural alignment. Each breath cycle becomes a line of code written back into the nervous system, drip-feeding the overwrite of stress reflexes.

Psychophysiology: Rhythm as Regulation

Our breath has rhythm, and rhythm teaches the nervous system what to expect. When breathing is jagged or unpredictable, the brain reads chaos. When breathing is smooth and consistent, the brain finds coherence. This rhythm functions as an internal metronome that regulates heart rate, brainwave activity, perception and emotion. This phenomenon is known as 'respiratory sinus arrhythmia', which (despite its clinical name) simply reflects adaptability and is one of the clearest biological indicators of how breath shapes emotional regulation in real time.

Tradition has always pointed to the same truth: steady breath = steady mind. Neuroscience now confirms it, showing that rhythmic breathing strengthens vagal tone, heart rate variability, attention and emotional regulation.[19] Cadence adds another gift. It helps us to meet novelty.

Novelty sharpens attention and raises arousal. It is how we learn. For a nervous system on guard, however, novelty feels more like a cold splash, and the breath quickens instinctively, ahead of thought. Rhythm becomes medicine here. A steady, reliable cadence allows the body to meet surprise without sliding into frenzy – to lean into what is unfamiliar without retreating. Cadence is not seconds on a clock or perfect ratios. It is the re-emergence of something the body recognises as its own. Rhythm is reclamation.

And then there are the pauses. Most people think of breath as inhaling and exhaling, yet there is another element: the post-inhalation pause, a hiatus that occurs after the inhale and before the exhale. Subtle but essential, this still point stabilises the airways, supports gas exchange and prevents the lungs from collapsing too quickly at rest. It also gauges how steady the system really is.

In states of dysregulation, that suspension disappears and breath becomes constant motion – always rushing to the next inhale; never lingering, never landing. Restoring rhythm means restoring pause; the space between the notes that makes the music come alive. In yoga, the pauses are where the mind falls quiet, and to rest there is to touch peace. This is what cadence offers: a rhythm your body can rely on and the stillness of coming home to itself.

Behaviour: The Breath Beneath the Breath

Behaviour is the most intimate and revealing dimension of breath, because it tells the story your body has been writing in breath since the day it learned to defend, to perform, to adapt or to belong.

Behaviour is the language spoken beneath words; the choreography you follow without remembering when you first rehearsed the steps. Consider the way your breath stalls when someone cuts you off mid-sentence; the way it thins to nothing when you are pressed against the possibility of being wrong; or the clipped rhythm that sweeps over after years of performing at full stretch. What lingers in the breath are imprints – fossils of experience the body absorbed and never quite released.

Behavioural breathing is memory made physiological, and your rehearsal turned reflex. Repeated patterns etch grooves that become embodied stories, inscribing not only what happened but how body remembered it.

Over time, a breath held in readiness becomes inhalation-dominant, always drawing in and holding on. The exhale dwindles to a short, effortful emptying, and the cycle swings like a pendulum that never quite finds its centre. Sometimes it is accompanied by sighing: breaths that shorten, then try to reset themselves with a sharp release.

You cannot out-think behavioural breathing. The cleverest students are often the ones who struggle the most, because they are searching for the solution in logic rather than in listening or the slow apprenticeship of allowing. In the rare moments when no one is watching, the breath reveals what it has been carrying. Most of us are simply too overstimulated to sit long enough to be alone with breath.

When the inhale finally softens and the exhale can depart without effort, the body reallocates its resources. What was once bound to vigilance is released into repair, into connection and into the possibility of choice.

When Breath is the Bouncer

In my early twenties, I put my pencil skirt into storage and took off to travel for a full year. One of my first stops was London, where I spent too much on a bright yellow blouse at Portobello Market. The shop assistant, equal parts charm and glitter, told me it was 'pure Parisian cool'. I believed him.

A few days later, I wore it to a nightclub in Paris. The bouncer took one look, muttered 'jaune' ('yellow') like it was an insult, and waved me away. I spent the night wandering the streets, glowing like a human highlighter.

Breath can be like that bouncer. You'd think that once oxygen is in the blood it would automatically reach your cells. But how you breathe governs whether that oxygen is released or stays bound to the blood. Breath is the gatekeeper – not only of oxygen, but of how you feel.

When your breath is low, slow and gentle, oxygen moves freely. But when your breath shows up out of style and out of step, it is waved off before it can cross the rope. Your cells are inside wondering where the hell the party's at.

It does not matter how encouraging your thoughts are; if your breath is irregular, then your body will follow its lead. Cognition rarely overrides entrenched breathing habits, and physiology usually wins. Breathing pattern issues are not always dramatic. More often they are quiet and subtle – a breath that cuts short and never settles into completion; a sigh that interrupts every few minutes as chemistry seeks to recalibrate; an exhale that presses out with effort instead of emptying with ease; or a mouth that slips opens at rest and bypasses the nose while drying the airways. Each on its own may seem unremarkable, but gathered over weeks and years, they reveal what the body has been rehearsing without witness. To notice them is to become your own breath detective, reading the margin notes your physiology has been keeping.

When Breath Patterns Speak

Standing at the checkout of a clothing store, surrounded by beautiful garments draped on posing mannequins, the saleswoman leans over the counter and asks, 'So, what do you do?'

I tell her, and she lets out a theatrical huff. 'Oh, I need to work on my breathing, I always forget. I should be taking bigger breaths.'

To prove it, she draws in a double inhale through her nose, throws her chest forward and exhales, letting a loud dramatic 'erghh' out of her mouth.

Now that you understand the deeper rhythms of functional breathing, it is easier to see why so many patterns slip by unnoticed. What many people believe to be 'healthy breathing' is so deeply ingrained that it often reframes dysfunction as good practice and sometimes pushes the body even further off course.

The kind of chest-heaving breath the saleswoman acted out resembles what researchers call the 'physiological sigh' – a reflexive pattern later popularised by Dr Andrew Huberman – though in the studies it is performed as one long, extended exhale through the mouth rather than a noisy collapse.

Hook someone up to a capnograph and ask them to perform the so-called physiological sigh – a double inhale followed by one long controlled exhale through the mouth. The trace tells the story instantly:

carbon dioxide levels drop. Sighs have a natural purpose when they arise reflexively; they briefly reinflate alveoli and help trapped air move, restoring more efficient gas exchange. However, string them together and the effect changes. Instead of restoring balance, you begin to wash out carbon dioxide. The chemistry drifts quickly towards hypocapnia (lower-than-normal carbon dioxide levels), and the sensations that follow – potentially lightness, tingling, or a floaty feeling of detachment – can easily be confused for calm. But is that what they really are?

A 2023 Stanford study published in *Cell Reports Medicine* showed that practising cyclic sighs for five minutes a day improved mood and lowered respiratory rate across four weeks.[20] The findings were striking, but the study never measured carbon dioxide levels. The omission is important, given that many stressed individuals already over-breathe and sustain chronically lower-than-normal carbon dioxide levels. Repeating sighs for minutes on end as a daily practice can push levels even further below normal.

Herein lies the confusion. Many people struggle to tell the difference between genuine relaxation and dissociation. As we saw in the Breath Reset in chapter 2, one is a settling into the body, and the other is a slipping away from it. A sigh can carry you either way, and when repeated over and over, it will also carry you further from homeostasis, regardless of mind–body connection.

Understanding Breath

Start with the exercise from chapter 1. Sit for one minute and watch your breath without changing it. Notice where it begins, where it pauses, where it wants to rush. Now try some small changes. Can you soften the edges without forcing the rhythm? Can you feel the pause at the bottom of the breath and again, without forcing it, extend that pause ever so slightly? Perhaps say to yourself, 'I have enough oxygen here; I can wait patiently for the next breath to arrive.'

Ground Truths

- Biochemical regulation is about reducing fear in the space between breaths.
- Good breathing begins with softening your breath.
- Behaviour is the key dimension in controlling your breath.

Chapter 5

The Past Is
in Your Breath

Rewiring Memory Through
the Body's First Language

The body often reacts before the mind has time to catch up. The reverse is also true: psychology follows physiology. That dialogue usually runs in the background as the unseen hand of impulses that control us, but in the breath, it becomes visible and tangible.

Breath is the meeting point where patterns surface and change can begin. Breath realigns us with the present moment and loosens the grip of long-standing physiological habits laid down long ago. It offers both a record of the past and a chance to write something new.

The Body's Early Signal: Breathing Patterns and Emotions

As I mentioned in chapter 3, your body begins preparing for an emotional response *before* your conscious mind even registers it, starting with your breath. Not only that, but the way we breathe is *embedded* in emotion. It is not a passive reaction but an active component of the physiological and neural architecture of emotion itself. When an emotional state arises – fear, joy, anger, sadness – its breathing blueprint is not an after-effect but part of the response itself, woven into the body's activation.

Neuroscientist Jaak Panksepp theorised that emotions are not abstract mental states but biologically grounded systems, each with its own physiological signature, expressed through changes in breath, posture and vocalisation.[1] In his work on affective neuroscience, he defined seven 'primary process' emotional systems – SEEKING, RAGE, FEAR, LUST, CARE, PANIC/GRIEF, and PLAY – and he insisted on writing them in ALL CAPS because he regarded them as fundamental, and shared across all species from humans to cats to rats. Unlike the cerebral cortex (which is linked to higher thought), these circuits, according to Panksepp, arise from ancient, subcortical structures such as the amygdala and hypothalamus. You can see them in the clenched jaw and forceful exhalations of RAGE, the shallow gasps of FEAR, the sobbing breath of PANIC/GRIEF or the panting of PLAY.

From this perspective, breath is not just a follower of emotion but part of its architecture: an early signal of state shifts and a thread you can follow to better understand your experience. It becomes an early warning, revealing dysregulation before it escalates. Once recognised, breath is also a way to alter the course dysregulation might otherwise take.

So, what does this all mean? In short, your breath is not just flowing down the river of your emotional life – it has got both oars in the water and is steering the whole boat.

It lets you bypass the mind's overthinking and speak directly to the body in a language it understands: sensation, rhythm and presence. It is rather poetic and 100 per cent physiological.

Decades of affective neuroscience point to this: the body's emotional circuits often fire *before* we become consciously aware of an emotion.[2] Breath is part of that activation, and part of the solution.

How This Relates to Trauma and Perception

Understanding how breath influences emotional states offers powerful insights into trauma and perception. When the body experiences trauma, its interoceptive system becomes altered, either through heightened sensitivity or disconnection.[3] This distorts how we perceive the world, causing everyday sensations to be misinterpreted as signs of danger, even when no real threat exists.

Interoception is your body's ability to sense what is going on inside. It is the feeling of your breath, your pulse, your heartbeat, your temperature, your muscles, your gut.

It is not just passive awareness. It is a continuous feedback loop between body and brain that shapes how you feel, react and decide.

When interoception is coherent, you can respond with clarity. When it is noisy or scrambled, reflexes take over. And when it is distorted through trauma or chronic stress, the world is read through a lens of protection rather than presence.

For example, someone with heightened anxiety may sense their heartbeat so intensely that it feels like a heart attack. Someone who has experienced abandonment may interpret a lack of eye contact or a weak handshake as rejection. In both cases, the brain is processing ordinary signals through the hypervigilant lens of past trauma, rather than accurately assessing the present moment.

Learning to notice subtle shifts in our breathing patterns can help us drop out of our heads and into our bodies. Slowing the breath refines those signals, making them more accurate guides for the brain.

How This Happens

Tiny moments, like a spoonful of porridge or an offhand comment, weave into the fabric of perception. Some dissolve and others cling on tightly.

Take Daniel, whose memory did not fade.

It was an ordinary Tuesday afternoon in 2015. Daniel was stretched out on the couch, half-watching TV, when the coffee table lurched. A porcelain cup rattled in its saucer, as if it were trying to escape.

Then the floor dropped. It felt like a trapdoor swinging open. Stability was gone. Glass splintered. A picture frame shot from the shelf, shattering at his feet.

And Daniel?

'I froze,' he told me later. 'Time stopped. My body locked up and I was not thinking, I was not even breathing. When it ended, I raised my hands to touch my face and check I was still there. Was I bleeding? I couldn't tell. All I felt was my heart pounding against my ribs. The silence afterwards was deafening.'

The 6.5-magnitude earthquake lasted less than a minute. But for Daniel, it never really ended. His brain pressed RECORD, and that moment burnt itself into his nervous system.

Months later, safe in his office, standing in line for coffee or sitting in traffic, his body would hit PLAY before his mind caught up. A flicker of motion, a slight vibration, a sudden noise and bam, he was back there. Not in the present and not in the past – just stuck inside a body that believed the danger was still happening.

When the Body Becomes the Trigger

Daniel was not reacting to the earthquake. He was reacting to its memory, replayed as if it were unfolding in real time. Think about the last time you were triggered. Did your body react first? What did it feel like?

While catastrophic events like earthquakes leave lasting imprints, it is often the subtle everyday experiences, especially from childhood, that cut the deepest and are the hardest to untangle.

It took me decades to realise I was over-attuned to people's mood shifts, constantly scanning for the slightest shift in tone or body language. In trauma research, this is a hallmark of 'hyperarousal', where the nervous system is scanning for threats in places where none may exist.[4] All I knew was that it made me incredibly intolerant when someone was in a bad mood. Other people's problems just did not seem like real problems, so I would think, 'Buck up, get over it, and get on with it.' And if they did not? I'd simmer.

This was not the result of my career in law, nor of one big traumatic event. It was a fairly constant state of alertness I had learned to live with. I never realised how much it had shaped my responses to the world until I found myself in a relationship where I became hyperaware of my partner Josh's moods. I started feeling like I was walking on eggshells, blaming him for his humanness (something I definitely couldn't control) instead of looking inwards to understand what was happening inside myself.

Many people go to therapy and say, 'But I had the most blessed childhood, loving parents, and nothing was wrong.' Yes, that is true for me too ... but neuroscience shows that it is not only overt trauma that imprints the nervous system. Subtle dynamics in attachment, tone or mood can shape vigilance just as powerfully.[5]

How Trauma Lives in the Body

Trauma is not stored as a single story but as physiological patterns. Its signature can move in more than one direction. At times, trauma sharpens the system into hyperarousal; the breath quickening and muscles tensing as attention narrows into scanning for threat. At other times, it pulls the system in another direction, towards dissociation, where sensation is dampened and awareness detaches from the body. Many people oscillate between the two, cycling from agitation to shutdown as the nervous system struggles to find equilibrium.

Neuroimaging studies show that in dissociation, the insula (the brain's hub for interoception) becomes hypoactive, muting ordinary cues of breath, pulse and visceral sensation.[6] Circuits that normally integrate the body state with self-awareness lose coherence, leaving experience fragmented. What emerges is not simple numbness but distance: fog, detachment, or the unsettling sense of life unfolding behind a glass wall.

Recovery does not begin by forcing a return to sensation but by establishing safety.[7] Breath offers one entry point here. It's an avenue that can be titrated with readiness, allowing awareness to re-enter the body in tolerable steps. In this way, breath is far less about technique and more about re-establishing the conditions for presence.

Intellectualising (Survival Through Logic)

One way the nervous system adapts is by retreating into thought. Analysis and intellectualisation take the foreground, creating distance from bodily sensation. In this mode, the prefrontal cortex exerts control, dampening signals from the limbic system and erecting a barrier to emotional processing. The mind feels active, even sharp, but the body remains cut out of the conversation.

Fawning (People-Pleasing for Safety)

This adaptation is often overlooked, yet it can be as fundamental as fight, flight or freeze. In this adaptation, safety is maintained by anticipating and appeasing others, becoming over-attuned to shifts in mood or tone. In this state, the nervous system learns to equate conflict with danger, treating harmony as the only guarantee of safety. What may appear as compliance or agreeableness on the surface is, at its core, a survival strategy.

Functional Freeze (Masked Survival Mode)

Some people do not collapse entirely, but neither do they feel fully alive. They move through life fulfilling what is expected of them. On the inside, however, everything feels flat, muted and disconnected from the self and the world. Even moments that should evoke joy arrive dulled, as though the colour has been drained from life. Here the nervous system has learned that full presence is unsafe and so withholds vitality, keeping life at a distance as a strategy of protection.

Dissociation (When Presence Feels Unsafe)

Dissociation is the nervous system's ultimate escape route when no other option remains. When overwhelming stress exceeds capacity, awareness detaches from sensation and emotion, creating distance from the body's experience. People describe this phenomenon in different ways: as if they were watching themselves from above, or as though everything around them had slowed to half-speed, or that the world itself had lost its sense of reality.

When intensity becomes too much to bear, the body turns away from what it cannot process. The embodied memory of the event is held in suspension, outside the natural sequence of beginning, middle and end. Dissociation makes endurance possible, but what is endured remains unfinished. The fragments wait, raw and unresolved, then break through later as if the moment were still alive. A vibration underfoot, the slam of a door or the whiff of a familiar scent can hurl the body back into the same surge of survival energy. Breath establishes both contact and communication within the body, providing the signalling conditions for what has been held in suspension to begin mobilising.

Why Trauma Gets Stuck

What persists after trauma is not a clear picture but a body state. Breathing quickens, blood chemistry shifts as carbon dioxide drops and pH rises, muscles hold taut under sympathetic charge and adrenaline drives the heart into a faster, more erratic rhythm. These conditions become bound with the memory itself.

The nervous system does not store experiences as neutral files. It carries them with the imprint of the state in which they occurred. Later, when physiology even partly resembles that original state, the trace is re-evoked. The altered neurochemistry, heightened arousal, disrupted breathing rhythms and hormonal surges under which the memory was encoded are the same conditions under which it is most easily recalled.

The Brain's Real Problem: It Is Terrible at Context

Your brain is fast to react and slow to discriminate. It does not pause to weigh evidence or to place sensations in time.[8] What it registers may come from this week, this month or decades ago. A trace of familiarity is enough to tip the system towards defence, and what emerges feels immediate even though its roots may lie far in the past.

Survival responses are not bound by time. The remnants of an earlier experience can rise and shape the present as though nothing has changed. The body reacts, the mind scrambles for meaning, and both are sucked into an old, often distorted version of reality that has never been fully resolved.

Developing Interoceptive Awareness

Now that we've seen how breath shifts before emotion, we can practise noticing these early cues in the body.

How finely tuned is your interoception? Objective measures are useful, but self-perception can be deceptive. The more the mind believes it is in control, the more likely it is to assume it is 'in tune'. However, awareness of the body does not always follow intelligence.

To explore this, we'll use a simple exercise: heartbeat counting. This practice develops awareness of internal signals and shows how accurately you can sense the rhythm of your own heart, and how that rhythm relates to your breath and emotional state.

Some people find it difficult to detect their heartbeat, and often the same difficulty arises with subtler cues like shifts in breathing under stress. This makes regulation harder because the body's early warning signs are missed. Others are acutely aware of their heartbeat and may misinterpret normal fluctuations, such as a slight quickening, as a sign of danger. This can fuel anxiety, creating the sense that something is wrong even when no real threat is present.

Heartbeat counting reveals where you fall on that spectrum: how closely connected you are to your internal state and how you interpret it. That insight, in turn, shapes how you regulate both your breath and your emotions.

A word of caution: if tuning into your heartbeat feels overwhelming, triggering anxiety or a sense of 'too much', it is okay to skip this practice for now. Your nervous system may not be ready to turn inwards in this way yet. The section on trauma responses above offers context for why this might be the case and how such avoidance is protective, serving a purpose until you are ready. You can return to this exercise when it feels possible to approach it with curiosity rather than fear.

Understanding Breath

The Heartbeat Counting Exercise: Taking Interoceptive Awareness a Step Further

If it feels safe, give this a try:

Settle into a comfortable position, either sitting or lying down. Without placing a hand on your body, bring your attention to your heartbeat. Count how many beats you can feel in 30 seconds.

Then, check your actual pulse for the same period, using your wrist or the side of your neck. Compare what you sensed to what you counted.

What We're Looking For

- If the count falls within roughly three-quarters of your actual pulse, it suggests a healthy degree of interoceptive accuracy.
- If it felt like a struggle to feel the heartbeat at all, it may indicate a disconnect from bodily signals.
- If the heartbeat was felt strongly and brought discomfort or anxiety, awareness may have been heightened yet dysregulated, with the brain rendering internal signals in a way that felt unsafe.

Wherever you fall, this feedback offers a valuable glimpse into how your nervous system perceives and interprets internal cues.

If You Feel Ready, Experiment

The next time your heart begins to race, pause. Slow your breath and notice the heartbeat again. See if you can sense it begin to steady. Even a fleeting moment of awareness can shift the body's trajectory and give you a sense of agency. These small experiments lay the groundwork for restoring regulation through the body.

Ground Truths

- Breath is shaped by emotion, but breath also shapes emotion.
- The body initiates an emotional response before the mind becomes aware of it.
- To keep you safe, the nervous system makes predictions based on past patterns – and it can react to those predictions rather than to the reality of the present.

Part II
Breath Resets

Chapter 6

Crossing the Threshold

From Recognising Patterns to Rewriting Your Response

In Part I, we traced the current of breath, seeing how it not only follows stress but binds to it, conditioning the body's memory of survival. Observation was the first step. Now comes the harder work of crossing into adaptation. Here, breath is no longer only a witness to old patterns; it becomes the medium through which we enter them again, feel their force and begin to rework them.

We will be using breath to recondition the patterns that shape how you meet effort, surprise and yourself.

From here, the chapters move us from insight into practice; from recognising the nervous system to deliberately re-patterning it. The work unfolds through five pillars. These five domains are most affected by chronic dysregulation and most open to the shaping influence of the breath:

- **Awareness:** Refining sensitivity to internal cues and softening the grip of automatic reactions.

- **Connection:** Sustaining presence in relationship with the body and others.
- **Sleep:** Restoring the cycles that allow repair, integration and reset.
- **Gut:** Supporting digestion, circulation and the two-way dialogue of the gut–brain axis.
- **Movement:** Aligning breath with stability, energy and adaptive posture.

These are not separate topics but interconnected dimensions of function, each shaped by breath. Elements such as interoception, emotional load and resilience move through them, linking one to another.

Part II offers a framework for reshaping how breath engages physiology, perception and behaviour – the level at which durable change becomes possible.

From Recognition to Relationship

When I was 12, my sister and I joined a day-long horse trail in the Australian outback. We spent hours riding steady-footed stock horses through red dirt country, cooking kangaroo over a fire and watching the horizon stretch beyond where words could reach. It felt like magic until we realised we were lost.

As the light faded, our guide admitted we'd wandered off course. The trail was gone, the star map no longer made sense. We had a choice: keep navigating by logic or trust the horses to lead us. Eventually, we dropped the reins. We let them follow terrain they knew better than we did. And they brought us home.

I return to that moment often, especially when I am working with breath. There are times in life that demand direction, structure and control. And there are times that call for something else: releasing the reins and trusting what the body already knows.

The first half of this book was about structure. Breath reflects the systems that condition you, your chemistry, your posture and your perception. You have learned to observe the breath and perhaps begun to sense its shifts, its absences and the way it mirrors stress. But observation is only the beginning. This chapter marks the turn from passive noticing to active retraining.

Now you will begin working with breath in real time, tracking how it responds under load, how it reflects internal states and how it shifts with the landscape of context and perception. Breath can be altered by will, yet it is retrained most deeply through sensation; by what is felt as much as what is done.

At the Edge of Reaction

In the instance of a trigger, the body can outpace thought, as though the response were already set. However, even in that rush there is a seam – a moment when sensation rises before it crystallises into reaction. Meeting that seam with breath allows the course to shift. Entering the body allows you to feel what stirs open space within the cascade. In that opening, physiology can turn, and behaviour with it.

A trigger is the moment where principle meets the body. The invitation is simple in form though never simple in practice – to pause inside the surge, notice what is moving in the body and allow sensation to register before the mind begins to assign meaning. This is the practice I return to with clients, and with myself, in the briefest moments that can tip a system into escalation if they are not caught.

The shift can be traced in physiology. In a trigger, vagal tone typically drops and the dialogue between body and brain changes. Signals surge upwards from below, cortical systems that lend perspective fall quiet and reaction arrives almost fully formed.

Sensation is the first link in a chain, stirring emotion, which colours thought and sets behaviour in motion. Here is how it unfolded for me in a recent moment.

My partner Josh woke up stressed about the mess in the kitchen. I understand this, mess can feel overwhelming – but when he walked into the room, his body language struck me like a hot flush, flooding me with discomfort. My first instinct was defence, the thought rising, 'Does he not see how much I already do?'

My body tensed, and before I realised it, I was scanning for the smallest shifts in his mood. The chain was already in motion: sensation registering as tension, emotion rising into anxiety, thought attaching the story, 'I must be under attack, he must be blaming me', and behaviour following on its heels.

I snapped, 'The mess is not my fault.'

The escalation was already underway, and I had snapped, convinced I was being blamed, when in truth he was simply overwhelmed. The threat existed only in the story my body had rushed to construct, and when I realised this in the moment, I softened, turned towards him and simply asked what was going on.

He exhaled, the weight spilling out of his breath, and admitted the pressure he was under. His stress was not about me, and by no longer defending against it as if it were, I could listen and make room for him, and in that room both of our systems found the ground again.

Breath Reset

When a trigger rises, use this reset to interrupt its momentum and return to presence.

Step 1: Pause

Take a single breath. Let it mark a pause before the mind rushes to interpret.

Step 2: Feel

Turn attention to sensation: the tightening across the chest, the breath becoming staccato, the shoulders subtly curling inwards and upwards. Simply notice without analysis. This widens the space between signal and story.

Step 3: Shift

Emotion is sensation with momentum. Feel it metamorphose as you stay with it. This is how the nervous system learns it has more than one path.

The pattern that once led automatically to reaction begins to loosen. As it loosens, another response becomes possible – one that unfolds more deliberately, with care.

With repetition, attention leads more readily into sensation, and response begins to shape itself at the level of reflex.

Chapter 7

Awareness

Before You Know, You Breathe

I was eight when I learned that being sick meant being different. With conjunctivitis, my eyes were swollen and tender, barely able to open through the thick, crusty film that clung to each lash. In the back of our 1992 Ford Laser, my mum tried to pry my puffy eyelids open. The sting of the eye drops made me flinch, and I screamed and squirmed in protest until a stranger peered in and asked, 'Is she okay?' I felt a smug satisfaction in my small defiance. A tiny revenge for the terror my mother was inflicting on me.

A week later, on Show and Tell day at school, someone brought in a teddy-bear-like puppy. As it bounded around the circle, I leaned back too far and plunged my hand straight into its food bowl, squishing the mush between my fingers. The smell of wet food clung to my skin, mingling with the faint scent of the puppy's fur. When it was my turn to share, I had nothing. Then my teacher, jokingly, said: 'Of course you don't, Junky-Vitis.'

I do not recall anyone laughing. Maybe it was just for her. But I was old enough for my cheeks to burn. My shoulders shrank inwards. My guts folded in on themselves, trying to disappear. I gripped the stupid dog bowl and stared down, throat constricted, belly taut. What I did not understand at the time (though what my body knew at once) was that feeling comes before analysis or rationalisation.

The Body Feels First

Awareness begins as a murmuration rising through the body's hidden infrastructure. The vagus nerve ferries a constant stream of chemical and mechanical messages, the insula stiches those fragments into a felt texture, and the anterior cingulate prepares the body to act before thought has arrived. By the time the prefrontal cortex forms an idea, the stage has already been set.

To notice this sequence is to encounter experience at its source. It is less a matter of constructing thoughts about the body than of inhabiting the raw data as it emerges, prior to narrative or belief. In that liminal space, awareness shows its true leverage: sensation is unyielding, while meaning (the brain's interpretation of it) can be revised, rewritten and renewed. The stories carried forward in consciousness are pliable, but beneath them runs the pulse of sensation as the bass note.

Awareness does more than reinterpret sensation; it can reshape the body's own decoding of sensation. A signal once registered as pain, as I have witnessed in those living with spinal cord injury, can, through new experience, be reclassified as tolerable and even safe. Staying close to what you feel and doing it often allows the body's language to grow more fluid, until even the raw alphabet of sensation can be redrafted into another tongue.

When the Nervous System Filters Reality

The reticular activating system (RAS) acts as a gate, deciding what is allowed through into awareness and what goes unnoticed. Its bias shifts with the body's state. When respiration moves in slow, measured cycles, the gate swings wider, admitting a broader field of perception where the world feels more spacious, nuanced and available. When breathing becomes rapid and irregular, the gate narrows. Subtle cues, such as vocal tone shifts, changes in body language or a pause between words are magnified, swelling out of proportion, while the wider scene recedes into shadow.

The same circuits that pace each breath are interlaced with chemistry, modulating the release of norepinephrine, a neuromodulator that heightens alertness. When breathing quickens, norepinephrine rises, sharpening vigilance and compressing the sense of time. In those moments, the contours of reality are warped by physiology itself. Breath sets the bias and the brain completes the story, sometimes even inventing a danger to match the signal it has already received.

When Awareness Breaks Down

Trauma not only alters the intensity of sensation but also bends perception at its roots. Predictive circuits begin to weight old signals more heavily than present ones, so the body responds less to what is happening and more to what has already happened. The insula and amygdala amplify this loop, drawing the past into the present until experience is filtered through a lens of memory. What appears to be overreaction is the nervous system rehashing history, replaying it through the immediacy of now.[1]

Clinical research underscores this point. In a randomised trial of trauma-informed yoga, Bessel van der Kolk and colleagues asked women with chronic post-traumatic stress disorder (PTSD) to practise simple postures and breathing while attending closely to bodily sensations.[2] Heightened bodily awareness enabled participants to detect subtle cues that signalled distress and to discern their emotions with greater accuracy. Just as importantly, the practice of noticing and tolerating these sensations, rather than turning away from them, improved emotional regulation and significantly reduced PTSD symptoms.

When the Familiar Is Not Safe

The nervous system is governed less by what is beneficial than by what has been repeatedly rehearsed. Familiarity, not goodness, is the gravity that holds everything in the nervous system in orbit. A body long accustomed to stress may find rest not soothing but dissonant, a state that feels unearned or unsteady, or somehow strangely hollow. Quiet can carry the flavour of what once followed it, and ease can feel more like an absence to be braced against than a presence to be welcomed. What is most practised becomes what is most trusted, even when it narrows possibilities or binds a person to the very patterns they long to outgrow.

For someone raised in volatility, the body learns that stillness precedes rupture, and so it continues to treat quiet as a prelude to disruption. In adulthood, the same nervous system may resist peaceful states, drawn back towards the textures of tension it has recognised as home.

Lasting change requires a careful reintroduction to the states the body has learned to mistrust, offered in doses small enough to be integrated. With each rehearsal, the unfamiliar begins to lose its edge and the nervous system gradually broadens the landscape it can inhabit with more ease.

The Breath as Feedback

Breath enters directly into the brain's loop of prediction, delivering streams of data from the body while simultaneously being shaped by what the brain expects to find. Prediction is continuous: the brain is always forecasting what sensation should feel like, then comparing these expectations with what arrives. If the input matches expectation, the loop confirms the old story. If the signal departs from expectation with enough force, the brain is compelled to revise its model; if not, the old story holds.

Respiration is one of the strongest drivers of this cycle. Chemoreceptors track shifts in carbon dioxide, sending signals that ripple upwards into perception, where they are translated as comfort, unease or urgency. When breathing continues in its familiar pattern, expectation and input reinforce each other – the breath carrying unease, which primes the brain for danger while the brain sharpens the breath's unease.

Practice can alter the raw data the brain relies upon. Subtle adjustments in breathing recalibrate the data that enters the system, tilting the baseline from which perception is composed. Breath is one of the strongest contributors to that bass note we mentioned earlier, the steady undercurrent of sensation beneath thought. With training, even that undertone can be tuned to another key.

The Window of Tolerance

Psychiatrist Dan Siegel coined the term 'window of tolerance' to describe the zone in which the nervous system remains balanced, flexible and responsive.[3] Within this range, you are able to meet challenges without losing presence: emotions rise and fall without overwhelming you, attention is steady and the body responds rather than reacts.

When pressure mounts beyond what the system can integrate, the window narrows and the nervous system tends to swing towards one of two poles: hyperarousal or hypoarousal. In hyperarousal, activation escalates – restlessness, agitation, vigilance and quick reactivity dominate. In hypoarousal, energy collapses, leaving you flat, numb, disconnected or shut down.

No one lives inside the window of tolerance at all times. The intention is to build capacity around it; to recognise where you are, to widen what can be tolerated and to move towards the edges, stretching and contracting, without losing yourself.

Breath Reset

The Window of Tolerance Diary

Awareness, at its most useful, means becoming attuned to your physiology, responses and rhythms as they unfold. This practice invites you to track your internal state across the day, so you begin to develop fluency in the signals your body is already sending.

How to Track Your State

Using a notebook, a journal or a visual graph, check in with yourself at least three times a day – morning, midday and evening. At each point, ask:

- *What was happening just before this check-in?* (Who was I around, where was I, what time was it, what did I eat?)
- *What do I notice in my body right now?* (Consider your breath, posture, muscule tone, temperature or internal sensations.)
- *How would I describe my emotional state?*
- *Which general state fits best?* (Am I in my window: regulated,

responsive, present? Am I hyperaroused: overactivated, tense, agitated? Am I hypoaroused: flat, disconnected, shut down?)
- *Did anything support a shift towards balance?* (Consider movement, rest, conversation, connection, quiet or breath.)

You can use colours or symbols if it's helpful, but this is not about making the diary look perfect. The goal is to make it real, trackable and honest. Over time, the act of tracking itself becomes a form of training: your window expands, your nervous system gains range and you start noticing triggers before they trip you up.

Chapter 8

Connection to Safety

When the Mind and Body Stop Communicating

Picture this: your mind and body are in couples therapy. The therapist leans forward and asks, 'When was the last time you two really felt each other?' Your mind stares blankly. Your body exhales audibly and mutters, 'Mind doesn't even notice me anymore.'

It is funny, but for many people, this is closer to reality than we'd like to admit. The mind and body go about like distant roommates, coexisting but completely out of sync. The brain is busy managing daily demands, while the body keeps signalling for attention, venting through nerve endings and muscle fibres, only to be met with radio silence.

Interoception is the bridge that brings them back into conversation. It is the foundation of any breath-informed reset, because you cannot heal what you cannot feel. When interoception is dulled, signals arrive muted and feelings blur or never quite register. Presence becomes effortful, because the very channels carrying sensation are faint. Re-establishing that line of communication is where integration begins.

Fluent in Psychology, Disconnected from Physiology

I recently worked with a client who was highly self-aware, health-conscious and immersed in personal development. One night, she found herself in bed with a tight chest, tingling down one arm and the looming fear that something was seriously wrong.

The next day, she went to the doctor, convinced she might be on the verge of a heart attack. After a few quick questions, he dismissed her: 'I think you are just anxious.' And because she clearly presented as someone invested in her own health and wellbeing, he leaned back into his chair, tilted his head to one side casually and added: 'But I think you already know that.'

Naturally, she was thrown. *Why would he say that? If I knew that, would I be here?* She did not *feel* anxious. She did not *identify* as an anxious person. Maybe just 'a little stressed'. There was a lot going on, after all, but she'd never zoomed out far enough to register just how much. Like the frog in slowly boiling water, unable to feel the rising heat until it is already overwhelmed, we simply cannot perceive our own internal environment when the baseline keeps shifting.

The doctor handed her a prescription for anti-anxiety medication. She was horrified, and that is what brought her to a mentorship with me. In our first session, we went through an assessment, and what I saw was a pattern I have come to recognise – especially in intelligent, self-aware people who spend a lot of time in self-development spaces. They are fluent in psychology but still disconnected from their physiology. Here's what I mean:

- Processing emotions mentally but not actually feeling them in their body.
- Overthinking the *why* instead of noticing *where* the sensation lives.

- Saying 'I guess I have a lot on' while insisting they are not that stressed.
- Skipping rest, over-exercising and normalising lack of sleep.
- Over-explaining feelings instead of sitting with them.
- Turning to self-help podcasts and talk therapy at the first sign of emotional discomfort.
- Knowing their trauma response inside out but still not honouring what their body needs in real time.

The more we worked together, the more I realised she could recite her trauma patterns like a textbook, even though she did not have a baseline capacity to feel safe inside her own skin.

Healing Is About Reconnecting

Autoimmune conditions arise when the immune system loses its tolerance for the body's own tissues. What should be recognised as *self* is flagged as *other*, setting off cascades of inflammation that damage the very structures they are meant to protect. Autoimmunity is, at its core, a failure of self-recognition – the body losing track of its own identity. Seen in this light, healing is a process of reorientation, a slow reteaching of the body to recognise itself.

In traditional medicine, a return to wholeness has always been the epicentre of healing. In yoga, health is both the absence of disease and a deep, unshakable connection to every part of who you are, from the seen to the unseen. As the Ancient Greeks said: 'Know thyself, and thou shalt know the universe and the gods.' They understood what modern science continues to validate: self-knowledge is not an end point, but the doorway through which all other relationships are entered.

Messages Left Unread

Every friendship group has that one indispensable friend; the one who plans the dinners, sets the table and actually invites people over to chortle, chat and connect. Yet in Western society's push towards hyper-individualism, disengagement is frequently reframed as emotional intelligence, and solitude becomes the sanctioned face of self-care, even when it masks a deeper disconnection. The indispensable friend is still at the table, waiting and wondering when opting out became the highest form of self-respect.

Now turn that metaphor inwards.

Your body is that friend, faithfully showing up, waiting for the others to arrive. Your mind slips out the back door to chase deadlines and your emotions linger as unopened messages. Your breath answers with the bare minimum, one-word, all caps 'OK'. Meanwhile, your nervous system keeps relaying signals, each one played out in the body but never fully brought into awareness. Biology does not stay quiet when ignored. Inflammation can break the surface as rashes, misfired signalling clouds into brain fog and autonomic storms erupt as panic attacks. The immune system lashes out in flare-ups and even the scaffolding of the body buckles as tasks that should feel manageable become crushing and legs give way, as mine did, beneath stress. What we call 'mystery symptoms' are often nothing mysterious at all, but the biology of neglect and the cost of messages left unanswered.

I did not reconnect with my body until I hit breaking point, when it was screaming through rashes and pins and needles. No doctor ever said, 'Your mind and body are out of sync. Let's work on that.' But for a breath specialist, that is exactly what needs tending.

If you have ever looked around and thought, *How on earth did I end up in this not-me life?*, the answer is not some cosmic mystery. It is right under your chin. When the mind–body connection fractures, the signals slip beneath awareness, holding back and gathering momentum until they can ram forward and break through.

Safety First

In any breath reset, establishing safety and grounding are the foundation. Awareness may bring you to the threshold, but without safety in the body, the nervous system cannot absorb or integrate new learning. This is Nervous System 101: state-dependent learning and conditioning. If your body does not register safety, your brain will not revise its patterns, no matter how many times you try to reframe your thoughts or 'choose calm'.

As they say in aeroplane safety briefings, 'Put your oxygen mask on first.' Safety is the condition that allows the brain to update; without it, old patterns hold. And safety is not universal. What settles one body may disturb another, which is why I do not claim to know how safety should feel or how sensations should be interpreted.

If a client says, 'I feel tight in my chest,' I do not jump to fix it. I get curious. I might ask, 'Can you tell me more about that?' Because their words matter.

Sometimes what they describe is mechanical – the diaphragm gripping, ribs compressing and drawing inwards. At other times, it speaks of chemistry or breathing behaviour – air hunger and a sense of never getting a satisfying breath. In those cases, I cannot know from words alone whether the driver is poor chemoreceptor tolerance or a conditioned sensitivity to the sensation of air hunger, but the language points me towards where to look. And sometimes the description carries the tone of anxiety, so that the constriction seems less physical than affective.

Each kind of description opens a different door, but none of them stand alone; mechanics, chemistry, behaviour and emotion are always woven together, and the language a person reaches for gives me a thread to follow. From there, I can assess more closely – mapping their breathing patterns, running assessments and tracking how those patterns are feeding into the physiology of stress.

For some people, though, the first foothold of safety has nothing to do with breath at all. Instead, it has to do with external environment, and you can imagine how difficult it is to practise breathing when you do not feel safe. Sometimes the trigger is a person, sometimes it is the unease that comes with aloneness and sometimes it is in the smallest details, like the lighting in the room, the angle of the blinds, the background soundscape and whether music is on or off.

If a person believes the man across the street is a peeping Tom, they will not feel safe lying down with their eyes closed. Whether he is simply a quiet neighbour minding his own business is irrelevant. What matters is not objective safety so much as perceived safety, and we must always meet people in the reality of what their nervous system registers rather than the abstract of what we think is true.

Yes, over time we can recondition these associations, working with the ingrained belief that 'I am not safe to relax'. External cues become the stage set for cultivating a felt sense of safety by providing the reliable context in which the brain can revise its predictions.

Breath Reset Preparation

Before beginning a formal practice, curate your space into a sanctuary of safety. Read a book in that same room, light a non-toxic candle, play music or lean into intentional silence and choose ambient cues that say, 'You are safe here.' Even the smallest details can help create safety in your environment.

The Titration of Stillness

Before we go deeper, it bears repeating: stillness does not always feel soothing. For many, it feels exposing, irritating or even threatening. The body has learned that stillness is when something breaks through, and sometimes that 'bad' thing is simply the flood of thoughts that arrive in silence. This can look like resistance to rest. Underneath, it is the raw sensation of being propelled to move: *Move. Now.*

So, the body complies. At 11pm you are on the treadmill or scrolling or cleaning or fidgeting; doing anything but sitting still. Motion has become paired with regulation, the state in which the conditioned self continues to know itself.

To recover from this state, exposure to stillness can be titrated – measured in teaspoons small enough to be tolerated, until the body trusts that stillness, too, can hold.

Tools for Creating Intrinsic Safety: Yoga Nidra and Non-Sleep Deep Rest

Yoga nidra and non-sleep deep rest sit at the centre of my own practice. Both reach deep into the circuitry between mind and body, altering the way stillness is registered.

The traditions diverge – with yoga nidra arising from yoga, and non-sleep deep rest framed through neuroscience and popularised by Dr Andrew Huberman – yet their effects converge. Both foster a stronger connection between mind and body, heightening interoception while easing sympathetic arousal and tilting the system towards parasympathetic recovery. In that shift, the space between sensation and reaction can widen, and sleep often improves in both quality and its ability to restore.[1] These states also touch cognition, with brief dips into non-REM activity that mirrors the slower brain-wave patterns of deep sleep and supports declarative learning and memory while deepening the body's sense of restoration.[2]

These practices build intrinsic safety – a sense born inside the system when the body knows it can rest.

In yoga nidra and non-sleep deep rest, brain activity drifts towards the slower frequencies of sleep while conscious awareness remains online. The nervous system enters patterns characteristic of deep restoration, yet awareness continues to register experience. It is a rare convergence: brain states of recovery and learning active at the same time as conscious perception. In that overlap, patterns of stress and meaning begin to reorganise, leaving behind a changed relationship to rest. For this reason, I place yoga nidra and non-sleep deep rest as the apex practices: what shifts in those liminal states continues long after the session ends.

What Is Yoga Nidra?

Yoga nidra is often referred to as 'yogic sleep', though it is not sleep in any ordinary sense. In the practice, the body lies still while awareness remains, directed inwards through a structured process that quiets the surface mind and opens access to deeper layers of experience.

Attention drifts through successive stages, from the obvious terrain of muscle and skin towards subtler strata: the breath, the images that surface, the traces of memory and the subconscious material that stirs beneath ordinary awareness. Different methods weave these elements in their own ways, but the intention is the same: to draw the mind steadily inwards until the boundary between what is conscious and what is concealed begins to thin. That permeability, more than rest alone, gives yoga nidra its particular potency.

In contemporary yoga teaching, it is often said that one hour of yoga nidra can restore the body as deeply as several hours of deep sleep,[3] a claim popularised by Swami Satyananda Saraswati in the 1970s and one that has since spurred scientific interest.[4] Electroencephalogram (EEG) research shows that yoga nidra induces a unique state of consciousness in which the brain remains awake while certain regions exhibit slow-wave activity,[5] a pattern sometimes referred to as 'local sleep'. In a recent controlled trial, four weeks of daily practice improved sleep efficiency, reduced wake-time after sleep onset by about 20 minutes and increased delta-wave activity during deep sleep.[6] So while yoga nidra is not a substitute for sleep, it can enhance sleep quality and often feels subjectively like deep rest.

The Patterns We Are Unwinding

In yogic philosophy, the deep impressions that shape our behaviours and beliefs are known as 'samskaras'. These live in the unconscious, silent yet powerful, and begin to shift when they are touched by awareness. Yoga nidra creates a bridge into these inner layers. In the unconscious, samskaras remain latent. In the subconscious, they are shifting and moving towards the surface. In the conscious mind, they can be seen, felt and, at times, released.

What emerges may be luminous or unsettling, but whatever takes shape is always an invitation to heal.

Modern science and non-sleep deep rest frameworks speak in different terms: 'implicit memories', 'conditioned responses' and 'entrenched neural pathways'. These terms describe how the repetition of thought, feeling or experience etches itself into the brain, shaping behaviour in ways that often remain unseen.

Though yoga nidra and non-sleep deep rest may overlap, their intentions are not quite the same. Non-sleep deep rest seeks recovery and recalibration, while yoga nidra reaches further. Its aim is not only to reshape habits but to expand awareness – to draw the subconscious and unconscious into dialogue with waking life; to foster insight and integration; and to open a path towards wholeness and spiritual fulfilment.

Where non-sleep deep rest restores, yoga nidra transforms. It offers not simply rest but a journey inwards – one that invites connection, harmony and the possibility of waking into a deeper dimension of being.

A Personal Vow

At the beginning and again at the end of yoga nidra, you may be invited to set a sankalpa – a vow spoken internally in clear, simple language. It is always present tense, brief and affirmative, voiced as though it is already true. The body can help anchor it, perhaps through the trace of a smile, the softening of the shoulders or any small gesture that makes the words tangible as they are spoken.

You do not need the Sanskrit. A sankalpa is simply a promise repeated until it weaves into the fabric of daily life. One of my teachers set the vow 'Every day, in every way, I feel better and better'. He even had us march around the room saying it aloud, the words circling until they sank beneath the surface and became believable. It still makes me smile and ... it worked! Repetition leaves its mark.

The secret is to choose one vow and stay with it. Six months, a year or even longer. The power comes from letting the words sink in, over and over, until they are no longer just spoken but lived.

Respecting the Tradition

Yoga nidra is an ancient practice with rich spiritual and philosophical roots. The form presented here is accessible and therapeutic, designed for nervous system re-patterning in modern life, yet its origins reach into traditions that explore kriya, subtle body practices, and states of oneness that are beyond the scope of this book. If you feel called, I encourage you to explore those traditions, too, guided by teachers who carry them forwards. In some lineages, the practice is pared back further, whereby no imagery is suggested, since even sound and symbol are thought to keep the mind tethered to objects. Here, awareness itself is the focus; resting without content.

Approaching the practice with humility, curiosity and respect ensures that when our own intention is primarily therapeutic, we remain open to the wider dimensions that yoga nidra, in its many forms, continues to reveal.

Breath Reset

Yoga Nidra

Ideally, practise for at least 20 minutes, three times per week, for significant nervous system benefits. If that feels challenging, begin with 10 minutes of mellow movement like gentle stretching or yoga-inspired movement to transition you into 10 minutes of yoga nidra. Gradually build up to 20 minutes or longer.

Step 1: Preparation

Lie comfortably on your back in a quiet space. Use pillows under your knees or head if that feels supportive. Allow your body to feel heavier and more supported by the ground beneath you, incrementally giving yourself over to gravity.

Close your eyes softly and take a few slow deep breaths through your nose, letting the exhale passively release. You are signalling to your system that a change in state is coming, inviting your body–mind to let go. Imagine you are closing all the open computer tabs in your brain and body, preparing yourself for a full reset.

Step 2: Your personal intention (sankalpa)

Choose a personal intention – a clear, positive statement that feels good to you right now, such as:

- 'I am resting deeply and healing fully.'
- 'Every day, in every way, I feel better and better.'
- 'My mind is clear and steady.'
- 'I am healthy and strong.'

Repeat your intention gently, three to five times, letting yourself truly feel its truth in your tissues.

Step 3: Rotation of awareness (body scan)

Begin the rotation of consciousness by letting awareness travel slowly through specific points in the body. At each point, linger for a moment before moving on, creating a lulling rhythm of attention unfolding. Remember, there is nothing to 'fix' or alter. Inhabit each place, feel it as it is, and then continue the journey.

Start at the centre of your forehead. Bring awareness to the right eyebrow ... the left eyebrow. Right eyelid ... left eyelid. Right eye ... left eye. Right cheek ... left cheek. The nose ... the upper lip ... the lower lip ... the chin.

Move to the hollow of the throat. Right collarbone ... left collarbone.

Right chest ... left chest ... the centre of the chest. The navel ... the lower abdomen. Right hip joint ... left hip joint.

Right thigh ... left thigh. Right ankle ... left ankle.

Now feel the whole body as one field of awareness, unified and at rest. As attention flows through these points, the senses begin to withdraw and the mind naturally settles, preparing for deeper exploration.

Step 4: Using imagery and sensations

As the mind relaxes into a hypnagogic state – that is, the threshold between waking and sleep that sits beneath the usual surface distractions – give your mind space for subtle or dreamlike images to appear. You are not making them happen; they may arise on their own. If your mind needs something to rest upon, you might conjure:

- gentle waves lapping at a quiet shoreline
- warm sunlight spreading through your body
- the sound of a flowing river or gentle rain
- a stream of white light entering through the crown of your head, flowing downwards to ease and brighten every cell.

Let these images come and go without forcing anything, simply allowing the mind to be lured more deeply inwards.

Step 5: Repeat your sankalpa

Mentally repeat your intention three times, reaffirming it clearly to yourself as your subconscious mind listens openly.

Step 6: Gradual return

Slowly become aware again of your body resting against the ground. Notice the sense of being supported and held.

Begin introducing tiny movements, perhaps tracing your thumbs against your finger pads or wiggling your toes. Visualise these movements first, then allow them to manifest softly in your body.

Stretch your arms overhead, inducing a full-body yawn if it feels good, opening your body into space.

Let your eyes flutter open, and when the moment feels right, sit up slowly. Stay in the afterglow long enough to notice what feels alive inside you – perhaps clarity, steadiness or quiet strength. The deeper measure of this practice is often revealed in the hours and days that follow.

What If Stillness Feels Hard?

If dropping straight into stillness feels difficult, know that is completely natural. When the body stops, sensations or restlessness often surface, and at first it feels easier to move than remain. Begin where you can, starting small (10 minutes is enough initially), and if it helps, start with a little gentle movement before settling down. Over time, your nervous system adapts; consistency is what makes the most profound difference.

The Threshold of Deep Rest

In your early experiences with yoga nidra or non-sleep deep rest, it is common to drift into sleep. That is natural, though once sleep takes over the practice itself is paused. With practice, however, you begin to remain aware even as the body slips into a sleep-like state. Classic yogic texts describe several layers within this inner landscape: the waking state, or jāgrat avastha; the dream state, or swapna avastha; the deep sleep state where awareness still rests intact, known as sushupti avastha; and turiya (literally 'the fourth'), which is pure consciousness that underlies and transcends the other three.[7]

In yoga nidra, practice often moves through waking into dream-like imagery (swapna), sometimes brushes against the stillness of sushupti, and ultimately gestures towards turiya. Many of us have touched these thresholds – they are there in the moment you 'wake up' inside a dream and recognise it as such, or the sudden drop felt just as you are falling asleep. These liminal spaces – half-in, half-out – are thresholds. When the body is still, the breath is quiet and the conscious mind is dissolved yet awareness remains, *that* is the state of yoga nidra.

This state reveals itself when awareness lingers in stillness and the nervous system feels safe to let go. Then the practice becomes less something you do than a state you enter – vast, unified and free.

Chapter 9

Connection to Context

The Feedback Loop in Motion

In a healthy connection, your mind and body are in constant conversation. This is a feedback loop designed to keep you balanced and responsive to life's demands. When signals flow smoothly, the body sends its messages, the mind interprets them, and together they shape a precise response to the moment. This loop runs both ways, each direction capable of creating order or disorder.

Bottom-Up Processing: When the Body Takes the Lead

You do not have to think *I am nervous* for your heart to start racing. You do not have to decide to sweat. The body moves first and the mind catches up later.

Picture yourself about to give a speech. When I was young, we were told to 'picture the audience nude' to help us relax. I am not sure it ever helped. What does happen, clothed or unclothed, is this: your heart pounds, your palms get moist and your mouth goes dry well before you have had a single conscious thought.

I recently bid at a house auction, and the same thing happened. I'd been rehearsing my 'deep pockets' look: fast bidding, no hesitation, paddle ping-pong, pursed lips. But then adrenaline staged its own performance. My pupils dilated. My body was still buzzing hours after the gavel fell, and sleep was impossible. That is bottom-up processing. The nervous system detects a potential threat, fires its signal to the brain and the brain assigns meaning. A pounding heart may be read as power or as danger. The meaning comes later; the body has already made the first move.

Top-Down Processing: When Thought Becomes Physiology

The brain cannot always distinguish between what is imagined and what is real; it responds to whatever it believes. Lying in bed, the house is silent around you, but your thoughts flicker into worry. *Did I leave the stove on? Did I reply to that email? Why am I not asleep?*

Even before you move, the body has shifted with the vague electricity of being on guard. Nothing in the room has changed, yet the whole system tilts, rerouting its energy as though summoned by some unseen signal.

The same anticipation seeps into movement. A coach calls out, 'This workout's going to be brutal,' and before the first set is begun, the body has already rearranged itself for load-bearing, with muscles primed, attention narrowed and energy diverted quietly into the tissues that will soon be called upon. This is anticipatory activation, a form of feedforward processing in which the brain prepares the body in advance.

Feedforward processing, in its proper rhythm, equips you to

anticipate and act. But when it turns inwards, rehearsing stress that never materialises, it becomes a loop of pre-emptive depletion, a body fatigued by futures that never arrive.

The Precision of Integration – Until It Falters

When the mind–body loop functions well, it demonstrates precision engineering: the body senses, the mind interprets and the body adjusts in kind. Yet this coordination is never assured.

Stress, trauma, injury, the slow erosion of purpose (*who am I?*) or the relentless conditioning of performance, especially in elite sports, can bend the loop out of shape, leaving the system overwhelmed and misaligned. What once moved with clarity now falters, the messages distorted, the body misread, until the conversation loses coherence and dissolves into noise, the way a clear signal might degrade into static.

The Biopsychosocial Divide

The mind–body connection is never only about thoughts and physical sensations – it is always braided with a third element, which is the environment around you. In modern psychiatry, George Engel named this 'the biopsychosocial model'; a framework that highlights how body, mind and the world continually shape one another.[1] The body (or 'bio') is home base, made of muscles, hormones, organs, asymmetries and quirks, the physical substrate that carries every experience. The mind (or 'psycho') processes thoughts, emotions and beliefs, sometimes with clarity and sometimes caught in a loop of overanalysis and self-doubt. The environment (or 'social') is the surrounding field of relationships and culture, architecture and climate, noise and light, daily stressors and supports, each exerting pressure that can recalibrate physiology towards resilience or reactivity.

These are woven through one another, each shaping and reshaping the rest. Disturb one part of the system and the whole structure wobbles, like a cafe table sitting upon uneven bricks.

This is why a morning argument can become a midday headache, and why the shadow of a looming deadline keeps the system wired long after night has fallen.

Yet just as stress compounds, so too does regulation. The patterns you practise are the ones your body learns to trust.

When you end a workout with slow breathing, the nervous system learns to pair exertion with release and strain with recovery. When you regularly drop into yoga nidra in the middle of a busy day, the body learns to move more reliably from high activation to deep rest, until recovery is no longer a privilege reserved for sleep but an expected rhythm of waking life.

What Your Body Learns While You Are Not Paying Attention

What you practise is never just the breath itself, but the internal and external conditions wrapped around it. Internal conditions are the body's physiology, blood gases, pH, autonomic tone and the breathing pattern at play. External conditions are the field around you, including light, sound, temperature, posture, timing, ritual and even the nervous system of the person guiding you. Breath is the linchpin here, continuously translating between the body's chemistry and its surroundings, and stamping both into the nervous system.

The Origin Story Gives Context: The Wim Hof Method

Ever wondered why women traditionally give birth lying flat on their backs? It is not because it is natural or particularly effective – it is partially because King Louis XIV wanted a good view. He insisted his mistresses deliver their babies on their backs so he could comfortably watch. The king's whim became the medical norm and stuck around, despite clear evidence that lying supine slows labour and increases discomfort and risks.

This shocking piece of trivia is a striking example of how power, culture and context shape practices, even those clearly at odds with our biology. The same goes for breathing techniques. Take the three-part breath that I mentioned briefly in chapter 1. Contrary to popular belief, it was not created by ancient yogis. It gained popularity during the Industrial Revolution when respiratory illnesses and collapsed chests were common, and expansive breathing became a symbol of vitality and survival.

And then there is Wim Hof's method, which began in the aftermath of personal tragedy. After his wife's death in 1995, Hof turned to intense breathing, long breath-holds and cold exposure. These practices were not gentle self-care rituals but urgent tools to pierce emotional numbness and recover a sense of being alive.

Origins matter, because internal states and external context profoundly shape how a breathing practice lands in the body. What feels vitalising and life-giving for one person may feel overwhelming or destabilising for another. To know a method's history is to understand its inherent tone, whether energising, grounding, transformative or demanding. That knowledge helps you ask, with clarity rather than imitation, 'Is this what I need right now? If so, how much and how often?'

My Personal Experience with the Wim Hof Method

I have personally explored aspects of the Wim Hof Method, though not through his full three-pillar approach. My cold exposure and ice bath practices typically included gentle cadence breathing, consistent with Wim's own guidance for calm breathing during immersion, rather than the rapid hyperventilation used in his breathing sessions.

My pranayama training, especially in practices like bhastrika, carries a superficial resemblance to Hof's technique – rapid breaths followed by retention – but the underlying intention and physiological effects diverge in important ways.

Here's a quick overview:

- **Pranayama** emphasises efficiency of breath. Even in vigorous forms like bhastrika, the practice is contained and deliberate, usually nasal and abdominal-diaphragmatic with use of the bandhas (the energetic locks we will come to later). Carbon dioxide levels do fall, but not to the extremes seen in the Wim Hof Method. The stillness that follows pranayama is cultivated through rhythmic cadence, inward-directed focus and awareness.

- **The Wim Hof Method** explicitly employs intentional hyperventilation (usually 20–30 rapid breaths per round) taken through the mouth or nose, sharply lowering carbon dioxide (hypocapnia) and enabling much longer breath-holds. This produces pronounced hypoxia (low oxygen), which has been shown to temporarily reduce inflammation, enhance immune responses and lift mood.[2] In one pilot study of athletes, blood oxygen saturation fell as low as 45–60 per cent by the third round of Wim Hof breathing.[3] This drop mirrors what has long been recognised in freediving physiology, where suppressed carbon dioxide signals allow oxygen to plunge to blackout levels before the urge to breathe is felt.

Understanding these differences clarifies why each practice can be powerful, but with distinct thresholds for safety and benefit, and with after-effects that shape how your system responds in the hours, days and even weeks that follow.

Short-Term Gain, Long-Term Strain?

Significant hyperventilation, as practised in the Wim Hof Method, sharply reduces carbon dioxide levels and triggers cerebral vasoconstriction (blood vessels in the brain narrowing). This limits oxygen delivery despite high blood oxygen, and can produce dizziness, fainting or cognitive fog.[4] Managed hypoxia – when oxygen saturation falls after a prolonged exhale hold – has been shown to produce short-term physiological effects, including marked sympathetic activation and anti-inflammatory changes in controlled settings.[5] Repeated bouts of intense hyperventilation do more than create transient shifts – they recalibrate ventilatory control and chemoreflex responsiveness, tuning how the brain and body respond to changes in carbon dioxide and oxygen. These mechanisms are well described in respiratory physiology and are also discussed in the literature on dysfunctional breathing.[6]

From a yogic perspective, rapid breathing techniques – whether Wim Hof's or bhastrika pranayama – were designed as targeted interventions, not daily routines. The tradition understood that the fire needed a container. To enjoy Wim Hof's immediate lift in mood and resilience safely and sustainably, it is best followed with slower, subtler practices such as cadence breathing, gentler pranayama or air hunger practices to restore blood gases to a healthy baseline and support long-term nervous system resilience.

Rachel's Story: From Wim Hof to Functional Breath Retraining

Rachel, a yoga teacher in Australia, spent 18 months devoutly practising the Wim Hof Method. She described it as a kind of 'circuit breaker' – yet on days without practice, the same background anxiety quickly returned.

When Rachel and I began working together, we stopped her daily Wim Hof practice and replaced it with gentle cadence breathing, progressing from inhaling for three counts and exhaling for six, eventually extending to four and eight counts. Without making other significant changes right away, her nervous system began shifting to move with greater ease between activated and calmer states across the day, reflected in longer restorative periods on her Oura Ring (a wearable device that measures sleep and recovery). At the time, she was solo parenting her son and recovering from a lengthy illness.

Rachel described the shift beautifully:

As a yoga teacher, I always struggled with the identity conflict that I should be able to easily regulate myself, but couldn't. After just eight weeks, I can hardly remember how it felt when my ribs were stuck tight, and I struggled to breathe even while consciously trying to relax. It really made me realise how crucial it is to match the right practice to the right state. Understanding context and practising in small doses has been truly life-changing, giving me genuine confidence, reassurance and resilience. My nervous system is finally experiencing true calm.

Rachel's story shows that transformation is not about doing more, but about choosing the right practice to meet an individual's specific needs and context. Daily Wim Hof gave her bursts of relief, but it was the subtler cadence breathing and functional retraining that shifted her baseline, building a nervous system that could regulate itself rather than leaning on continual intervention.

Foot in the Door or Fuel on the Fire?

There is no doubt that 30 hard-and-fast mouth breaths have a powerful effect. For some, it provides exactly the jolt they need: a surge of adrenaline, dopamine, serotonin and the body's own opioids floods the system, clearing brain fog, sharpening focus and creating a profound sense of release. In one landmark study, trained participants injected with endotoxin (which can cause a strong immune response) showed reduced inflammation and reported fewer flu-like symptoms under controlled conditions.[7]

Mindset shapes the outcome, too. In Wim Hof Method trials, participants who expected to feel better mounted stronger anti-inflammatory responses and higher adrenaline surges.

This practice can be transformative; nowhere more so than in states of numbness, when the nervous system has folded inwards and emotional range feels out of reach. The sympathetic surge jolts the body into movement, breaking through stagnation and returning colour to what had dulled. For people physiologically trapped in that freeze, breathwork of this kind can act as a lifeline, melting the ice and cracking open the door to recovery.

For those who are chronically stressed, adding more stimulation (more breath, intensity and adrenaline) risks reinforcing the very pattern they are trying to escape. The so-called Type A achievers – shorthand for high-drive people with a restless nervous system – may feel the method working because it mirrors their baseline, turning stress into something that masquerades as productivity. Over time, intensity can become a dependency: the high mistaken for transcendence and the adrenaline surge misread as wellness.

Chasing States: Why We Need Integration, Not Addiction

I never tried the Wim Hof Method during the peak of my law career, but I can imagine craving that immediate state shift and relief from relentless stress. At one point, I stayed in an ice bath so long I ended up with chilblains. It was a stark reminder of how quickly intensity can slip into compulsion. Experiences like high ventilation breathwork or extreme cold exposure can foster dependency because they create temporary states we long for but cannot sustain without external support.

This is not traditional addiction but a subtler, attachment-based dependency. People return to breathwork events built around high ventilation because they reliably deliver the charged states they crave. Without integration through grounded sleep, functional breathing patterns and a regulated nervous system, these experiences risk reinforcing dependence rather than building resilience.

The difficulty is that this dependency often feels familiar, and familiarity easily masquerades as safety. For someone accustomed to operating at high speed, breathwork that accelerates the system feels like home. The nervous system translates arousal into productivity, control and even healing, but the pattern being rehearsed is the same one that needs disrupting.

The deeper question is what your breathwork is actually teaching your nervous system. Is it cultivating long-term resilience or subtly creating dependency? Or is it binding you to a new form of dependency and attachment disguised as healing?

Is the Wim Hof Method Good or Bad?

People often ask me, 'Is the Wim Hof Method good or bad?' My honest answer is always, 'It depends.' Specifically, it depends on the state your nervous system is in when you practise.

No breathing method is inherently good or bad – what matters is what it reinforces. The more useful question is to ask both what state you are in when you practise and what your nervous system is wiring into that state. Are you practising from a sense of safety, empowerment and capability, or from a place of being pushed, flooded and merely enduring?

The aim of breathwork is not to elevate one method above the rest, but to cultivate a nervous system flexible enough to move between states without relying on intensity to feel alive. What we are training is flexibility expressed as range and adaptability rather than tolerance alone.

State-Dependent Learning and Breathwork Addiction

Neuroscience helps explain why the state you are in makes all the difference. State-dependent learning shows that experiences are encoded in relation to the nervous system state present when they occur – that is, what the body feels and what the brain tags alongside it. Practices like rapid breathwork or cold exposure unleash potent neurochemistry including dopamine, adrenaline, serotonin and beta-endorphins, the body's natural opioids.

Beta-endorphins generate a rewarding surge, easing pain while amplifying pleasure. Over time, the brain learns that rapid breathing or intense cold reliably deliver this euphoric state, creating a pull to return again and again. This is not a chemical addiction in the classical sense, but a subtler form of emotional dependency.

If your baseline state is chronically overstimulated, practices that amplify the reward pathways may only strengthen those patterns. The deeper question is what the nervous system is learning each time you return to that state, even when it feels good.

Integration means choosing practices that instil adaptability, so resilience becomes embodied rather than borrowed from intensity.

The Science of Expectation

Psychoneuroimmunology (a long word for a simple idea) studies how thoughts, emotions and expectations shape immunity and nervous system function. It shows that belief is not fluff but a physiological amplifier. Research has found that optimism can boost anti-inflammatory signals in the bloodstream,[8] while negative expectation can provoke symptoms even in the absence of cause, known as the 'nocebo' effect (placebo's darker twin).[9] Ritual, emotional meaning and trust in a practitioner also heighten outcomes, amplifying the very processes that bring about change.

This pattern is visible in research on the Wim Hof Method. As described earlier, the landmark endotoxin trial showed that people trained in the method mounted a strong immune response.[10] Those effects persisted even when Hof himself was absent, ruling out the idea that his presence or charisma produced the effect, and confirming that the method itself, once learned, drove physiological changes. A later brain imaging study added another layer: expectancy and belief activated brain networks involved in pain relief, interoception and autonomic control.[11]

Together, these findings suggest that physiology is real and reproducible, but the meaning and expectation you bring to practice shape its power. Belief, when paired with embodied action, becomes a signal to your nervous system: 'Get ready for something good.'

Context Conditions the Body

Expectation is not the only amplifier – the neurobehavioural dimension is just as decisive. Breath bends to its surroundings, taking shape not only from what is happening inside the body but from the climate its practised in. The temperature of the room, the ambiance of the lighting, the music that drops you in or brings you out, the posture you hold and the nervous system of the person guiding you; even the collective energy in the room. Cold exposure can feel like torture when the body is braced against it, but the same cold, recast as a chosen challenge, shifts the entire hormonal response, transmuting punishment into resilience. A vow in yoga nidra works in the same way – a ritual gesture that seals the practice into memory like wax pressed with a signet. These cues, subtle as they may seem, leave their mark. You are never simply doing a technique; you are training the associations your nervous system will carry forward. What you pair together, you wire together.

How You Feel Shapes What You See

The nervous system does not reveal the world as it is – it reveals the world as your body feels it to be. When the system collapses into hypoarousal, the signals that normally rise from the body – such as the variability of the heartbeat, the shifting rhythms of breath and the subtle feedback from the gut – begin to thin out, as though the channels of interoception have narrowed to a trickle. In that muted state, the brain's internal map loses contour and colour, and the texture of experience flattens: decisions blur, emotions grow indistinct and even the passage of time feels distant or diluted. Life continues to unfold, yet you may feel as if you are scrambling through it in slow motion, or else watching from behind a pane of glass.

Breath can act as a portal to redraw the map in real time. Many of the breath resets you will meet in this book are designed to increase vagal tone, restore pliancy to the oscillations of the heart and send upwards the unmistakable messages of safety on which clarity depends. Other practices work by a very different mechanism. The more forceful techniques amplify sensation until numbness is interrupted, sometimes as a jolt that drives awareness back into the body, or sometimes as a wave so strong it risks sweeping awareness away altogether. This is why some people report intensity as a lifeline or a shock that reawakens presence, while others experience the very same practice as a dissociating slide further away from themselves. The difference is not simply 'wired' versus 'numb'; it lies in the histories we carry, the stories that shape our perception and the meaning we assign to the return of feeling.

The Wim Hof Method was not born as a clinical protocol but shaped in part by loss, layered onto a life already devoted to testing human limits through extreme feats of endurance. Hof turned to breath, to cold and to sheer will as a way of reclaiming his vitality. These practices later carried into world-record performances that captured global attention. For someone collapsed into absence, such intensity may become the spark that restores presence – but for someone already stretched thin by anxiety, the same force may aggravate fragility, stripping away the very drive required to recover. None of this is black and white. The fulcrum is always the same, whether the system returns to regulation afterwards or learns to come home to another state. Each practice leaves a trace and, over time, traces accumulate into a baseline. The state you return to again and again becomes the bedrock on which the story of breath inscribes itself deeper into the body.

Repetition and Reflection

Research using functional magnetic resonance imaging (fMRI) has shown that during extreme cold exposure, Wim Hof shows heightened activity in the periaqueductal gray, a midbrain region involved in pain suppression, defensive responses and altered states of consciousness, which is also active in dissociative states such as analgesia and trauma-related shutdown.[12]

In other words, Hof's ability to override discomfort may share neural pathways with dissociative coping.[13] That does not invalidate his method, it simply frames the kind of adaptation it reflects and what that might mean for those who take it up.

I am often asked if I teach the Wim Hof Method, or people assume that because I teach breathwork, I must use it. It is arguably the most widely recognised breathwork practice today, though conscious connected breathing and rebirthing breathwork are quickly gaining ground. For those who practise the Wim Hof Method, the effects are tangible.

Yet attachment always signals something deeper at play. Techniques like the Wim Hof Method are undeniably powerful, but they are also popular, commercialised and deeply personal. Once a practice becomes entwined with identity, it becomes more difficult to step back and ask what it is actually reinforcing.

The issue is not that intense breathwork has no place – far from it. For the right person at the right time, it can be profoundly life-changing.

However, state and context matter. If you consistently pair high-intensity breathwork with equally intense mornings, your system may learn to rely on stimulation to find familiarity, associate regulation with effort, and learn to access calm only on the other side of intensity.

That is not inherently wrong, but neither is it neutral. This is the subtlety of state-dependent learning: your breath becomes both a bridge and a blueprint. A morning routine can reinforce physiological patterns just as powerfully as a trauma response. The aim is not to abandon breathwork but to keep asking whether your efforts are helping you access a broader range of states fluidly.

Breathwork is most powerful when it enlarges your capacity to feel, to regulate and to rest without drama. Connection does not always enter through the doorway of intensity. Sometimes, it emerges from softness and subtlety; the breath that arises unbidden arises when your nervous system no longer needs convincing that it is safe.

Breath Reset Reflection

You have just explored how breathwork interacts with state, context, identity and the stories your nervous system tells itself about what is safe, what is familiar and what is needed. Before you move on, take a moment to pause and ask:

- *What state do I tend to reinforce through my current chosen practices?*
- *Is my current state helping me expand or keeping me in a loop that once served me but no longer fits?*
- *What is my body learning from this pattern?*
- *Can I allow safety without needing to earn it through intensity?*

Chapter 10

Connection to Real Life

Training Your Breath Where It Counts – In the Messy Middle of Real Life

Breath is a teacher, and the body is always listening. This chapter is about carrying that lesson into the unpredictable theatre of daily life, where pressure and wonder intermingle, and where resilience is not cultivated in retreat or in rehearsal but in the immediacy of experience itself – in the thick, shifting currents of real life.

Why the Brain Clings to Stress Like Velcro

The body is always reaching for balance, adjusting blood gases, temperature and blood pressure from moment to moment in the ceaseless pursuit of homeostasis. Yet the brain does more than record those shifts – it predicts them.[1] The brain prefers patterns it has seen before because predictability itself feels reassuring. A system may be strained or even corrosive, but if the strain feels familiar then the brain will still claim it as safe.

This is how cycles of hyperarousal take root. The physiological cost may be high, but the pattern is recognisable and the nervous system confuses recognition with stability. Dysregulation can wear the mask of equilibrium – a familiar set point the brain comes to accept even when true balance is absent.

Older traditions grasped this intuitively, and today's research echoes it: the nervous system leans towards what it already knows, even when what it knows erodes the health of the nervous system.

Most of this training happens beneath awareness. Breath shapes itself to posture, to mood, to environment – shortened at a desk, hurried in social situations or conflict, restless late at night – until the rhythm fixes itself as automatic. Over time, breath grows subtly effortful, each one as if dragged from a body already under effort, like paddling against a current that never yields. The labour is small but relentless, and the body pays for it in energy it never gets back.

Those repetitions do not just tax the muscles of breathing; they ripple upwards, reinforcing vigilance in the nervous system and carving deep tracks in the brain's default networks.[2] Like channels carved into sand by the outgoing tide, these patterns are easy to slip into, even when they carry the body away from balance. Breath retraining opens the possibility of another route, each repetition cutting a new line through the sand until ease becomes the path of least resistance.

Why Training Breath in Real-World Conditions Matters

The gap between a beginner surfer and an experienced one is not strength but perception. The novice paddles blindly into the break, arms burning as the waves toss them under, board slipping away with every roll. The seasoned surfer waits, studies the current conditions and chooses the right moment. Once they are out the back and a wave comes, they sit in the right spot and with two strokes they are picked up cleanly, conserving energy for the ride.

Athletes train the same way. They know a skill must hold under pressure or it does not hold at all. Basketball players rehearse buzzer-beaters with the clock counting down. Sprinters drill their starts to the crack of a gun. Boxers spar in timed rounds that mirror a fight. Gymnasts perform entire routines with music, judges and distractions until the routine survives any potential chaos. Mastery is never just technical; it is mastery under fatigue, noise and urgency.

The nervous system learns breath in context, linking the breathing pattern of response to that level of arousal and calling it back when the same state arises again. Breathing responses learned in moments of strain are stored within that state, and they surface again whenever the body enters it. Slow, steady breathing in a quiet studio has its place, but it does not prepare you for the text message that makes your stomach drop, the slammed door in an argument or the glance that sends you spiralling.

Two principles explain why: exposure and active inference. Exposure means deliberately recreating the internal states and the external pressures that tend to unseat you, and staying with them long enough for something new to be rehearsed.[3] Active inference describes what happens when that rehearsal produces a surprise.

The brain is a prediction machine, continually forecasting what the body will feel next. When the body answers differently, the forecast falters. That mismatch captures the brain's attention, and if safety is present, the system begins to update.[4]

What is Bhastrika?

Any breathing practice can, in theory, work with prediction, sensation and exposure, because every alteration in breathing, whether in depth, pace, pathway or pressure, gives the brain a new signal to compare with its forecast. Bhastrika pranayama is a striking example, not because ancient yogis set out to run experiments in predictive coding, but because the practice they developed for entirely different aims (such as moving lifeforce energy, burning through distraction and preparing for meditation) also generates the very sensations modern science associates with prediction error, including dizziness, tingling, warmth and breathlessness.[5] In fact, modern studies show that bhastrika alters blood flow to the brain, underscoring just how powerfully these practices shift physiology.[6] In this sense, bhastrika sits at the crossroads of tradition and neuroscience, illustrating how different frameworks can point to the same embodied truths.

In practice, bhastrika pranayama (Sanskrit for 'bellows breath') is a vigorous technique named after the pumping air that feeds a blacksmith's fire. Each cycle is powered by a sharp abdominal contraction that drives the air out, followed by a deliberate expansion to draw it back in. Inhalation and exhalation are equal in length and pace, producing breaths that are both deeper and faster than those of ordinary breathing. Traditionally, the practice was repeated until fatigue set in, followed by prolonged retention with bandhas, intended to circulate prana and open a space in which the mind could steep itself in meditation.

Similar patterns surface in modern freediving and methods like Wim Hof's, where rapid breathing can be used to offload carbon dioxide and extend the capacity for holding the breath.

This adapted version in the Breath Reset at the end of this section omits the traditional breath retention and instead uses bhastrika as a way to evoke the sensations we often associate with hyperventilation or panic. Encountered briefly and with intention, this practice stirs mild ripples throughout the system, a light buzz across the skin, warmth rising in the chest and a faint shimmer of breathlessness – the nervous system switches into a higher gear for a moment before settling back into steadiness. These sensations become a form of exposure. The nervous system is given a chance to reduce fear of its own internal signals, to update its predictions so that they no longer read as danger but as temporary states, and to gradually build resilience and accuracy in how those signals are interpreted. Over time, this shift can lessen anxiety and expand tolerance for the body's natural variability.

Because bhastrika relies on rapid, intentional abdominal movements, the diaphragm may fatigue quickly, especially in those with weaker diaphragmatic strength or pre-existing dysfunctional breathing such as chronic hyperventilation. When this happens, people often compensate by lifting the shoulders, neck or upper chest. However, these are accessory muscles that, over time, can reinforce the patterns of inefficiency that the practice is meant to disrupt. For that reason, bhastrika is best approached with discernment, particularly if your breathing mechanics are already compromised.

Without the traditional breath-holds, risks related to pressure build-up and prolonged shifts in oxygen or carbon dioxide are significantly reduced. Still, the practice is not suited to everyone. Those with high blood pressure or cardiovascular disease should keep it short and gentle. For people with epilepsy, vertigo or balance disorders, rapid breathing may worsen symptoms and is best avoided.

For most, brief exposure to bhastrika without breath retention carries minimal risk. If you live with specific health conditions, it is best to seek guidance before beginning. The practice should be avoided in the middle of panic or when you feel unprepared. Sensations usually settle with rest, but if they escalate into chest pain, faintness or distress that does not ease, then this is not the right practice for you. For those who live with anxiety or chronic over-breathing, bhastrika can be therapeutic exposure, but it should only be entered from a calm baseline, beginning with very short rounds that are extended gradually as tolerance grows.

Breath Reset

Brief Bhastrika as Interoceptive Exposure

Step 1: Set-up

Sit comfortably with your spine upright but relaxed, feet grounded or legs crossed. Keep your mouth closed so the breath moves rapidly through your nose. Inhalation and exhalation are equal in length: the belly expands during inhalation and contracts on exhalation.

Step 2: Practice (60 seconds)

Contract the abdomen sharply on each exhalation, expelling air through the nose. Allow the abdomen to expand immediately on inhalation, drawing the air back in. Continue this rhythmic, equal-length pattern for one minute at a pace that feels sustainable. Mild sensations such as tingling, warmth, or light-headedness are expected and intentional in this adapted form.

Step 3: Recovery and integration (2–3 minutes)

After one minute, stop. Return to slow, gentle nasal breathing. Notice the sensations as they fade. If grounding is needed, rest a hand on your chest or abdomen.

Step 4: Reflection

Stay with the sensations that remain. Remind yourself: *These sensations are temporary shifts in chemistry, safe to encounter when the ground beneath me is steady. I am creating new associations with these signals.*

Progressive Hypocapnic Exposure

After the body has grown used to the lighter shifts of brief bhastrika, the practice can be carried further into progressive hypocapnic exposure, where the same chemistry is sustained for longer and the sensations gather more force. The breath is opened through the mouth, drawn in and released in a looping rhythm that steadily lowers carbon dioxide. Even within a single minute of this practice, the body begins to answer more strongly. Here the sensations take on a sharper edge, closer to the sensations the body often mistakes for panic, including breathlessness tightening more insistently, a rush in the head, skin prickling with greater intensity and the heartbeat thudding more loudly than usual. Held safely and deliberately, these sensations become an opportunity to meet what once felt unmanageable.

In ordinary life, these signals often pull the system into panic. However, when they are summoned intentionally and contained with steadiness, the nervous system begins to read them differently. The brain expects danger and when collapse does not follow the forecast falters. This is active inference in motion. The mismatch between what was expected and what unfolds becomes the ground for new learning. Each repetition adds weight to the evidence until the same sensations no longer drag the body underwater but pass like swells that can be ridden and released.

With practice repeated over time, the internal tide shifts. The racing of the heart feels less like an alarm and more like the pull of water moving with unusual force. The lightness in the head becomes a brief unmooring rather than a threat of capsizing. The tingling across the skin is recognised as a transient change in circulation, no more dangerous than the foam at the crest of a wave. Some sensations soften quickly, others linger, but together they widen the range of experience the body can inhabit without fracture, expanding its capacity to move with stronger currents and return intact.

This work belongs in moments when the baseline is steady and curiosity is alive. It is not suited to hearts or lungs under strain without the guidance of a professional. Entered with care, it becomes a place to meet stronger waves without being swept away, where each return strengthens the quiet confidence that the body can dive deeper and surface again, carried by the same breath that once seemed to overwhelm it.

Do not use this practice if:

- you are currently highly anxious, panicked or feeling overwhelmed
- you have severe heart or lung conditions (unless medically cleared)
- you are emotionally unprepared or feeling dysregulated
- you are unclear about which sensations trigger your anxiety or panic.

Breath Reset

Progressive Hypocapnic Exposure (Intentional Over-Breathing)

Step 1: Set-up

Sit comfortably with your spine relaxed but upright, feet grounded or legs crossed. Open your mouth and breathe fully into your abdomen in a smooth, continuous rhythm. Eliminate pauses between inhalation and exhalation so the breath feels like a flowing loop. This depth and continuity lower carbon dioxide and intentionally bring on the sensations of light-headedness, tingling, warmth or mild breathlessness.

Step 2: Practice (60 seconds)

Maintain this rhythm for about a minute. Notice sensations as they arise. Stay present and curious, feeling them fully.

Step 3: Recovery and integration (2–3 minutes)

Close your mouth and return to slow, soft nasal breathing. Allow sensations to fade. If grounding helps, rest a hand on your chest or belly.

Step 4: Reflection

Acknowledge that these sensations were created intentionally and do not signal danger. Remind yourself: *These sensations are safe, temporary and within my capacity to handle.*

High-Ventilation Breathwork: Stress on Purpose (Hormetic Stress)

Everyday stress finds you, whereas high-ventilation breathwork calls it in deliberately. Practices such as holotropic breathwork, the Wim Hof Method and conscious connected breathing differ in lineage and intention, yet each works through the same lever: you breathe far beyond the body's metabolic need.

The same cascade you have already met unfolds here but is sustained for longer. Carbon dioxide falls below demand, cerebral blood flow narrows, the brain moves into relative hypoxia (low oxygen) and sympathetic activity surges with noradrenaline release.[7] Some studies suggest this shift heightens gamma-band oscillations, which are rhythms linked with integrating sensory input and updating the brain's predictions.[8]

Physiologically, hyperventilation creates shifts that can be framed as compensatory, as the body works to defend blood pH and rebalance gases. Experientially, however, it is not felt as quiet correction but as immersion, with skin buzzing, balance tilting, perception distorting and emotions breaking loose in unexpected waves. For some, this arrives as insight or release. For others, it tips into dissociation or even a sense of identity dissolving. The chemistry is constant, but the meaning of the experience is shaped by the frame that holds it.

Clinically, therapists sometimes use brief voluntary hyperventilation as interoceptive exposure, reproducing panic physiology so patients can reframe their response. Neuroscience calls it the 'hypocapnic challenge' or 'hyperventilation provocation', in which carbon dioxide is deliberately lowered through fast breathing, symptoms are provoked, and the system is observed.[9] In the lab, these exposures usually last a minute or two under supervision, whereas in breathwork circles they may extend to an hour, stretching the same chemistry across a far greater timeframe.

Prolonged practice brings further risks. Sustained alkalosis alters blood gases, electrolyte balance shifts, and the system produces muscle cramps, faintness or (in rare cases) seizures. These are the reasons medical protocols are brief and supervised, and why readiness matters, testing for stable heart rate variability, consistent restorative sleep, easeful nasal breathing at rest, and simple breath tests that reflect tolerance. With those foundations in place, the body is more likely to absorb the stress as hormetic challenge rather than collapse.[10]

Physiologically, high-ventilation breathwork unfolds in two arcs. The first is the surge with sympathetic drive climbing, heart racing and energy pouring through the tissues. The second is a return as parasympathetic tone rises, stress perception eases and clarity breaks through like the sky reappearing after a storm.[11] Studies suggest that in careful hands these practices can reduce rumination, ease depressive symptoms and support regulation, though the research is still in its early stages.[12]

For those already living with chronic over-breathing, in states of panic, anxiety or trauma, adding intensity can reinforce the very pattern it seeks to loosen. Functional breathing is the foundation, and only once that ground is steady does it make sense to treat breathwork like a sprint – something you do occasionally and deliberately, and always with a clear way back to baseline.

Kapalabhati

In the older yogic texts, kapalabhati (literally 'skull-shining breath') was not filed under pranayama at all, but under kriya – a cleansing act. The descriptions were strikingly physiological: clearing impurities, stimulating digestion and peristalsis (gut motility), strengthening the diaphragm and abdominal core and generating inner heat to stoke the metabolic fire. These effects were offered as essential purifications, preparing the body and mind for deeper pranayama.

To modern eyes, kapalabhati looks deceptively simple. A dynamic hug of the abdomen drives the air out, followed by a soft rebound that draws it in. Fifty pulses, sometimes more, each one forceful on the exhalation and passive on the inhalation. Within moments, warmth rises, the diaphragm tires, and the body tingles with an energetic current.

Physiologically, it lies on the same spectrum you have just walked through with bhastrika and other high-ventilation practices. Rapid cycles of breathing tug carbon dioxide lower, especially when tidal volume rises, and the sensations emerge in familiar ways. However, there is nuance. Traditional teachers argued that much of the air in kapalabhati moves only through the anatomical 'dead space' of the nose, mouth and bronchi, rather than drawing fully into the lungs. In that reading, blood gas chemistry is disturbed less than in other rapid-breathing techniques. If the diaphragm is strong and engaged, the practice may stay closer to its classical description. If not, accessory muscles take over and chemistry can swing further than intended.[13]

In the classical form, kapalabhati was followed by bahya kumbhaka – a retention after the inhalation, often sealed with the bandhas. In this adaptation, the pause comes after an exhale. The shift is small yet significant, with the breath held on empty, lowering intrathoracic pressure and easing strain on the vessels, as carbon dioxide rises just enough to stir the sense air hunger. With repetition, the chemistry continues to lean towards hyperventilation, the body replaying, with shimmer and hum, a pulse that can bring clarity yet can also press at the edge of tolerance.

Why practise this now, in a world of late-night streaming and endless scrolling? Not for Himalayan enlightenment, but for what the sensations can teach us. Entered with readiness (meaning a steady baseline breathing, good diaphragmatic strength and solid sleep and recovery in place), the practice becomes a contained stressor – a hormetic flicker the nervous system can absorb as training.

Still, it is not for every body in every moment. If blood pressure runs high, if the eyes and brain are vulnerable, if the gut is inflamed or anxiety is already threatening to spill over, kapalabhati can amplify strain rather than ease it. Gentler practices may lay better foundations.

Approached with steadiness, this practice is less about 'skull-shining' than about finding clarity in the everyday sense: a wakefulness that comes from a body briefly stirred and then steadied again, edges sharpened, currents running a littler cleaner and the breath reclaiming its role as both cleanser and teacher.

Avoid this practice if you have:

- high blood pressure or cardiovascular disease
- history of stroke or brain tumours
- vertigo, dizziness or balance disorders
- glaucoma or elevated intraocular pressure
- stomach or intestinal ulcers, gastro-oesophageal reflux disease (GORD/GERD), gastritis, diarrhoea or inflammatory gastrointestinal conditions
- chronic systemic inflammation or autoimmune conditions
- chronic hyperventilation or severe anxiety (introduce gradually and only when baseline breathing is steady).

Breath Reset

Kapalabhati with Exhale Suspension

Step 1: Set-up

Sit comfortably with your spine upright, chin slightly drawn in, the back of the skull long and lifted. Stay relaxed in your body, with your gaze soft. Take a few gentle nasal breaths to prepare.

Step 2: Practice (30–50 breaths + exhale suspension)

Rapid breaths: Contract your abdominal muscles dynamically to sharply expel air through your nose. Let inhalation happen naturally as your abdomen relaxes.

Continue with rhythmic rapid breaths for around 30–50 cycles, building gradually if you are new to the practice.

Exhale suspension (bahya kumbhaka): After the final exhale, inhale gently to a comfortable fullness (without strain), then release to a natural resting exhale. Pause here, holding the breath at this suspension point, at the base of the exhale. Stay curious and relaxed, leaning into sensations without force or strain.

Release: When you feel a moderate to strong urge to breathe, inhale softly through your nose. Rest briefly with easy nasal breathing before the next round.

Step 3: Repeat

Complete two to four rounds or stop earlier if you feel fatigued.

Step 4: Recovery

After your last round, linger in the after-effects with slow nasal breathing for 2–3 minutes. Stay close to the sensations as they dissolve and notice any shifts in your inner landscape.

Chapter 11

Sleep

Navigating the Limits of Nervous System Activation

A few years after stepping away from my law career, I returned to Thailand for yet another extended stay, this time fully immersed in an intense yoga therapy training. For three months straight, my days stretched across 11.5 hours of asana practice, yogic breathing, meditation and lectures on everything from Ayurveda and kundalini yoga to tantric yoga and yoga nidra. Each day brought new insights into the mysteries of mind, breath and body. The sheer intensity of these practices left my nervous system humming, often pushing me right to the edge – energised, hyperalert and wide awake well before the sun came up each morning.

I vividly recall standing on the balcony of my bungalow very early one morning, around 5am, looking out across a sea of vibrant green and earthy browns. The trees seemed to pulse, their colours vibrating with such intensity they appeared almost psychedelic, like a vision from a mushroom journey. My entire body overflowed with ecstatic aliveness. I was desperate for the day to begin, almost agonising over the impatient joy I felt. Have you ever been so in love with life that sleep itself felt like an interruption? My two-year-old daughter experiences this nightly, but as an adult, it struck me as wild, foreign and intoxicating.

Intrigued by these ecstatic states, I carried my stories to my teacher, Dr Mihaiela Pentiuc, a Western medical doctor, yoga therapist and life-long meditator whose presence in a room seemed to anchor everyone who entered. A meditation guided by Maha, as we called her, was unlike meditation with anyone else. It was infused with a presence and precision that made silence feel almost tangible, as if she was holding the atmosphere itself. Quietly, I hoped she would name what I had touched as spiritual progress, to confirm that the visions and the electric joy flooding my body were signs of deeper awakening. After all, only months earlier, on the brink of burnout, I had struggled to stay upright in practice, sliding again and again into sleep during meditation or yoga nidra, my body desperately clawing back a mountain of lost rest. Instead, Maha listened, her eyes unwavering, and then offered a perspective I had not expected: rajasic depression.

Initially, I bristled. Activated depression? The phrase sounded like a contradiction in terms. But Ayurveda's concept of rajas began to clarify the puzzle. This Sanskrit word describes a state of heightened stimulation, passion and restlessness, energising but inherently unstable – a fire that burns bright yet quickly runs out of fuel. It was exactly how I felt: joyful yet unsustainable, exhilarated yet ungrounded.

As the practices dug deeper into me, my nervous system grew raw, every signal amplified, the smallest ripple echoing through me until it felt as though the air itself was pressing in. With this came altered states that were as startling as they were illuminating. In one class I will never forget, a voice appeared in my mind, as crisp as if spoken aloud, yet it was not mine. It was the teacher's words, arriving long before she spoke them aloud, as if her inner dialogue had travelled directly into me and waited there, fully formed, until sound caught up. We finished in headstand, and as she counted silently, each number appeared within me with perfect accuracy, until the final 'zero' resounded both inside and out in flawless unison. For a breathless instant there was no separation at all, only the eerie sense that thought itself had bridged the space between us.

Another day, I lost my keys somewhere along the ride to the yoga school. Realising this upon arrival, I set off to retrace the long, winding route home on foot. For more than an hour I trudged along a dusty dirt road, motorbikes flying past, because no one walked on Ko Phangan. Then, without warning, something inside me tugged hard enough to stop me in my tracks. I felt pulled to a random patch of roadside scrub – no landmark, no logic, just an insistence from within. I pushed into the bushes and there, beneath a small thorn bush, half hidden in the dirt, lay my keys, exactly where intuition had drawn me. It was miraculous and yet curiously unsurprising – less like an explosive revelation and more like stumbling across something I had known all along.

Such experiences of fleeting telepathy, uncanny synchronicities and inexplicable attunement began to arise with greater frequency – markers of perception growing porous in ways that unsettled and intrigued me. However, even in their wonder, I came to see that these profound micro-expansions of perception, for lack of a better phrase, were not the same as becoming a balanced, embodied human being. Deprived of rest to replenish, of grounding to hold, of the oscillation where arousal is balanced by recovery, the insights remained only sparks, dazzling in the moment yet untethered and ultimately without meaning.

I was bumping up against the important realisation that the very practices I had relied on to expand awareness were also leaving me adrift, increasingly detached from everyday life and from the simple weave of human relationships. What began to emerge was a truth I had overlooked – that the essence of a truly embodied yoga practice is not measured by ecstatic states or extraordinary perceptions, but by the way those inner expansions are grounded into the fabric of daily life, deepening rather than diluting connection with the world around me. In practice, this meant allowing insights to take root through the most ordinary of anchors – through sleep that restored and replenished;

through the capacity to ride emotions and energies with ease; through the ability to move fluidly along the whole spectrum of the human state, from the sharp edges of arousal to the quiet settling of rest, and all the subtle shades in between.

Managing my arousal through rest and rest-adjacent practices – particularly the steadying influence of breathwork – became essential in guiding me towards equilibrium. These were the tools that turned intensity into something I could carry without burning out, and that allowed heightened awareness to be transformed into something sustainable and genuinely integrated. At the centre of it all was better sleep – necessary, restorative and non-negotiable.

The Gatekeeper of Deep Rest

Maybe you have never considered yourself to be someone with a sleep problem. You get to bed. You fall asleep. You stay there. Of course you wake up once or twice in the night, but isn't this what everyone does? You chalk it up to stress, or the moon, or that one glance at your phone at 3am. There is nothing dramatic about your sleep, certainly nothing worth naming – yet something is off. You wake up flat and foggy, as though the body has been horizontal for hours without ever switching off, present in bed but absent from repair.

Most people imagine sleep as passive: a kind of nightly shutdown where the body lies still while the mind goes dark. Sleep, however, is anything but passive. It is active, intricate and exacting. These are the hours when the body recalibrates; when the brain not only files memories but rinses itself clean; when the nervous system toggles between standing down or staying on guard. And threading through all of it, shaping the outcome in ways most of us never notice, is breath.

In clinical settings, you will meet plenty of people who sleep straight through the night but still show every sign of broken recovery – and again and again, the missing link is breath. Decades of research confirm that breathing patterns shape not only how we sleep but whether the body permits repair at all.

This chapter is not only for those with diagnosed sleep apnoea or clinical sleep disorders. It is for anyone who has avoided a sleep study even when you suspect you should do one, who wakes unrefreshed, who drifts in and out through the night, who lies down for hours yet rises as though they have barely slept. Because sleep is not one thing. It is thousands of tiny negotiations, and breath sits at the centre of every one.

Sleep is a living system, complex in its design, adaptive in its cycles and entirely state-dependent. It is shaped by more than routine or sleep hygiene – it is steered by chemistry, by breath and by the nervous system's capacity to shift state. Lying down to rest does not automatically create a restful breathing pattern. The body does not default to optimal breathing just because it is horizontal. Stillness on it is own does not create safety.

In sleep, breath is governed by the brainstem respiratory centres, not the conscious mind. If a system has been conditioned by stress to stay alert, it will not register stillness as rest. You may lie motionless, but beneath the surface the body continues to scan, unsettled and restless. This is what happens when stillness has been learned in the wrong context – hours locked at a desk while thoughts loop, nights in bed with the mind circling the same story, or the breath hopping and skipping as you scroll or wait for a reply.

Under these conditions, the body draws its own conclusion, interpreting stillness as a signal that something is about to happen. Unless that association is retrained in the chemistry of sleep itself, it will not disappear when the lights go out. Each state of consciousness keeps its own ledger, and unless you balance it in that state, the debt remains.

In sleep, the brain stem's responses are exquisitely state-sensitive.

Once consciousness falls away, safety is governed by older, more primitive systems. During sleep, we become more sensitive to carbon dioxide. This is an adaptive safeguard that ensures the body acts if balance begins to drift. However, when life has been lived in a state of high arousal shaped by chronic stress, trauma or persistently elevated norepinephrine, those same systems grow jumpy, so even the smallest shift in breath chemistry can set off alarms.

Your survival system is just doing its job – an adaptation written deep into the body – but unless your system trusts the chemistry of sleep, your survival system will interrupt a full night's rest. Your conscious mind is offline, yet the body is still listening, not to thought but to signals.

That is why breath retraining for sleep cannot happen only in daylight. It is ideally also practised in a state that mirrors sleep, so the body can relearn safety in the very moment it usually resists it.

If your breath turns erratic, if your airway narrows, if your brain becomes hypersensitive to carbon dioxide, if your nervous system does not trust the chemistry of stillness, then sleep fractures and recovery unravels. You wake each morning carrying the same weight you went to bed with the day before. For the nervous system, fragmented sleep and chronic stress blur into the same experience – a body that keeps watch when it longs for release.

That is why we are here: because if your breath has been shaped by adaptation, it can also be reshaped for trust, for rest and for repair.

Snoring and Sleep-Disordered Breathing

Snoring is often brushed off as harmless, but it is one of the earliest and most overlooked signs of sleep-disordered breathing. It means the airway is narrowing, airflow turning turbulent, the nervous system already stepping in to compensate. Snoring is not just sound; it is a physiological warning that breath (and recovery) may already be compromised.

On the spectrum of sleep-disordered breathing, snoring often sits at the entry point. It can progress to upper airway resistance syndrome (UARS) or obstructive sleep apnoea, where breathing repeatedly stops or becomes abnormally shallow during sleep. Even before that threshold, the extra effort of turbulent airflow can fracture sleep, elevate stress chemistry and block full restoration.

I grew up with some awareness of this world. My father's best friend from university, Dr Peter Farrell, went on to co-found ResMed, now a global leader in sleep apnoea care. He was not designing prototypes himself, but he recognised the promise of technologies that could help people breathe better during sleep, and he had the vision to bring them to the world. My dad has told me about those conversations, such as how little was understood about sleep at the time and how extraordinary it was to watch a friend help shape a field that barely existed.

When I began working with clients, I started to understand how often sleep-disordered breathing goes unnoticed – not because the signs are not there, but because they are subtle and easy to miss. Too many people have normalised exhaustion as simply 'how life is'.

Even in sleep, the nervous system does not switch off. It scans the inner landscape, tracking chemistry and state as breath follows in step. With each moment, the body weighs whether to descend into repair or to linger at the surface, light enough to keep watch.

Homeostasis at Night

In the depths of slow-wave sleep, the body returns to balance. This is the phase where thought recedes, muscles become heavy and the autonomic nervous system leans firmly towards parasympathetic sway. Breathing slows and steadies, heart rate decreases with variability shaped by vagal tone, and blood pressure settles into its most stable range.[1] It is a nightly recalibration and repair written into our biology.[2]

During this phase, the brain's glymphatic system opens wide, flushing metabolic waste and leaving neural circuits clearer for the day ahead.[3] Immune defences are strengthened as inflammatory markers fall and infection-fighting cells circulate more effectively.[4] At the same time, stress reactivity is reset: the nervous system restores vagal tone and recalibrates thresholds of arousal, preparing the body to meet waking life with resilience.[5] By morning, you do not rise renewed by change but by design.

What Being 'a Light Sleeper' Really Means

As you drift towards sleep, breathing slows. This is good – a sign the nervous system is shifting into parasympathetic rest.[6] Yet for some, the body misreads this slowing as instability. REM, or rapid eye-movement sleep, is the phase when the brain remains highly active even as the body lies still, the closest state to waking. REM typically occupies around one-fifth of an adult's total sleep time, and its episodes lengthen as the night progresses. In both REM and non-REM sleep, the brain's control of breathing changes; ventilation eases, carbon dioxide rises slightly,[7] and arousal systems linger at the edge of wakefulness. Normally this safeguard is silent, but in bodies shaped by chronic stress, anxiety or trauma, even the smallest rise in carbon dioxide can breach tolerance thresholds.[8]

When this happens, the arousal centres fire. The amygdala, the brain's sentinel for salience and emotion, lights up, scanning the body's signals and tilting the system back towards waking.[9] Instead of sinking into deep sleep or stable REM, the brain pulls the brake: *Wake up. Something's wrong.* These momentary activations, called micro-arousals, unravel the fabric of sleep.[10]

Sometimes this plays out as fragmented nights, shallow rest or abrupt pulls back to the surface of sleep. In REM, it may surface as vivid or emotionally charged dreams that rouse the body just as the brain begins to process them.[11] If you wake to pee during the night, you may notice the timing – often it is straight from the middle of a vivid dream. You might spend eight hours in bed, yet the system never descends into its deeper cycles of restoration. You rise feeling foggy, restless and uncertain that you have slept at all, because the nervous system never received the all-clear to let go. This is often the invisible root of so-called 'light sleep'.

Breath Reset

The Patterns Beneath the Numbers

A sleep journal can help you discover how your system already responds to breath, rest and rhythm. You do not need a fancy template – any notebook will do. If you prefer structure, there are plenty of printable trackers online. What matters is your intention and attention.

Draw up a simple table: days of the week down the side, and headings for the following across the top:

- the time you got into bed
- the time you woke up (and how often)
- the rituals, movement or breathwork (if any) you did beforehand
- how you felt on waking – were you groggy, clear, wired, flat?
- any major mental, emotional or physical events the day before.

What you are offering your system is something it may not have had for a day, a year or even a lifetime: the chance to feel heard. A wearable won't give you that, because this is not data. It is *subjective awareness* – noticing what you did for 7–10 days, and what followed.

What to Do with What You See

Do not overhaul everything. Start with degrees of change and incremental shifts that seem to help. Tweak one thing. Notice the bio-effects. This is the 1 per cent rule: tiny refinements, one grain at a time, until the effects compound.

That is how the nervous system recalibrates and relearns. The nervous system shifts the breath, and breath cascades into sleep. The quality of sleep then becomes the next day's input: rest, recovery and restoration feed forward through the body.

What Is Sleep Apnoea?

If you are not familiar with them, there are three main types of sleep apnoea:

- **Obstructive sleep apnoea:** The airway relaxes or collapses during sleep, physically blocking airflow even while the body keeps trying to breathe.
- **Central sleep apnoea:** The brain pauses its signal to breathe. There is no obstruction, only a temporary loss of respiratory drive.
- **Mixed (or complex) sleep apnoea:** A combination of both, sometimes emerging during treatment or in long-standing cases.

Sleep apnoea is not the only problem that interrupts breathing during sleep. You can experience fragmented breathing and nervous system arousals without meeting the clinical threshold for a diagnosis.[12] The spectrum is broader than most realise. You might not stop breathing completely, but your breath can still falter.[13] You might not wake up gasping, yet your brain can still work overtime through the night. Subtle dysfunctions in breathing – mechanical or chemical, and always shaped by state – do not need to be dramatic to be worth noticing. Over time, they disrupt the architecture of sleep, leaving nights lighter and less restorative than they appear.

What Contributes to Sleep Apnoea?

Sleep researchers have identified four physiological traits – which they call 'phenotypic traits' – that shape the likelihood of sleep-disordered breathing.[14] Patrick McKeown has helped bring these concepts into wider awareness outside of clinical settings,[15] translating them into everyday language for those exploring the role of breathing in health. Not everyone has all of these traits simultaneously, but individually and collectively, they influence your body's ability to breathe efficiently and remain asleep throughout the night. They are:

- **Pcrit (critical pressure):** The threshold of pressure needed to reopen an airway once it has collapsed. Mouth breathing, a heavy neck angle, extra tissue around the airway and sleeping position can all increase the pressure required, making collapse more likely.
- **Loop gain (ventilatory control sensitivity):** If your system is overly sensitive to carbon dioxide, it creates a feedback loop of instability that appears as over-breathing, then under-breathing, then apnoea, and the cycle repeats.
- **Airway muscle tone:** As we age, or with certain neurodegenerative conditions, the pharyngeal muscles in your throat weaken. Less tone means more collapse, even without excess weight.

- **Arousal threshold:** Some people wake too easily, startled by even small chemical shifts before the body can self-correct. Others do not wake soon enough, leaving the system hypoxic before it responds.

You do not need to hold every detail of the science. Simply recognising that sleep-disordered breathing is far more than snoring can help you understand what your body is signalling.

....

Sleep Disruption in Women: What You Might Not Know

In women, sleep-disordered breathing often presents differently from the classic male pattern of loud snoring, clear apnoeas and heavy daytime sleepiness. Symptoms may be subtle: quieter snoring, brief pauses in breathing that pass unnoticed, trouble falling asleep, restless or fragmented nights or a lingering sense of exhaustion that no amount of rest seems to satisfy.[16]

Research suggests this difference is partly physiological. Women, on average, tend to have a lower arousal threshold, meaning their nervous systems wake more readily in response to small internal shifts, like small increases in carbon dioxide.[17] These micro-arousals can be so frequent that they shatter sleep continuity without ever showing up as dramatic apnoea events. The sensitivity becomes even more pronounced during the luteal phase of the menstrual cycle, when progesterone levels rise. Progesterone is a respiratory stimulant and sleep disruptor. It can lighten sleep and increase reactivity throughout the night.[18]

In other words, the same subtle chemical shift that might push a man into obvious apnoea could simply wake a woman up.

Add chronic stress or burnout and you have a perfect storm: a nervous system stuck on high alert, leaving a woman struggling to fall asleep, waking frequently through the night, and too often dismissed as 'just a light sleeper', 'just anxious' or 'just hormonal'.

This is where the gap lies: because the signs look different. Women are consistently under-diagnosed. Current research and clinical guidelines highlight this gap, calling for a far better recognition of gender-specific symptoms.[19] Culturally, sleep apnoea is most often still treated as a 'male condition', and women are more likely to downplay or deny their symptoms, even when exhaustion quietly erodes their days.

As a result, many women are handed quick fixes such as melatonin, meditation apps or mouth tape instead of thorough assessments of airway function, breathing chemistry or sleep architecture. While mouth taping may support nasal breathing, it is not universally appropriate, particularly for women with a history of apnoea, cardiovascular problems or night-time panic. The real work lies deeper, in re-establishing safety in the nervous system, reclaiming stillness and returning the breath to its role as an anchor for rest.

The Edge of Sleep

We begin retraining the breath at the threshold of sleep; the pivot point when wakefulness begins to yield and the chemistry of evening gathers its momentum. Of course, preparing for sleep starts much earlier than when you get in bed. From the moment you wake, every choice becomes part of the descent. The day is a sequence of cues – morning light, movement through the day, coffee before noon (or not at all), screen curfews, post-work 'breakers' and gentle wind-down rituals – all of it guiding the body towards a quiet landing at night.

Let us narrow in on the threshold itself – that fragile passage between waking and sleep. In this interval, the breath-holds sway: it can conduct the body towards rest or keep it hovering in muted vigilance. Most nights, it follows whatever rhythm the day has carved into it. 'Training' here means offering a counterbalance to the residue of the day. To meet that moment differently is to give the body a clearer signal; one strong enough to tip the balance towards sleep rather than circling at its edge.

Breath Reset

The Edge-State Breath Reset

This practice uses cadence breathing to align the rhythm of the breath with the chemistry of sleep.[20]

Step 1: Get into bed

Dim the lights. Keep yourself warm. Let the room grow quiet.

Step 2: Begin cadence breathing

Inhale softly through the nose for 3 seconds. Exhale through the nose for 6 seconds. Add a hum (known as humming bee breath or brahmari pranayama) by taking your tongue to the roof of your mouth behind the front teeth, keeping your lips sealed and teeth slightly parted, sounding 'OM' on the exhale. The hum boosts nitric oxide and enhances relaxation. Feel the vibration in the skull, a resonance that can feel like a quiet massage through the head and nerves.

Step 3: Settle into rhythm

Stay with this for several minutes. Let the lengthened exhale draw you downwards, each cycle tilting the body closer to sleep. If the cadence feels short, stretch to 4 seconds in and 8 seconds out, without increasing the air volume.

Step 4: Let go of the count

When the rhythm feels established, drop the numbers. Allow the breath to carry you on its own, flowing with ease and quietude.

Step 5: Drift

Continue for at least 5 minutes or longer if comfortable, gradually progressing towards 15–20 minutes of sustained practice. If sleep comes sooner, let it.

This is state-dependent retraining – re-educating the system at the very edge of consciousness.

Sleep and the Limits of Breathwork

Recognising the Boundary Between Practice and Medical Care

Before we move forward, let us pause. We've been tracing the ways breath shapes sleep – how it steadies physiology, trains rhythm and helps the body access the chemistry of repair.[1] Breath is powerful, but it is not a universal fix. As I noted in chapter 1, advice can miss the body when it assumes every difficulty yields to practice. It is important to recognise the boundary: where breath belongs, and where it must step aside to work in concert with medical care.

Because breath touches every system, it is sometimes spoken of as though it could solve them all. In reality, breathing practices can recalibrate chemistry, re-pattern stress-shaped responses and help the body recover rhythms it has forgotten. They can take the edges off panic, lower heart rate and restore a quiet consistency in sleep onset. However, there are limits. Breath alone cannot keep a collapsed airway open at 3am when REM sleep slackens the muscles in the throat. It will not resolve atrial fibrillation or rebuild the architecture of a failing valve. It cannot substitute for respiratory drive when the brain stem fails to send the signal, nor can it prevent oxygen from falling when the airway closes completely.[2]

The distinction to draw is simple: breath supports the system that breathes, but if the system itself is compromised when the airway collapses or the neural signal fails, it cannot carry that weight on its own. Still, this does not diminish the role of breath. Breath can prepare the terrain beneath all of these systems, toning muscles so collapse is less likely, stabilising breathing before sleep, lowering carbon dioxide reactivity and reducing the sympathetic load that destabilises breathing during sleep.

Think of it this way: breath will not, on its own, replace continuous positive airway pressure (CPAP) machine – but it can make the body more receptive to therapy. Breath alone will not resolve atrial fibrillation; the big shifts there come from comprehensive risk-factor work, especially sustained weight loss, which can cut the burden dramatically and sometimes restore long stretches in sinus rhythm. And while breath can steady the terrain around disordered breathing, it cannot substitute for missing drive in central sleep apnoea; here, the aim is to stabilise control of breathing and widen the carbon dioxide reserve with supported therapies. Sometimes breath is not the cure – it is the bridge that lets the cure take hold.

All this matters for another reason: people often hesitate to seek medical support, wary of labels, devices or interventions that seem to place them into a category of illness. Sometimes, though, the very act of learning to breathe differently creates the ripe soil needed for the next step to take root. Breath is not the answer to every problem, but it is often the bridge.

When to Seek Medical Evaluation

Remember, sleep-disordered breathing does not always announce itself. You do not need to be waking in panic or gasping for air. More often, the signs are subtle – compensated for until the system can no longer keep up. A formal sleep assessment may be warranted if any of the following apply:

Structural or Clinical Indicators

- Diagnosed cardiovascular conditions such as atrial fibrillation, heart failure or resistant hypertension.
- Known or suspected moderate-to-severe sleep apnoea.
- Obesity (BMI ≥30) with symptoms such as snoring, fatigue or observed apnoeas.
- A history of childhood tonsil or adenoid surgery with ongoing breathing or sleep issues, including persistent mouth breathing.

Functional or Pattern-Based Indicators

- Loud, positional snoring (especially worse when lying on your back).
- Dry mouth, nasal congestion or headaches upon waking.
- Excessive fatigue despite 7–9 hours of sleep.
- Observed breathing pauses, choking or gasping during the night.
- A STOP-BANG score of 3 or more (see the calculator at mdcalc. com).[3]
- Persistent fatigue, poor focus or disrupted sleep despite 4–6 weeks of personalised, consistent breath practice.

If these signs are present, I recommend working one-on-one with a qualified breath specialist. They can help tailor practices, track your progress and guide you towards the right medical support if it becomes necessary.

When Breathwork Can Help

Breath is most effective when the dysfunction is functional rather than structural. These are situations where the system is unstable but still trainable, and they include reduced airway muscle tone that falls in the low-to-moderate range, heightened loop gain in which the system overreacts to carbon dioxide shifts, a low arousal threshold where sleep is fragmented by reactivity rather than obstruction,[4] carbon dioxide sensitivity shaped by chronic over-breathing, and the more mechanical contributors such as nasal congestion, mouth breathing or sub-threshold snoring that does not meet the criteria for apnoea.

In these circumstances, breath retraining works as a stabiliser. It improves pharyngeal muscle tone and recalibrates carbon dioxide response, dials down sympathetic reactivity so arousal is less likely to fragment sleep, and supports nasal patency and airway stability. The net effect is resilience at the sensitive edge of sleep, where stability is the difference between drifting through the night and waking unsettled.

Breathwork will not prevent the natural relaxation that arrives in REM sleep when muscles slacken beyond their ability to hold the airway open. Even so, it does raise the baseline, building tone and stability that make collapse less likely. It is not the whole answer, but it is a vital layer and often the one that allows the body to sink into deeper repair.

Knowing Your Edges

An edge is a vantage point – the place where you begin to see yourself clearly; where breathing stops being background and becomes deliberate; where stillness sharpens sensation into focus and the body reveals what it is ready to release and what it still holds to cope. Some edges soften, the breath widening until what once felt locked now opens; others remain, repeating with the same insistence as ever. Both are 'biofeedback' – the body's way of showing you its habits in real time.

Breath practice is the art of leaning into those edges, listening for which ones yield like tiny doorways cracked open, ready to be stepped through. One door at a time, then another, until over months and years a map begins to take shape; an inner cartography that lets you find direction inside your own physiology and build a more intimate relationship with your body from within.

A Note on the Willingness to Get Help

Readiness is not a switch, it is a stage. Maybe you have suspected apnoea for a while. Maybe someone has mentioned it, or you have looked up CPAP, or you have hovered on the edge of a referral but not followed through. That is not necessarily avoidance. Readiness often unfolds more like fruit ripening than a sudden knowing.

People delay seeking help for many reasons. Some are practical: time, access, cost and uncertainty about where to start. Others are emotional: fear of the results, dread of being told to lose weight or anxiety about sleep becoming medicalised. For women, as we saw, there is often an added layer: the stereotype of sleep apnoea as a 'male' condition, which leaves many real cases overlooked. And sometimes none of those apply.

Recently my partner Josh reminded me what this feels like. He had been putting off seeing someone about a shoulder injury from jujitsu, convinced they would tell him to stop training and commit to weeks of rehab. When he finally went, the advice was a handful of exercises that strengthened his shoulder without keeping him off the mat. The next day he was training again, not with dread but with a renewed enthusiasm for exploring ways to build his strength.

The story we tell ourselves about how hard it will be may keep us from discovering how much relief and possibility may be waiting on the other side of help.

The Stages of Change

Hesitating before change, circling around it and finally stepping forward are not accidents. Behavioural science has mapped this process for decades in the Transtheoretical Model, often referred to as the 'Stages of Change Model', which traces the arc of human effort across six stages.

'Precontemplation' is when change is not yet on the radar. 'Contemplation' is when an idea is present but uncertainty holds it at a distance. 'Preparation' is the gathering of information, the weighing of options and the imagining of first steps. 'Action' is when the shift begins. 'Maintenance' is when the new pattern begins to feel like part of everyday life. And 'relapse' is when old patterns return, reminding us that the path curves back as often as it moves forward.

The path is rarely straight. People loop, stall, revisit and linger between stages. Some spend months in contemplation, turning it over in their minds and testing it against their fears. Others launch into action only to find themselves pulled back, then forward again with a clearer sense of direction. When sleep has been compromised for years, even the thought of change can feel overwhelming, as if you were being asked to climb a mountain without having slept the night before. That weight is not a verdict on your effort. It is a sign you are already somewhere on the path, and what carries you forward may be less about willpower than finding the kind of support that makes the next step possible.

Making the Next Step Feel Possible

Sometimes it takes only a single night – one stretch where breathing settles into quiet regularity, sleep runs its full course and the body wakes as if it has remembered something ancient – to show that change is possible. The nervous system does not need months of flawless practice to reset its bearings. It needs a glimpse, a reminder of what regulation feels like, and from there it can begin to reorient towards that memory.

Breathwork is never the whole answer. It is layered and personal and shaped by the layers of habit and history carried in each body. These practices can offer a framework and an understanding of where breath fits, how it shifts state and where its edges lie. Beyond those edges, support takes on other forms, including guidance, devices, medicine – the scaffolding that upholds the body while it relearns its own balance.

If you have practised with care but fatigue persists, sleep remains fragmented or focus is fuzzy, the message is clear: the body requires more. And that is when the next layer of support comes in.

Chapter 12

....

Sleep and Stillness

Why Sleeping Through the Night Does Not Always Mean Rest

You can log eight hours in bed, drift off quickly, never wake once, and still rise in the morning feeling heavy, unenthused and unrefreshed. You can look calm, sound calm, even insist you *are* calm, while underneath the body is running a different program. Awareness at the level of thought won't often reveal it. Unless we tune into the body directly, we miss the undercurrents within the body even when the mind perceives things as normal.

I hear it in the clients who tell me, 'I sleep through the night, but I wake up exhausted.' Or 'I do not feel stressed, but I cannot sit still.' One woman admitted, 'I meditate, but I do not think it is doing anything.' Dozens confess, 'If I do not exercise every day, I go crazy.'

What they describe is a system that leans on movement to keep itself regulated because stillness feels uneasy – sometimes unbearable. They are not consciously anxious, yet the body keeps its guard, even as the mind rests.

Sleep is not one thing but a sequence. It slides first into Stage 1, a brief drift from waking where consciousness loosens. Stage 2 follows, deeper and marked by bursts of sleep spindles and the high-amplitude K-complex waves that act like guards, protecting against disturbance and beginning the work of memory consolidation. Stage 3 is slow-wave deep sleep, the stage of heavy repair, where tissues knit, hormones rebalance, the immune system mobilises[1] and the brain's plumbing – the glymphatic system – flushes out waste like a night crew hosing down the streets after the day.[2]

From there, the cycle flows into REM, when the body is paralysed in atonia while the brain lights up with activity. Eyes dart beneath the lids, dreams unfold and another kind of repair takes over: memory consolidates, learning takes root[3] and emotions are metabolised instead of carried raw into the next day.[4] REM sleep is the psyche's editing room, turning fragments of experience into story.

Lose slow-wave sleep and the body carries yesterday's strain forward; lose REM and the psyche frays. Disordered breathing, micro-arousals and a nervous system held too close to activation can shear these stages short,[5] leaving sleep that looks complete from the outside but is unfinished within. And when the reset does not complete, the effects compound.

Around you go, wired but tired, busy but brittle, never quite arriving back at yourself.

Breath, Carbon Dioxide and REM

Carbon dioxide levels, and how well your body responds to them, play a powerful role in shaping the depth and stability of REM sleep. Research shows that a moderate rise in carbon dioxide during stable non-REM sleep acts on the brain stem's REM-OFF neurons. These neurons usually suppress REM sleep, but as carbon dioxide rises, they quiet down. This lifts the brake and allows the REM-ON neurons to activate, carrying you into this vital stage of sleep.[6]

REM sleep is not optional. This is the stage when your nervous system resolves emotion, integrates memory and restores physiological balance.[7] However, if your sensitivity to carbon dioxide is high, even the natural night-time rise can feel destabilising to the system. Central chemoreceptors may flag the shift, sometimes triggering micro-arousals small enough that you do not notice, but which are disruptive enough to pull you away from REM sleep before its work is complete.[8]

Training your breathing may help change this response. Early evidence suggests that practices such as slow breathing and gentle pauses after the exhalation can reduce chemoreceptor reactivity, improving tolerance to the normal rise in carbon dioxide.[9] By reshaping how the nervous system interprets its own signals, these techniques may allow the rise in carbon dioxide to be woven into the rhythm of rest rather than treated as a reason to wake.

Breath Reset Reflection

Ask yourself: *What if 'fine' is not my baseline but a cover; armour I wear because my system never finished its repair? What if my breath is caught in the same loop, repeating what my body never had the chance to complete in the night?*

When Stillness Feels Like a Waste of Time

What if the reason you cannot sleep is not mental or even structural, but that your system simply does not recognise stillness as safe? One client, Betina, came to me thirty-two weeks pregnant. She had burned herself out during her first pregnancy and described her postpartum experience as horrendous. She was determined not to repeat the same experience, but noticed herself slipping back into the very patterns that had undone her before: always moving, always doing and never able to sit still. Betina's system resisted the biochemical shift required to arrive at calm. Her breathing was being steered by a nervous system state locked into a subconscious strategy of avoiding stillness, and the same reactivity that unsettled her during the day also intruded on her nights, disrupting the rise of carbon dioxide that helps signal the transition into REM sleep.

What I see again and again are people who cannot sit still because their physiology resists the biochemical shift required for rest. They do not realise that what appears as calm can in fact be the body holding itself in check. I notice it in high-performing clients, in movement-driven people, in those who appear 'fine' by every visible measure, yet beneath all the hurrying, their system rarely allows itself to yield to recovery.

Betina was one of those people – in her mid-thirties, sharp, capable, high-functioning by any standard, with no obvious breathing dysfunction or surface signs of dysregulation to the untrained eye. However, when I suggested our program include yoga nidra, which is designed to retrain the nervous system's relationship with rest, she hesitated.

'I don't really see the point,' she said. 'It feels like a waste of time, and I'd rather be doing something.'

Betina's ego mind equated movement with progress, and she had no felt reference for stillness as valuable. In her system, rest signalled stagnation or even vulnerability.

For Betina, busyness was regulation and motion was the protector of her feelings. This is the part most people miss: dysregulation does not always erupt in chaos. It can wear the face of composure or of stoicism, of a life propelled by momentum, precision and control. Like many who appear calm, Betina's connection to herself and to life gave the impression of composure, but in truth it was a closed fist rather than an open palm.

That image of a fist, from my dear friend and Zenthai Shiatsu creator Gwyn Williams, captures it exactly.

Carbon Dioxide, Acid Sensitivity and the Urge to Move

We saw this urge to move clearly in Betina's story. Her body resisted stillness, driven by biochemical discomfort beneath her composed exterior. Chronic over-breathing lowers carbon dioxide, and over time, this can deplete bicarbonate, the buffer that helps regulate blood pH.[10] When the breath slows and carbon dioxide rises, a system with reduced buffering capacity registers the shift as agitation, anxiety or internal pressure.[11] To escape that discomfort, the body stays in motion. Movement becomes a way to offload carbon dioxide and avoid the chemistry of stillness.

This may explain why so many high-functioning, anxious or Type A people are always moving, doing and pushing. Type A is not a fixed personality but often a nervous system state, and the real drive is not towards action itself but the narrow state range that action sustains.

The Cost of Constant Motion

This subtle compulsion to stay in motion often goes unnoticed, because from the outside everything looks fine. The breath may look steady, the exterior composed, yet a poised rigidity in the chest or a hidden holding pattern tells another story – one of quiet vigilance, where stillness feels less like rest and more like vulnerability.

It reminds me of the old fairy tale of the girl in the red shoes, compelled to dance and dance until she collapsed. In a culture that worships doing, it is easy to mistake this pattern for success. We praise relentlessness and determination, rarely pausing to ask what the body is working so hard to resist.

When Control Becomes the Coping Mechanism

Control is often where high-functioning clients want to start. They say: 'Give me the technique. Tell me what to do, and I'll do it.' However, the very mindset that drives performance is also the one that blocks repair.

Breath reflects our relationship with control as much as our ability to influence our own state. Breath is a feedback system, mirroring how we meet effort, emotion and safety. For many high-functioning bodies, that system has been shaped by years of pushing through, and is propelled by perfectionism, urgency and a constant need to hold the reins and steer.

Clients come ready to 'do the work', ready for effort. However, the real challenge begins when the doing ends and the stillness starts to speak. They want structure, cadence and something to master. This is the paradoxical energy of an evening yoga class in the heart of Sydney: a room full of bodies desperate to unwind, yet accessing that release through the only mode they have – 'go'. To meet them there, I speak to the same drive that fuels their doing, reframing stillness as a skill to be honed rather than an absence of action.

The breath that holds you together may not be the breath that frees you. Before it can be retrained, the breath has to be met. Not forced. Not corrected. Simply tended to, as you would tend young herbs in the garden. This is especially true for people who use control as self-protection. The body cannot be commanded into softness; it can only be given the conditions where softening can emerge.

Breath Reset

A Practice for Those Who Hold On

If stillness feels foreign or even unsafe, the work begins not by imposing technique on top of the breath but by resisting the urge to control it. Welcome yourself in exactly as you are, without needing to fix or alter a single thing.

Begin to feel. Where does your breath go when you are not thinking about it? What moves, what does not? Does it feel controlled by the breathing muscles, or in sync with them? Is each cycle long or short, inhibited or free-flowing? When you stop trying to change the breath, subtle patterns may reveal themselves. An inhale may want to stretch past what the mind believes is 'natural' or 'relaxed,' and an exhale may cut short and sharp and feel difficult to allow effortlessly.

Allow the exhale in particular, since it corresponds to the slowing of the heart and the rise of parasympathetic influence. When the parasympathetic influence is inhibited by chronic activation, the exhale is stifled. Retraining how to allow it can take time. Be patient – it may mean a few weeks of feeling frustrated that it will not yet 'let go'.

Now turn to the emotion, or energy in motion, revealed in the pathway and pattern of your breath. Each emotion carries its own breath frequency and blueprint. Imagine magnifying your attention until you can sense the subtle degrees of feeling expressed through the breath in this moment.

Ask yourself: 'What is the breath revealing about the emotions I am carrying?' There is no need to name them. Contemplation is a seed, and you do not need to track its growth. Simply place it in the tender soil of awareness and trust that your presence is enough to help it grow. It is the eyelash you blow a wish on and then forget.

One day, you will move towards a fuller experience of breath: a little longer, a little softer and a little slower because your system welcomes it. You listen, and only then make your next move. This is how we begin to remember what it feels like to relate to the most essential part of who we are.

Reflection

Ask yourself: *Am I always in motion because I am thriving or because stillness feels unfamiliar? When I pause, what sensations rise that I usually move past?*

The Infamous 3am Wake-Up

If you regularly wake up around 3am, wide awake and still tired, frustrated and strangely wired, you are experiencing something incredibly common, though not particularly well understood. It might feel normal simply because so many people share the same story, but common does not mean inevitable – and it certainly does not make for a restful night.

So, why 3am? While there is rarely a single clear-cut explanation for something as nuanced as early-morning waking, a cluster of physiological shifts converge at this hour, making restful sleep more vulnerable.

At around 3am, your body is typically moving through the later stages of your sleep cycles, which occur roughly every 90 minutes. These shorter cycles are known as ultradian rhythms, the body's smaller clocks nested within the 24-hour circadian day.[12] Most people override them without realising by working at a desk without breaks or pushing through the whole day without pause. The cost of this is nervous system overdrive – the same overdrive that wakes you at 3am. Tuning into the peaks and valleys or weaving your practices intelligently into them helps recalibrate the system to its intrinsic nature.

Each sleep cycle includes both deep, restorative non-REM sleep and lighter, dream-rich REM sleep. Early in the night, REM phases are short, usually about 10 minutes. Later, especially after 3am, they become significantly longer, sometimes lasting 20–40 minutes. During these longer REM phases, your brain is especially active, processing emotion and consolidating memory, and your breathing naturally becomes more irregular.

At the same time, cortisol (the hormone designed to mobilise you gradually towards wakefulness) begins its morning rise. Ideally, it remains low for most of the night,[13] only trending upwards as dawn approaches. However, when chronic stress, subtle anxiety or disrupted circadian rhythms push cortisol higher prematurely, the nervous system leans towards alertness sooner than intended.

Your **circadian rhythm** is your body's internal 24-hour clock. It regulates your sleep/wake cycle, energy levels and bodily functions such as hormone release, digestion and temperature. It works by aligning your internal biological processes with external cues such as daylight, darkness, meals and activity patterns.

When this rhythm is balanced, you feel alert during the day and sleepy at night. Disruptions, such as inconsistent sleep schedules, chronic stress or late-night light exposure, can knock your circadian rhythm off balance, reducing sleep quality, energy, mood and overall health. As a result, you might feel wired when you should be resting and flat when you need to be alert.

This convergence of factors creates a subtle tipping point. In these later REM periods, the muscles supporting your airways naturally relax a little more, causing a slight narrowing.[14] Under normal conditions, this change is inconsequential. When the nervous system is already primed by stress or a premature rise in cortisol, even slight shifts in airflow can be enough to trigger brief awakenings.

Breathing also grows less regular in extended REM, mirroring the brain's work of emotional processing.[15] If your nervous system carries too much charge, the faintest ripple can feel like a surge. The brain stays alert, overreacting to every fluctuation until you are tipped out of sleep.

What this looks like in lived experience is familiar to many. You fall asleep without difficulty, only to find yourself suddenly awake between 2am and 4am, restless, mind switched on and turning over worries, stressors or even mundane to-do lists you know won't be completed in the middle of the night. You probably do not notice your breath; most people do not. What you do notice is being frustratingly awake when you should be asleep. Beneath that alertness, though, the breath has already shifted. In people prone to anxiety, research shows these shifts are even more pronounced, with breathing showing shorter inhales and more irregular pauses between breaths.[16] These patterns make rest more fragile and waking in the night more likely.

Minor disruptions accumulate night after night, subtly undermining your body's ability to recover. Fragmented sleep can contribute to fatigue, reduced stress resilience, heightened emotional reactivity and a kind of unease that leaves you puzzled about why your efforts to sleep well do not translate into feeling properly rested.[17]

As common as this experience is, it is not inevitable. Nor is it a sign of irreversible dysfunction. It is an indication that your nervous system and breathing patterns are ready for gentle recalibration.

Restful sleep returns through a broader, more intentional process. It involves actively managing your nervous system's arousal throughout the day, weaving in downregulation strategies at night, and gradually restoring flexibility by teaching the nervous system to anticipate downregulation after upregulation, so it learns that arousal can settle.

With time, these practices expand your nervous system's window of tolerance and increase your comfort with internal sensations like air hunger, making restful sleep more accessible and sustainable.

As your breathing evens out and your nervous system adapts, the inner climate shifts. The conditions that once primed your body for unnecessary night-time awakenings fall away, and sleep holds longer and deeper.

Burnout: When Your Body Is Forced to Stop

Disrupted nights can pass unremarked, quietly subtracting from you for weeks before the cost is felt. A few minutes shaved from deep sleep, a dream cut short or a repair left unfinished become small omissions that hardly register in the moment, yet accumulate all the same, layering one upon another until what was once a rough patch becomes routine and the body carries a backlog of unfinished nights. During the day, you may still show up and deliver, still smile on cue – but beneath the façade, repair has been pared back to the bone.

I'll never forget a friend of mine describing burnout as a professional dancer. She said it was the fantasy of being hit by a bus on the way to class, not to die or even to quit, but to break a leg badly enough that she would finally be allowed to stop. That is burnout – less a single collapse than a slow erosion of the body's repair systems over nights that no longer restore, emotions left unresolved, immunity thinning quietly beneath the surface. It dims, like lights on the body's switchboard going dark one by one.

In the blueprint of burnout, the nervous system does not simply speed up. First, it remains in overdrive, cortisol rising earlier or higher than it should,[18] sleep peppered with tiny awakenings that splinter REM sleep and shave depth from slow-wave rest.[19] For a time the body copes, carrying incomplete restoration forward into the day, but the deep, slow waves that once washed through the brain like ocean swells begin to flatten and REM sleep, which should have stitched memory and emotion into coherence, grows ragged and uneven.

With time, the balance tips further. The morning rise of cortisol weakens, hunger and satiety cues arrive like faint signals from a radio out of tune[20] and fatigue blurs into something more like an absence. Awareness pulls back and the system retreats into a quieter shutdown that is still outwardly functional but inwardly conserves what little remains.

What disappears most insidiously is perception. Fatigue registers only when it tips into collapse, irritation bursts through without warning. Still, you keep going because the system prioritises outward performance over inward repair. This is a survival strategy that maintains the appearance even as the substrate hollows. This is why high-functioning professionals, athletes and parents alike often insist they are fine, even as their sleep, mood and breathing patterns tell another story. The nervous system edits out the evidence of burnout as a kind of protective blindness that keeps you moving forward while cutting you off from yourself.[21] If this sounds resonant, I recommend looking at the Emotionally Withdrawn Breath Reset Plan in chapter 18 for guidance on where to begin.

Sleep is the most honest record keeper, and in burnout it carries the signatures clearly. Nights are not always broken, but the cycles are thinned and shortened and coherence is disrupted. Without sufficient slow-wave sleep, tissues cannot fully repair, the glymphatic system clears less waste and hormonal tides that should rebalance at night drift out of balance. Without adequate REM sleep, the brain's emotional editing room leaves experiences raw, so conflicts linger, stress replays and the amygdala's salience circuits remain sensitised.[22] What looks like resilience on the surface can be a debt that compounds until it demands repayment.

And yet, somehow, rest becomes the very thing you resist. If your identity has been shaped by composure, productivity and the capacity to push through, then stopping feels out of alignment – as if pausing would unravel the scaffolding of your worth. Burnout is cruel in this way, because it erodes physiology but also entangles your sense of value so tightly with doing that recovery feels like losing yourself.

Burnout yields to advice like 'just rest more' no better than anorexia yields to the advice to 'just eat more'. Rest requires a felt sense of safety and in a system trained by years of overextension, safety is the one thing that cannot be accessed. Repair does not return by bargaining with the brain's reasoning and logic, but through direct experience.

Reconnecting with your body and breath through the practices in this book is a way through. Instead of overwhelming the system by shooting for a life overhaul (although that is a common route), you can create small, repeatable experiences in which the felt sense learns that letting go is safe. Each moment recalibrates awareness, teaching the body to recognise what it truly feels. Reconnection is the cornerstone of rest. Burnout is not the end of the road – it is an invitation to let external drive bow in service to a higher calling from your own intrinsic genius.

Breath Reset

The Pre-Sleep Protocol

A suggested sequence for shaping cues your nervous system can learn to trust.

Step 1: Dim the lights (but make it moody)

Light is the strongest circadian cue, and your brain is extremely sensitive to its shifts. As daylight fades, lower artificial lighting, swapping bright overheads for lamps in warmer amber tones or very dim red light. Your pineal gland reads these changes as nightfall, releasing melatonin, the hormone that whispers sweet lullabies like 'it is safe to let go'. With less to process, the brain stops scanning for input and begins to fold inwards towards rest.

Step 2: Shape your soundscape (because silence is not always golden)

Sound guides the nervous system as much as sight. Whether it is ambient music, white noise or deliberate silence, your brain listens for signals of safety. Aim for a soundscape that sets a mood, not just background noise. Choose one and return to it nightly. Familiarity transforms it into a non-verbal signal that reassures your system it can unwind. Yoga nidra uses this same principle, creating a trusted auditory path into deeper rest.

Step 3: Anchor with scent (your limbic system's secret shortcut)

Scent bypasses the rational brain and travels straight to the limbic system (the emotional command centre). Use this pathway intentionally: select one natural essential oil such as lavender, cedarwood or neroli and reserve it for evenings. Consistency teaches the body to associate the scent with safety and softening. This is not aromatherapy fluff; it is neurophysiology. Over time, the aroma becomes a reliable cue that it is safe to let down your guard.

Step 4: Use movement to get still (because forcing it rarely works)

Sometimes your nervous system is not ready to drop straight into stillness, especially when it's under stress or burnout. Gentle movement provides the bridge: yin yoga, intuitive stretching or slow self-massage with a therapy ball can coax your body out of tension and into trust. If you have children, do this beside their bed and make it a shared ritual.

Step 5: Breathe softly, not forcefully (a subtle reset, not a push)

After movement, let breath be the final guide. Resist the urge to force the breath longer – that often just means taking in more air. Instead, let the breath refine. Imagine unspooling a ball of yarn so the breath becomes more threadlike. Keep it subtle and nasal, pausing gently at the bottom, waiting patiently for the next inhale. This quiet pause builds a touch of carbon dioxide while nasal breathing increases nitric oxide, deepening the relaxation response. Each breath that follows is relaxed and easy, no larger than normal. If you are ready, move towards subtle air hunger – the faint sense of wanting just a little bit more air while staying completely relaxed – to heighten the chemistry of release.

If you prefer a more structured rhythm, try breathing in for 3 seconds and out for 6 seconds, or in for 4 seconds and out for 8 seconds as taught in The Edge-State Breath Reset from chapter 11. Work your way up to 10–15 minutes of this rhythm.

Step 6: Repeat, repeat, repeat (because trust builds slowly)

A consistent bedtime routine works because it is predictable to your nervous system. Your body anticipates the familiar rhythm, responding with relaxation before you even realise it has happened.

Pair these cues with something small: a cup of herbal tea, a warm shower and 15–20 minutes of a good book. These are rituals your system recognises as a green light to rest. Remember, your body learns through experience, so begin this protocol tonight and let the routine do the teaching.

Emma's Story: The Journey Back from Burnout

Emma was 41 when she came to see me, managing a demanding role in corporate communications where her days were often consumed with 'putting out fires'. Recently remarried and navigating the complexities of a blended family, she was also quietly hoping to conceive through IVF. But chronic exhaustion and persistent anxiety were wearing her down.

At first, Emma described her sleep as 'fine enough'. However, a closer look revealed otherwise: morning tingling in her fingers (a common marker of chronic hyperventilation), new-onset snoring reported by her partner and weekend crashes she described as wanting to 'rot in bed'. Her memory had grown foggy over the past year – the same year she lost her brother.

Emma knew she had not fully processed her grief. Instead, she poured herself into work to keep moving forward. Her breathing was thoracic-dominant and, based on my assessment, she was well into the red zone of burnout. On examination, her tongue was visibly swollen with scalloped edges and almost no view of her airway, which are classic signs of reduced breathing space and obstruction. I immediately suspected obstructive sleep apnoea (OSA). Knowing the cardiovascular risks associated with untreated OSA, I referred her for a sleep study. While she waited, we began restoring nasal openness (called patency) and building functional breathing patterns, laying the groundwork for deeper reconnection.

The sleep study confirmed moderate OSA. Emma started CPAP therapy, cut out alcohol and adopted positional strategies to avoid back-sleeping and added myofunctional support. The shift was profound as she went from 16 breathing events an hour to 0.2, which is essentially normal. Her sleep became restorative and she started noticing early shifts in her weight and energy.

In an uncanny synchronicity, the very day she received her CPAP (a device she had been hesitant to try), she attended a funeral for a friend who had died in his sleep at 53 from untreated apnoea, just weeks before he was due to start CPAP himself. The message was not lost on Emma.

Emma's story highlights that meaningful wins are not just about changing breathing habits but also about having the clarity to seek the right medical support. For her, CPAP was the bridge back to herself when everything felt as though it was crumbling. From there, the deeper work of grieving her brother could begin, and she could step into the next chapter of her life: preparing to conceive.

Sleep as a Neurobiological Rehearsal for Safety

During sleep, the brain is not only resting but also rehearsing. Every night, respiratory rhythms, heart rate patterns and shifts in autonomic tone are registered and reinforced. The body treats these internal signals as data, consolidating them into the predictive models that guide physiology the next day.[23]

The breathing pattern sustained through sleep – including its rate and depth, the ease of exhalation and the pauses between breaths – becomes part of that imprint. These signals are registered with unusual sensitivity at night, when the brain is tuned more closely to internal cues than to the outside world. The signals influence memory processes, hormonal regulation and metabolic balance.[24]

Efficient and unobstructed breathing establishes itself as the expected norm with repetition. The system encodes sleep as a viable state, shifting the baseline expectation[25] so that the nervous system predicts safety, and strengthening the body's capacity to enter recovery during sleep to extend that stability into waking life.

Breath Reset Reflection

Ask yourself: *What if sleep is not something I fall into but something I prepare for with trust? What signals could I offer my body tonight to say, 'You are safe now'?*

Chapter 13

The Gut

The Depleted Forest Within

Your body is a habitat – a living ecosystem that once teemed like a rainforest filled with life. For most of human history, the gut sheltered hundreds of microbial species that evolved alongside the nervous system, fermenting complex plant fibres into fuel, calibrating immunity and sending signals along the vagus nerve that shaped internal states of safety, energy and resilience. Much of that ancient microbiome has since disappeared, eroded by the conditions of modern living.[1]

Industrial agriculture, hyper-hygienic living, fibre-starved diets, soils stripped of biodiversity and crops carrying only a fraction of their original phytochemical richness have together stripped the gut of diversity as surely as clear-felling strips a forest. Processed foods and pesticide residues add to the burden, while artificial light and constant digital stimulation intensify the physiological strain, thinning the body's internal forest until the loss is undeniable.[2]

Even foods sold under a 'healthy' banner are not immune to these forces. Produce may come from soils depleted of nutrients, while packaged foods dressed in greenwashed labels carry added sugars, oils and additives. Terms like 'natural' or 'organic' create a halo effect that obscures how little wholefood nutrition is actually inside. Add to this the cumulative load of modern toxins, and the pressure on the body's internal forest is depleted further still.

The result of all these changes is a silent extinction event in the rainforest within. The gut microbiome co-regulates the nervous system, influencing inflammatory tone and immune response, influencing the production of neurotransmitters and helping to guide hormonal rhythms that sustain metabolic resilience.[3] It influences not only how you respond to stress but how effectively you recover from it.[4]

The microbiome is part of the operating system of life, running beneath thought and intention at the level of cellular logic. When your internal ecosystem is disrupted, the capacity for self-regulation weakens – but it can repair. The internal landscape can regenerate just as external ecosystems do, and breathing is one of the most immediate ways to begin that restoration.

The **gut–brain axis** is the network of nerves that links your gut to your brain, with the vagus nerve at its core.

Through conscious breathing, you can influence vagal tone, inflammatory signalling, digestive motility and neuroimmune balance, creating the conditions for your internal ecology to rebuild.[5] This rebuilding is a state shift – a change that becomes apparent not only in how you feel but in the way your body regulates, heals and responds. The gut processes more than nutrients. It processes experience. And right now it is being asked to do that in an ecosystem stripped of its roots. To see what has been lost, and what can still be restored, we need to look back.

The Microbial Mirror

The remains of ancient humans, from the desiccated intestines of mummies to the compacted fossilised remains of ancient faeces, reveal something astonishing: their gut microbiomes shimmered with a richness and diversity rarely seen in the modern world.

Analyses of these ancient samples – whether drawn from the Caral civilisation in Peru or the frozen 'Ötzi the Iceman' found in the Ötztal Alps – consistently point to an internal ecology that was far denser, more varied and more resilient than ours is now. What we classify today as rare species such as cellulose-digesting bacteria, fibre-fermenting allies and certain spiral-shaped microbes, were then abundant. Whole lineages of life that coevolved with the human organism have dwindled – some disappearing altogether – and microbial species once threaded through traditional societies have now almost vanished from industrialised guts.

To grasp the magnitude of this loss, imagine the disappearance of elephants and wolves, of bees and the fungi that invisibly knit the forest floor together, all within the span of a single human lifetime. That is the scale of loss that has unfolded inside the human microbiome, a wilderness once lavishly alive now reduced to fragments of its former abundance.

This erosion is an event still unfolding in the present, inscribed in your own tissues with every meal, every exposure and every chemical burden. It arrives without spectacle, settling slowly into the body's foundations, altering the chemistry of digestion, retuning the way stress is absorbed and released and recasting the very capacity for recovery and repair. You may not clock extinction in conscious thought, but your nervous system is bearing this weight as an imbalance in its circuitry or resilience less supple than it once was. As research advances, a new vocabulary is taking shape – one that recognises these microbial communities as intimate co-regulators of mood, emotion, immunity and sleep rather than incidental passengers.

You might sense this shift in a volatile mood, or in anxiety unmoored from any single event, settling instead as a kind of low electrical hum under everything you do. It shows itself in recovery that never quite settles back to baseline, in digestion that gurgles and swells, and in sensitivities that ignite as if the body has forgotten the difference between friend and foe. The immune system begins to weaken with colds that recur and skin marked by rashes and irritations that surface seemingly without cause. These are reflections of a past abundance. The voice of an inner forest thinned to embers is now calling for renewal.

Psychobiotics, Breath and the Chemistry of Trust

A new term has emerged in the scientific lexicon: 'psychobiotics'. These are specific strains of bacteria, along with the prebiotics that nourish them, working through the gut–brain axis to influence mood, resilience and recovery from stress.[6]

For years, mood was seen as a top-down phenomenon, with the mind directing the body. Research now reveals that the current flows in both directions. Gut microbes are chemical artisans, producing neurotransmitters like serotonin, dopamine, gamma-aminobutyric acid (GABA – the brain's principal calming signal) and norepinephrine, which primes us for alertness. Gut microbes also generate compounds that tune the endocannabinoid system, which is the internal network regulating pain, appetite and mood. In fact, 90 to 95 per cent of your body's serotonin (the so-called mood-stabilising molecule) is synthesised in the gut.[7]

Certain microbial families, such as bifidobacteria and lactobacilli, act like local pharmacists within this internal marketplace, adjusting the brain's chemistry in ways that ripple outwards through your behaviour. Some strains increase GABA receptor expression, strengthening the nervous system's capacity for calm, while others dampen cortisol, steadying the stress response. Still others refine emotional regulation and flexibility, softening the edge of anxious or depressive states in both animal and human studies.[8]

The signals generated in the gut do not remain there – they travel along the vagus nerve, which is the two-way channel binding digestion, emotion and breath into one continuous exchange system. With each alteration of inhalation and exhalation, you influence more than the nervous system's surface calm. You alter the chemical terrain of the body, in turn moderating its inflammatory response, clearing the lines of communication between gut and brain, and restoring the balance that allows the body to recover more quickly from strain. Practices that strengthen vagal tone allow microbial signals to move with greater fidelity, creating an environment where psychobiotic signals are transmitted more clearly and microbial diversity can return.[9] In this way, breath is not merely a comfort to the mind but a regulator of the biological ground on which the mind depends.

Priming Your Gut–Brain Axis

Before moving into specific breath practices for gut health, it helps to set the stage. The following two warm-up exercises are designed to wake up the gut–brain axis, release held tension and prime the body for deeper regulation. We begin where regulation lives: right here under the breathing muscle at the crossroads of gut, nerve and diaphragm.

When I trained at the Agama Yoga School in Thailand, every session began with a sequence of warm-up exercises to awaken the energetic body. Exercise six was a small, focused massage just beneath the breastbone, at the gateway to the stomach. At the time I learned it through the lens of energy – a way of clearing stagnant forces from the body's centre. In time, I came to recognise it also as a mechanical way to stimulate the vagus nerve, strengthen gut–brain connection and ready the system for deeper balance.

Breath Reset

Gastric Reset

This practice awakens visceral awareness, enhances vagal tone and primes the digestive system for regulation.

Step 1: Find the point

Stand with your feet hip-distance apart. Make a thumbs-up with your right hand. Using the flat pad of your thumb, find the small hollow just beneath your breastbone where the rib cage parts, resting above the soft belly. This is the entryway to your stomach. Place your left hand over your right fist so you can guide gentle, even pressure into the tissues.

Step 2: Massage gently

With your left hand applying pressure through your right thumb, trace small, slow, anticlockwise circles about the size of a coin. Keep your breathing natural. Let your awareness nest into the point of contact, noticing sensations of warmth, softening or release.

Step 3: Lean into what you feel

Close your eyes if you feel comfortable. As you continue the circular motion, imagine your entire system yielding to the touch and your digestion responding to a deeper biological signal of safety. You may notice slight nausea, waves of emotion or unsettled sensations as tension begins to metamorphose. These are normal responses.

Step 4: Pause for awareness

Less is more. If the tissues soften and invite you deeper, follow with gentleness rather than force. Allow sensations, emotions or thoughts to arise without analysing them. Simply notice. This is the body speaking its internal language.

The Breath-Emotion Axis

If digestion begins with safety, what powers that signal? The diaphragm. True gut healing is not only microbial or chemical but also emotional, and it begins with the diaphragm. The diaphragm rests at the centre of human experience in its anatomical, energetic, emotional and neurological dimensions, and stands as the crossroads where body and feeling continually intersect.

In yoga, the diaphragm is described as the gateway through which prana (breath) enters and leaves; the passage of life energy itself. Taoist tradition calls it 'the middle gate' – the bridge between heaven and earth, spirit and body. Modern science speaks of the same truth in different terms, recognising the diaphragm as the only muscle governed by both conscious command and autonomic currents that run beneath awareness. This is the hinge between voluntary breath and involuntary survival.

When life presses in through grief or pain, through repeated stress or the slow accumulation of unprocessed experience, the body learns to brace. Muscles tighten first, and the grip soon settles into the diaphragm, the jaw and the psoas (the powerful hip flexor that connects spine and legs and carries the body into its stance of protection). Over time, the tissues adapt around the contraction where emotions congeal into structure as the nervous system records the response in memory and scripts it into posture, breathing patterns and watchfulness.

Release, when it comes, is just as layered. The diaphragm yields most clearly in crying – not the restrained trickle of silent tears that muffle the breath, but the convulsive kind that shakes the ribs, softens the belly and draws air unevenly down into the body's core. Crying like this is one of the body's most primal diaphragm releases – a reset that shifts vagal tone and rebalances chemistry. However, this kind of unguarded release has become rare. Many of us live with diaphragms held halfway between contraction and surrender. Breathing continues but never deeply; feeling stirs but only on the surface and life rolls on as disconnected as ever. The next practice is about making space for what has been waiting underneath.

Breath Reset

Diaphragm Release

This exercise is designed to soften diaphragmatic holding, enhance vagal tone and invite emotional and visceral regulation.

Step 1: Find the point

Find the bottom edges of your rib cage (the costal margins) with your fingertips. Use the opposite thumb to the rib side. Begin with the left thumb on the right ribs first, and gently trace along the inner curve.

Step 2: Enter with the exhale

With each exhale, apply light inwards-and-upwards pressure along the inside edge of the ribs. Pause on the inhale. Imagine peeling tissue off the bone. Breathe slowly and naturally. Let the tissues guide you. When they soften, they are saying *yes*. If you find a tender or emotionally charged point, pause. Stay close. Lean in with presence.

Step 3: Invite release

As you inhale, gently press your diaphragm outwards, allowing it to meet your thumb. On the exhale, let your thumb follow the softening, sinking in again. Find a rhythm of offering pressure and receiving feedback. Breath becomes dialogue. Be sure to respect the body's protective layers. Subtle release signals deep shifts in the autonomic system.

Step 4: Reflection

Stay with the after-effects of this practice and feel the subtle shifts in your upper abdomen and lower ribs that signal release.

I have called these warm-up exercises, and they do prepare you for practice, but their reach goes further. They shift the body in its structure, its sensations and its signalling pathways, opening the door to deeper state shifts. Focused visceral practices like gastric massage and diaphragm release enhance vagal tone, reopen gut–brain communication and create the conditions for balanced digestion, clearer emotional processing and energy that renews itself from within.

The State Beneath the Surface

Digestion is both mechanical and relational, coloured not only by what you eat but by who you are when you eat it, because your gut receives food in context and that context is your state.

You could be chewing the most nutrient-rich, organic, wild-foraged, fibre-rich food on the planet, but if you are eating on the fly, shovelling bites down at your desk or swallowing faster than you can chew, the gut will not read this as nourishment – it will read it as noise.

When regulation is present and you are truly tasting and appreciating each bite, the stomach releases acid at the required strength; the pancreas follows with enzymes; the small intestine receives food with ease; the gut–brain axis communicates, sending clear signals back and forth, and microbial allies flourish so that inflammation cools and immunity strengthens.[10]

At my yoga school, one of our daily practices was not on the mat but in the cafe, where we were instructed to chew each bite of food fifty times. Every single bite. At first it seemed absurd – our food cooled on our plates and our jaws ached as we sat on our shins in the diamond pose, a posture traditionally used to support digestion and strengthen weak abdominal muscles. For the first few nights, we chewed between fits of laughter. Gradually the atmosphere softened; the laughter gave way to silence, and in that silence we began to digest not only what we ate but also the weight of emotion stored in the body, the leftover momentum of the day and the subtle patterns of reactivity surfacing in the body.

As the evenings unfolded the practice shifted, no longer centred on chewing alone but on the quality of arrival. Bites stretched into ritual and meals slowed into meditation. The long arc of each day found its close in a nervous system reset carried from eyes to saliva, from breath to gut. In time, I came to see that digestion begins long before food ever reaches the stomach. It starts earlier – in the way you enter a meal, and in the state you bring with you.

How Are You Eating?

Let's ask a better question – not only 'What should I eat?' but 'What state am I in when I eat it?' Food nourishes only when the body is ready to receive it, and that readiness is carried in the way you enter the meal.

Your autonomic nervous system governs digestion, orchestrating acid secretion, enzyme release, gut motility, nutrient absorption and immune response. In a regulated state, these processes run in concert, each one supporting the next. When you are dysregulated or even simply distracted, digestion does not stop but is rerouted, with energy pulled away from breaking down and absorbing food and directed instead towards immediate response, because in the hierarchy of needs assimilation almost always yields to survival.

Food is the seed and your state is the soil. You can plant the finest seed available, but if you scatter it on hardened ground it will not take root – the wind will carry it away and it will sit exposed and unanchored. Plant this seed instead in softened, fertile soil and the picture changes. The seed is held, nourished and sheltered. Add sunlight (what the yogis call 'agni' – the fire of good digestion) and the conditions for growth are complete.

Your breath is how you tend the soil, loosening what has hardened, opening hidden channels and preparing the ground to receive. When you pause and begin with breath rather than another protocol or supplement, you create a dialogue between body and mind that runs beneath words. The pace and shape of breath mould the terrain itself, and that terrain decides whether nourishment will be absorbed or lost. To change the ground at its roots, we must pay attention to where signals first arise in the body and to the ways the gut registers tension, pace and presence before food is ever taken in.

The Gut Feels First

We've explored how emotional circuits activate before conscious awareness and how breath can help redirect that momentum. We've already encountered Jaak Panksepp's view that emotional life is rooted in ancient circuitry shared across species.[11] Those circuits do not originate in the thinking brain but in subcortical networks that interface with the autonomic nervous system. This wiring influences mood as well as motility, digestion and gut tone.

In other words, emotional circuits are biological events expressed first as mechanical signals processed below awareness and only later assembled into meaning. The first gateway of emotional regulation is state, and every signal from the gut helps set that state. The gut modulates how the body receives information and how the brain interprets it. To construct emotion, the brain listens for shifts in breathing and in the body's internal signals such as chemistry, microbial messengers and visceral tone, and from their interplay it composes feeling.[12]

An unsettled gut sends more than local distress. Inflammation, slowed motility or muscular tension are transmitted through visceral pathways as shifts in state,[13] and the brain interprets those shifts as uncertainty or unease even when nothing outside demands alarm. What feels like anxiety may be the echo of that miscommunication. What feels like fatigue may be the body diverting resources to immune vigilance or to neural repair. In both cases, perception bends around physiology, and the story you tell yourself begins downstream of these covert negotiations.

Distortions in perception rise from physiology first, for the body sets the terms on which the mind interprets the world.[14] Breath alters your perception of the world. A change in vagal tone, the restoration of digestive flow, and a release of inner resistance can each change the terrain the brain must read. As the terrain regenerates, the signal alters;

and as the signal alters, perception rearranges. The transformation takes place in biology, where new conditions allow a more connected kind of knowing to emerge.

The Gut as Trauma Site

When an experience overwhelms the system, whether acutely or chronically, the gut can enter a freeze state in which digestive movement slows, enzyme secretion is suppressed and blood flow is drawn away from intestinal functioning towards defence. If that state is sustained, it settles in as the gut's baseline. The interruption becomes a pattern and the physiology endures even when the external danger has passed.

In my work with clients, chronic inflammatory conditions such as eczema or rosacea often trace back to a convergence of microbiome imbalance (gut dysbiosis), immune dysregulation and an element of emotional holding, particularly around boundaries and unexpressed frustration. This may seem unlikely at first, but it becomes more coherent when you consider that the gut and skin are both boundary organs; meeting places between the internal and outer world. When those physiological boundaries are strained and emotional expression is suppressed or unavailable, the body often finds other ways to speak.

The **enteric nervous system**, often called the 'second brain', contains more than 500 million neurons that line the digestive tract. It works alongside the sympathetic and parasympathetic nervous systems of the autonomic nervous system. Although it receives input from the brain, it also initiates its own responses, creates feedback loops and can hold patterned reactions to stress long after the original danger has passed.

Beyond my own experience, the gut–emotion connection has been observed across many domains of research. People with PTSD or developmental trauma show markedly higher rates of gastrointestinal disturbance, including irritable bowel syndrome, inflammatory bowel disease and functional dyspepsia.[15] Trauma alters vagal tone, amplifying sympathetic dominance and weakening the body's ability to return to rest.[16] It impairs gut barrier function, increasing permeability and fuelling chronic immune activation.[17] The gut microbiome itself shifts under stress, losing diversity, fostering inflammatory species and disturbing the production of neurotransmitters such as GABA and serotonin.[18]

What emerges is a pattern in which vigilance, poor nutrient absorption and emotional volatility mirror microbial and neural imbalance. The gut inscribes stress, holding memory in folds and fibres, in signalling loops and microbial tides, forming an imprint that feeds back to the brain. However, the same tissues that store the past also remain capable of change, because biology is dynamic and renewal is woven into its design.

Bandhas: Restoring Core Rhythm

One of the most precise ways to reawaken core rhythm, recalibrate the nervous system and restore energy from within is through the bandhas. In yogic language they are called 'locks' – they are a set of subtle muscular engagements that channel energy, stabilise the core and stimulate pressure-sensitive pathways that send signals through vagal and phrenic circuits. In nervous system terms, the bandhas are mechanical inputs that modulate internal pressure and influence state.

The **phrenic nerve** controls the diaphragm, the primary muscle of breathing. It not only sends signals that control contraction, but also carries sensory feedback from the diaphragm back to the brain, making it vital for every breath you take.

Here's how the bandha system works:

- **Mula bandha** engages the perineum, anchoring the base of the core and adjusting visceral pressure upwards, which can influence autonomic balance.
- **Uddiyana bandha** lifts the diaphragm and draws the belly inwards, rebalancing phrenic output, enhancing vagal tone and extending tolerance to breath-holding by easing the urge to inhale.
- **Jalandhara bandha** settles tension in the neck and cranium, stimulates baroreceptors in the carotid arteries and provides stability through the cervical spine.

When performed together, the bandhas form a kinetic chain – an inner architecture that restores structural coherence and energetic flow. Imagine the body as a suspension bridge where mula bandha anchors the base, jalandhara bandha secures the top and uddiyana bandha lifts the centre into lightness.

This vertical alignment supports both posture and perception. It reclaims the body's ability to feel safety, stability and strength from within, and this reclamation begins in the gut. Although each bandha offers its own benefits, our focus here is on uddiyana bandha.

Having traced how trauma, digestion and emotional holding shape the gut, you are ready for one of the most potent physical resets in the Breath Reset Plan. Uddiyana bandha shifts pressure in the abdomen and chest, creating space for the organs, releasing tension in the diaphragm and activating vagal pathways that calm the system, all through the mechanism of suction and release. Practised with breath, it becomes a direct pathway to recalibrate the gut–brain axis, regulate vagal tone and reawaken the body's innate capacity to rise.

Uddiyana Bandha: The Energetic Lift

Often called the 'abdominal lock', uddiyana bandha is one of yoga's most transformative practices. In the hatha tradition, it is taught as a practice in its own right, used to cultivate and direct energy, to extend breath-hold capacity and to influence autonomic balance through vagal and pressure-mediated feedback.[19]

Physiologically, the practice works through a profound shift in pressure. Drawing the abdomen inwards and upwards beneath the rib cage creates a vacuum that lifts the diaphragm, alters intra-abdominal and intrathoracic dynamics, and activates vagal pathways known to foster calm and regulation.[20]

For yogis, the same mechanism has long been described as 'sublimation' – the transformation of dense, heavy energies into lighter, more expansive ones. In traditional language, it is the movement of vitality from the lower chakras (muladhara, svadhishthana) upwards along the spine towards higher centres of perception and awareness.

The suction and lift of the diaphragm, when practised with consistency, creates a tangible sensation of rising heat. With focused attention, practitioners can guide this ascent towards specific chakras. With discipline and devotion, this practice is said to awaken kundalini shakti (the dormant potential at the base of the spine) and open the door to altered states of awareness.

Nervous System and Breath Reset

Beyond its energetic power, uddiyana bandha is a time-tested way of restoring balance to the nervous system. When the abdominal wall is drawn inwards and upwards during a breath-hold at the end of exhalation (bahya kumbhaka), the diaphragm rises into its dome, phrenic drive eases and the urge to inhale subsides. In this quieter state, breath can be held longer, tolerance expands and parasympathetic influence rises.[21]

Uddiyana bandha makes breath-holding more stable by reducing the diaphragm's urge to contract. However, because it is performed after exhalation, when oxygen reserves are lower and carbon dioxide builds quickly, it often feels harder at first. As tolerance adapts, the same practice that once felt impossible becomes the key to longer and more easeful retention of the breath.

From this single action cascades a sequence of effects. Pressure receptors in the abdominal cavity are stimulated, vagal tone strengthens and the parasympathetic branch reclaims influence. The transverse abdominals and deep core are recruited into subtle but powerful engagement. As breath and musculature dance in rhythm, the organs receive a gentle massage, circulation improves and movement is restored where stasis once held firm.

Swami Sivananda Saraswati captured the breadth of this impact when he wrote, 'There is nothing which resists the practice of Uddiyana Bandha,' referring to its powerful healing effect on the abdominal and visceral systems.[22] In yogic tradition, the practice has been applied to ease digestive sluggishness, clear abdominal stagnation, strengthen the digestive and reproductive organs and support the upward movement of energy through the body. It is also described as a means of releasing emotional holding and teaching the diaphragm to let go of its chronic grip.

Breath Reset

Uddiyana Bandha

Practise on an empty stomach (wait 2–4 hours after eating).

Safety note: Avoid this practice if you are pregnant or managing high blood pressure, glaucoma, heart disease or recent abdominal surgery.

Step 1

Stand with your feet shoulder-width apart or a little wider. Bend the knees slightly, lean forward and rest your hands on your thighs just above the knees, fingers pointing inwards. Straighten your arms and lock the elbows so the upper body is supported without muscular effort. Relax the belly. Take three deep exhalations, lowering into a squat with each out-breath, only as far as is comfortable, rising naturally to inhale between rounds.

Step 2

After the third exhale, let the breath out as fully and comfortably as you can. If mobility allows, gently draw the knees towards your ribs to encourage a deeper release. Return to the standing position without inhaling. You are holding the breath at the end of the exhale. Keep the straight arms, elbows locked but soft, with your body weight supported by your hands on your thighs, and no unnecessary muscular effort.

Step 3

Perform a 'false' inhalation by expanding the rib cage slightly while keeping the throat closed. This creates a vacuum inside, and the belly naturally hollows and draws upwards under the ribs.

Hold this abdominal vacuum for as long as you can manage without strain or panic. Bring your awareness to the sensations that arise. You may notice heat in the abdomen, the subtle (or strong) pull of air hunger, a subtle pulsing through the core or a tingling that moves along the spine. You may wish to visualise energy rising upwards.

Step 4

When the need to inhale arises, gently release the suction, let the belly soften and expand, and draw the breath in slowly and smoothly. Remember to relax the belly before inhaling; if you do not, the diaphragm can be pulled higher, and the sensation may be sharp or uncomfortable. Once you inhale, hold the breath at the top for as long as you can without strain or panic, and stay with the sense of energy rising. When you are ready, exhale. Notice the effects. Take a few unforced breaths and then begin again from the top.

Tips

A mirror can help you see the hollowing of the abdomen, and it may take a few tries to get the feel of it. If standing feels too intense at first, try the practice seated, which often makes it easier to develop awareness and control.

Case Study: How Uddiyana Bandha Transformed My Skin, Health and Life

For two years I struggled with rosacea (a persistent, acne-like inflammation) that developed in the months after the birth of my perfect, heavenly daughter. Each morning, red bumps on flushed cheeks stared

The Breath Reset Plan

back at me, a constant reminder that something inside was unsettled. It made even simple joys, like taking photos with her, feel frustratingly out of reach.

Doctors told me it was an autoimmune condition that could not be cured. I knew that was not true. Having enjoyed clear skin most of my life, and growing up health-conscious with brown bread, fruit salads and the 'works' (including plenty of overcooked vegetables), I was baffled. How could my complexion reflect so much anger in the mirror?

This was not my first postpartum health worry. The rosacea followed a relentless bout of mastitis and a punishing parade of antibiotics. I tried everything from cabbage-leaf boob wraps to using an electric toothbrush to massage my milk ducts. Nothing worked. My little vampire was chewing my nipples off. If you have ever had mastitis, you know it is no joke.

Topical creams were useless and doctors blindly followed protocols, prescribing more antibiotics – ironically, the very thing causing havoc. Something felt profoundly off. I went deeper. I sought answers from a naturopath who asked the right questions and ordered a comprehensive stool analysis, which was incredibly illuminating. The results were shocking yet validating. My gut was overrun. This was not just a surface issue; it reached right down to the core.

Unbeknown to me, my gut had become a battleground. The balance of good bacteria had slipped away, and opportunistic microbes (five different species to be exact) had begun a rave in my intestines. No wonder my gut was sending up emergency flares. When my naturopath saw the results, she paused, looked at me, and simply said, 'Wow.'

Herbal remedies and dietary tweaks helped a lot, but not completely. I was still managing symptoms, and if I ate cheese or gluten? Heaven forbid. As I scrolled through blogs, I discovered more. Rosacea was not just linked to gut health but deeply connected to unresolved emotional stress, particularly stored anger. My dear friend and teacher Gwyn Williams often reminds me, 'The psoas is the deepest muscle of the body. It hides all the emotions you do not want to deal with.' I had never thought of myself as angry, but when I checked in with my body, I felt chronic tension in my psoas and the erector muscles of my back, the ones that lock you habitually into fight-or-flight.

My liver (the body's emotional clearing house) was holding onto something I could not quite name. Compressed beneath the tension on my right side, it felt like my skin was shouting what my body had not yet learned to express.

That was when I returned, with renewed conviction, to uddiyana bandha, a practice I had not danced with for a while. Every morning for three months straight, before the world could capture my attention, I stood on my yoga mat and practised this ancient technique for 12 minutes.

Uddiyana is visceral magic. As the belly hollows under a lifted diaphragm, the abdominal organs are compressed and stimulated. When the hold is released, fresh blood floods the gut, liver and spleen, flushing toxins, resetting digestion and loosening emotional knots. The alchemy of uddiyana is something you must experience for yourself.

Within weeks, my skin began to clear. The chronic tightness around my shoulders and ribs softened and I felt like I could smile in photos. I felt lighter, clearer and happier, the way you do when you finally recognise yourself in the mirror again.

Why Did Uddiyana Bandha Succeed Where Medicine Failed?

Healing the gut cannot be reduced to a capsule of probiotics or the removal of gluten from a plate. There is an art to digestion that extends beyond food and includes the assimilation of the emotions left unprocessed when life moves too fast. Emotions such as anger, sadness, frustration and grief do not dissolve through neglect but imprint themselves as changes in breath, vagal tone and microbial balance, weaving threads that bind emotion into biology. Uddiyana bandha reaches into those hidden recesses, releasing the tension that gathers there and restoring flow through breath, circulation and digestion.

What became undeniable for me was that gut, skin and emotional life belong to a single network. To address one without attending to the others is to miss the pattern entirely. Root healing comes from restoring the relationship between them, from moving close enough to see the nuances and far enough back to see the system whole, and from breathing and behaving in ways that re-establish coherence across it. That is the essence of the Breath Reset Plan: an understanding that breath is the golden elixir that can benefit every system of the body, gathering what was scattered back together into coherence, until we meet ourselves again in clear reflection.

Rising from the Core

The gut can be felt as both an archive and an engine, storing our metabolic memory while at the same time driving the chemistry of the present. In uddiyana bandha, the ordinary pressures are reversed, the organs are lifted and released, and a surge of information travels along the vagus nerve into the brain. A recalibration of perception can follow, as if the body were adjusting the lens through which it takes in the world.

Chapter 14

The Gut and Breaking the Bias of Survival

Expanding Your Threshold

Few people are motivated by the idea of a regulated nervous system alone. What they care about is the life it makes possible. Everything you do is limited by your threshold,[1] – the level of stress your system can safely manage. When you reach that point, the body shifts and dysregulation begins to spill outwards.

In business, you rarely earn only in proportion to your effort or skill. You earn according to what your nervous system feels able to sustain. If money rises past that felt threshold, it can register less like abundance and more like pressure – and the system will find ways to release it. In relationships, the same pattern plays out. When intimacy passes the level you can manage, the body anticipates loss or betrayal. You may want closeness consciously, yet still find yourself withdrawing before it deepens because physiology has already drawn the line.

'Threshold' is not an abstract metaphor. It is a biological reality, and the gut sits at its centre. Gut-derived signals travel along vagal and spinal sensory pathways as well as immune and endocrine channels,[2] and together they form part of the interoceptive stream that the brain

203

uses to construct its sense of safety or threat. When those signals become irregular through inflammation, altered motility or microbial imbalance, the brain defaults more heavily to prior survival models. In the brain's forecasting system, noisy input amplifies reliance on old templates,[3] and what emerges in experience may appear as anxiety, mistrust or withdrawal. The experience feels immediate, yet it is driven by forecasts pieced together from outdated information.

Anyone who has studied sales will recognise the same pattern. Just before someone commits to something big and new, they hesitate. Suddenly they have to ask their partner, check their finances or consult their astrology chart. They tell themselves they need more time to think – but to think about what? The information is already there. They are not getting clearer; they're simply stalling, because the nervous system does not yet feel safe enough to hold what is coming.

This is where breathwork and other body-based practices offer something different. You work at the deepest level of consciousness to clear up the signalling from body to brain. With clearer signals, the brain can update its predictions, and threshold expands[4] by shifting the body's conversation with itself. In that shift lies something even more worthy than regulation: a felt sense of safety and inner trust arising from within.

Unlearning the Self You Built at Threshold

The forecasts your body generates do more than colour perception in the moment. Repeated often enough, they crystallise into identity. What began as a short-term adjustment to keep the system within range becomes a familiar style of responding, and that familiarity is easily mistaken for personality.

Patterns such as falling silent in conflict, speaking over others to maintain power or holding rigid rules around food for control are recognisable examples. Most people trace them back to childhood, when the body first learned what it could and could not hold independently.

Therapy may untangle the origin of these patterns, but they can also be understood physiologically. They are reorganisations written into breathing habits, gut signalling, muscle tone and autonomic reflex – in some cases, this coding goes right down to gene expression. The brain receives this stream of input and weaves it into a story of identity. Over time, the provisional adjustment hardens, narrowing the system's range of possible responses in any given context.

Psychology has often classified these constellations as disorders or personality types. From a physiological perspective, however, they can be read more accurately as the residue of outdated predictions.

Personality vs Adaptation

Baseline personality is expressed through traits that are stable and effortless, and through dispositions that emerge without strain and remain relatively consistent across contexts. Curiosity, humour, empathy, creativity and a preference for either solitude or connection are examples of temperamental qualities that reflect a person's natural orientation rather than a response to pressure.

Adaptations, by contrast, are patterns that the nervous system generates when threshold is exceeded. They arise as short-term routes for reducing load and restoring a sense of stability. Independence can harden into isolation, speech can become rapid to prevent silence or compensate for an inability to settle internally, and aloofness can be misread as introversion. Such patterns can appear to be enduring traits of personality only when they are claimed as identity rather than recognised as expressions of a system in dysregulation.

Who Are You, Really?

Are you a perfectionist because drive is part of your temperament, or because your system learned that achievement was the safest route to approval? Do you see yourself as uncreative because expression was unsupported, or because that capacity was suppressed by rigid learning conditions until it no longer felt available? Do you prefer solitude because it is your natural inclination, or because withdrawal became the most reliable way to manage overload?

These are contemplations that act as a litmus for distinguishing stable traits from persistent conditional states. Making this distinction matters because once you see which aspects of identity are provisional, you can begin to loosen the confines of the self shaped by pressure.

Breath Reset Reflection

What is Beneath the Behaviour?

Think of a behaviour you have judged, whether in yourself or someone else. It might be procrastination, emotional withdrawal, chronic lateness, people-pleasing, scattered attention or overworking. Then ask yourself:

- *What nervous system state might be driving that behaviour?*
- *Could it be linked to a search for safety, for control, for connection, for validation or for invisibility?*
- *Is what you are seeing a survival response that has simply been mistaken for a personality trait?*

We often try to change the behaviour at the surface, focusing on the action itself while neglecting the state that is producing it.

When the state shifts, the behaviour often shifts with it. Behaviour is the nervous system speaking through action, and the invitation is to listen for the state beneath the story.

Case Study: Tiana

By the time Tiana walked into the yoga studio for our first private session together, 'ADHD' was the first word out of her mouth, blurted out as some cross between an apology for her behaviour and a badge of honour.

Ever since year 2 at school, teachers had colourful descriptions for Tiana: a hurricane in the classroom, bouncing around like popcorn in a hot pot, rambling at freight-train speed, and endlessly disruptive with her loud voice. At home, her parents were caught in their own loop of frustration, snapping, 'Can't you just settle down?', their own nervous systems becoming dysregulated in response.

Over eight sessions, a different story emerged. Tiana's presentation resembled hyperactivity, though it functioned as a specific adaptation to environmental stressors. Her nervous system had learned to rely on movement and stimulation to cope with uncertainty, inconsistency and the emotional unpredictability of her environment. In groups, she naturally became the centre of attention, but at the same time, she could spend days consumed by minor decisions, unable to move forward. Movement was her primary strategy for regulation, allowing her system to sustain the level of activation that felt most familiar.

There were practical factors shaping her, too. Born in late December, Tiana was nearly a full year younger than many of her classmates, thrust into structured classrooms at an age when her body still craved puddles, butterflies and free exploration. A large Canadian study of nearly one million children confirmed the significance of this timing: December-born kids were around 70 per cent more likely to receive an ADHD diagnosis than those born in January – not necessarily because their brains met the criteria, but because they weren't yet developmentally ready for adult expectations.[5]

Just as powerful a diagnostic factor were the conditions at home, which demanded their own constant adjustments. Tiana's parents had recently separated, leaving her caught between two contrasting homes, each with its own rhythms, foods, routines and emotional climate. Her nervous system adapted brilliantly, constantly on high alert, shifting rapidly from one stimulus to the next, forever adjusting and never settling.

Our initial work was to reframe movement itself. Instead of waiting until her nervous system had already tipped into an unsettled state, forcing restless fidgeting just to cope, we threw out the old playbook. Tiana was given permission to explore movement fully, leaping and skipping, stretching, moonwalking and dancing, even throwing herself about with the abandon of a wildebeest, while staying present with her sensations rather than slipping into unconscious restlessness. From that joyful place, real groundedness began to emerge more consistently and sustainably.

The next step was bridging the gap between Tiana's sense of safety in movement and her ability to find safety in stillness. Week by week, we introduced practices such as cadence breathing and yoga nidra. As her capacity expanded, we moved into the exposure phase, incorporating walking apnoeas (breath-holding during movement) and eventually static breath-holds without movement. Through progressive sama vritti pranayama – equal-sided breathing, building from a four-count to an eight-count on each part of the breath (inhale, breath retention, exhale, breath suspension – we stretched her comfort zone. Week by week, Tiana learned to feel safe across a spectrum of states, from active engagement to intentional relaxation, and from focused concentration to stillness with awareness.

By the end of our mentorship, she was practising trataka – a somewhat intense yogic practice of steady, unblinking gazing (in her case, at a golf ball). This training expanded her ability to focus, and she was amazed at how dramatically her mind quieted, finally giving her relief from her racing thoughts.

These combined breath and body-based practices brought Tiana significant breakthroughs: sharper thinking, greater emotional range and a genuine, comfortable ease within her own body. She discovered that sensation could feel safe, and that concentration delivered a quality of enjoyment she had never experienced before.

Why Insight Alone Is Not Enough

Talk therapy helps people recognise the connections between past and present and develop insight into the patterns that shape their behaviour. However, research shows that a map alone does not guarantee change.[6]

This tension was already clear in the early history of psychotherapy. Sigmund Freud argued that healing required looking backwards and excavating childhood, memory and the unconscious. His legacy moulded much of traditional talk therapy, which emphasises interpretation, insight and the origins of behaviour.

Alfred Adler, once Freud's closest collaborator, imagined something different. For Adler, while the past mattered, healing arose primarily through purposeful action. Humans, he argued, do not only repeat the injuries of trauma, they also act out unconscious goals directed towards belonging, contribution and meaning. Transformation, in Adler's view, came less from endless excavation of the past and more from clarifying one's orientation in the present and actively choosing a new direction.[7] Freud urged, 'Look back to understand.' Adler countered, 'Look forward and choose.'

Breath training aligns more closely with Adler's stance. It is purposeful, direct and experiential. It shifts patterns through lived experience rather than analysis alone.

Culturally, we have leaned towards Freud's model, assuming understanding is enough to produce change. Research now shows this assumption to be unreliable.[8] Insight can be powerful, but transformation often requires disruption – the kind of disruption that embodied practices such as breathwork are uniquely positioned to deliver.

What Is Personality?

'Personality' is a set of dispositions and capacities that emerge when physiology has access to regulation and range. It includes temperamental tendencies formed by genetics and development,[9] but it is not limited to those. Personality shows itself in the ways you can flex between states, hold coherence under change, and respond fluidly to context.

Traits and labels are often used to describe personality. While this language can be useful, it captures only a fraction of human capacity. When physiology settles and is no longer dominated by defensive configurations, a wider repertoire becomes available. You can move between the poles of capacity – whether from silence to speech, or from stillness to motion – as part of a natural alignment with the body's own cycles.

At its most authentic, personality is dynamic. It carries a recognisable thread shaped by temperament and development, but its expression is state-dependent and context-sensitive. The same dispositions can expand or contract and soften or intensify as physiology and environment change – and through it all, coherence is retained. Personality allows multiplicity without losing integrity. Personality broadens as safety deepens and the system regains access to range.[10]

Emotion Starts Below Awareness

Some theories describe emotion as something that arises from the body, while others see it as something the brain assembles from its internal signals. Jaak Panksepp argued that emotional life begins in ancient neural systems, conserved across species, that erupt into circuitry that drives behaviour before thought even arrives.[11]

Neuroscientist Lisa Feldman Barrett places the emphasis elsewhere. For her, emotion is not an ancient impulse but a construction. The brain does not detect an emotion waiting in the body; rather, it predicts one into being, drawing on interoceptive cues, memory and context to assemble experience from the inside out.

One perspective treats emotion as impulse, and the other as interpretation. These views diverge sharply, but both suggest that what we call 'emotion' takes shape before awareness, and that the gut plays a central role because of the influence it exerts over the brain's unfolding story.

In one interview, Barrett described sitting on a plane during turbulence and saying to her husband, 'I am experiencing increased sympathetic nervous system activity, likely due to a prediction error under uncertainty.' Not 'I am anxious' or 'I am afraid'. Barrett gave a clinical description of bodily change before emotion had crystallised. It sounds oddly mechanical, even absurd, yet in that strangeness lies her belief. Emotion is not something that simply happens to you. It is something the brain constructs, moment by moment, from the signals it interprets.[12]

Where Barrett's description of turbulence reduces fear to arousal, negative affect and prediction error, Panksepp would see it differently. In his view, the experience would have already triggered the FEAR system, and that circuitry would have surged into the body, tightening breath, sharpening arousal and colouring the experience with the unmistakable feeling of fright. For him, Barrett's account leaves out the very thing that matters most: the *felt* reality of emotion.

Whether Barrett was glimpsing a state before it solidified or translating her fear into theory, both perspectives remind us that emotion begins before awareness, and that the body's signals are the ground upon which every story of feeling is constructed.

Gut Signals and the Bias of Expectation

The gut orients not only present feeling but also the anticipatory horizon of the brain, conditioning what it believes is about to unfold. Signals carried through microbes, immune molecules and gut–brain pathways tune the confidence of the prediction itself, adjusting the balance between evidence and assumption.[13] When the stream of signals is steady, the brain entertains possibility and updates its predictions moment-to-moment. When disrupted, the weighting shifts and expectation becomes narrower, recycling anticipations that are vestigial.[14]

What is often taken to be character or temperament may be physiology at work, with signals from the gut tilting perception and setting expectation before awareness arrives, so that a world is half-built inside and then projected to the outside – a forecast seeded in the gut and taken as reality.

Because expectation is first sculpted in physiology, you can approach it through sensation itself, meeting the body at the place where forecasts are born and reshaped.

Breath Reset

Mind–Body Check-In

Close your eyes, if you feel comfortable doing so. Without needing to name it, ask yourself: *What kind of world is my body preparing me for right now?*

Invite the answer to rise, not in words but as sensation – raw, unshaped and older than language. The word 'sensuality' sounds full of encouragement to 'sense you all'. Can you be sensual in your attention? Feel what your body is predicting.

Next, take three gentle breaths through your nose, if nasal breathing is available to you. Let each exhale be light, breezy and effortless. Speak back to your sensations through breath rather than analysis. Let the inhale say, 'I am here.' Let the exhale say, 'You are safe to update.'

Subtle Breathing: Embodied Proof

To interrupt a predictive loop, the nervous system requires clarity; a shift in signal that it can register and integrate. Subtle breathing, grounded in principles from the Buteyko method, alters the chemistry of perception. By gently reducing breath volume and inviting a mild air hunger, it increases tolerance for the sensation of air hunger, helps the brain update its response so that this feeling is not reflexively equated with fear, enhances nitric oxide release and supports oxygen delivery to the brain and gut via the Bohr effect.[15] The breath becomes metabolically efficient, precise, quiet and aligned with the body's true demands.

This practice restores a relationship to discomfort, creating space for stillness, refined attention and the physiological conditions through which new predictive patterns can emerge. When combined with an inversion (like 'legs up the wall'), it can support digestive function by stimulating parasympathetic settling, softening abdominal tension and easing gas clearance, thereby enhancing both motility and vagal tone.

What follows is a technique at the centre of my own practice and one I teach often. It can be practised before meals to prime digestive readiness, or at least two hours after eating when the body is more available for internal work. It is equally powerful as preparation for sleep, reducing respiratory drive and signalling the system to settle.

This practice is not suitable for everybody. It should be avoided in pregnancy, particularly in the first trimester, and in the presence of uncontrolled hypertension, arrhythmias, glaucoma, retinal disease or recent abdominal surgery. This practice has been shown to benefit many people with asthma, improving symptoms and reducing reliance on medication,[16] but in severe or unstable asthma it should only be explored under professional supervision, since the deliberate induction of air hunger can provoke distress or bronchospasms if the condition is not well controlled.

This practice is also unsuitable for those living with COPD, or for those experiencing active panic, trauma responses linked to breath, or any condition where the sensation of air hunger provokes distress. Inversions such as shoulder stand or headstand require additional experience and should not be undertaken where there is neck weakness, cervical instability or acute disc injury.

Breath Reset

Subtle Breathing

Subtle breathing is not a gut-specific practice in origin. Its primary effects come through respiratory chemistry and neural recalibration, using tolerable air hunger and reduced breath volume to update the brain's response to sensation. However, these same mechanisms extend into the gut, modulating vagal tone, easing abdominal tension and improving motility.

Step 1: Posture and set-up

Lie on your back with your legs resting against the wall (or over a bolster, if that's more comfortable). Elevate your hips slightly with a folded towel or cushion to support blood flow and spinal alignment. Let your arms rest by your sides, palms facing up. Close your lips. Begin breathing quietly through the nose. If inversion is not possible, practise seated or lying down with your knees bent and feet grounded.

Step 2: Abdominal-diaphragmatic breath awareness

Inhale into the lower rib cage, aiming for a 360-degree expansion. Notice the front ribs move gently forward, lateral ribs flare and back ribs widen into the floor. The action is subtle, not obvious like a full movement. Exhale gently and notice the rib cage recoil towards the midline. Keep the chest and shoulders relatively still; easeful without being rigid.

Step 3: Refine the breath

Begin to reduce the volume of each breath – not with muscular effort or breath control, but by softening into less. The inhale becomes a soft sip at the nostrils. Imagine a teaspoon of breath being stretched like thread, unspooled and delicate. The exhale is so gentle that if you held your hand at the tip of your nose, you'd barely feel the air. If a tiny feather rested there, it wouldn't ruffle.

Step 4: Interiorise awareness

Let the breath become more and more subtle in a way that draws awareness inwards. Track it as sensation rather than sound. Imagine it shifting from breath as movement to breath as space. Let breath become less like air and more like presence.

Step 5: Subtly reduce

Continue to reduce breath volume without increasing the rate, aiming to find a manageable edge where you can surf your threshold without getting stressed, anxious or needing to gasp for air. Let the breath move from run to walk to crawl. Track its movement through the inner lining of the nose, the sinuses, across the floor of the skull and downwards.

If the urge to breathe more arises, try to relax. Wait for the next breath to arrive or be delivered. Rest in the space at the bottom of the exhale. If it is not there yet, be patient – it will come. Stay within a sustainable threshold. If the breath reduces too far and a larger breath comes, simply allow it, then let yourself breathe naturally for a few cycles before returning towards the soft edge once more, refining with patience and without force.

Let your body experience that less is safe. Remind yourself that you are okay, that you have plenty of oxygen and that you are changing your relationship to sensation.

Practice Duration

Begin with 30 seconds to 1 minute at a time, and then rest for 1–2 minutes, breathing naturally. Notice the contrast between subtle breath and your default rhythm.

Repeat one or two rounds if desired. End with 2 minutes of natural breath and stillness.

You can increase practice time as your system acclimates,

lengthening it in small increments of a few minutes at a time until 20 minutes or more feels natural in a single sitting.

What to Look For

- **Physical shifts:** Salivation, nasal clarity or drainage, warmth in the hands or feet, moisture in the eyes, mental quiet.
- **Subtle body shifts:** A drop in urgency, a sense of spaciousness, alertness without tension.

Optional Add-Ons

- **Legs up the wall (viparita karani):** Supports digestive rhythm by improving circulation, calming the nervous system and helping release trapped gas. Remain for 5–15 minutes while practising subtle breathing.
- **Shoulder stand or headstand (for experienced practitioners):** May further support digestive reset by compressing and decompressing the abdominal cavity. Practise only if you are confident in your technique, and not necessarily while performing subtle breathing. These are advanced postures that require stability, not subtlety.

As always, listen to your body. If your breathing becomes strained, let it return to its natural rhythm. Lasting change comes through consistency rather than intensity.

I have taught this practice to people of all ages, backgrounds and states of health, and I have witnessed firsthand how context and timing shape the outcome. When this practice is introduced too early or offered to the wrong person at the wrong moment, it can provoke anxiety or panic. Breathwork is never a uniform medicine. However, when it arrives at precisely the right point in someone's journey, I have seen it quietly and profoundly reshape the whole texture of their life.

As I write these words, an email has just arrived from a student in my Advanced Breath Instructor Training. Her reflections feel fitting to share here:

> I love this practice so much, Brooke. When I first began the training, I remember seeing that it lasted 20 minutes and thinking, 'There is no way I could sit still that long, I am too busy, I'd get distracted. Ten minutes, maybe, but not twenty!' Yet here I am, just a few months later. Today, while my daughter napped, I returned to this practice seeking something nourishing and restorative. Though I have been doing brief subtle breathing sessions before bed, today was my first time diving fully into the 20-minute practice. I did not just get through it, I cruised through it and felt I could have stayed even longer! It amazes me how this work deepens over time, teaching patience, persistence and tapas [commitment]. Feeling the gradual yet undeniable benefits is powerful beyond words. Thank you.

The benefits of this practice can reach into many systems of the body, and the gut is often among those that respond noticeably. As breath patterns normalise and the body learns to remain even in the presence of mild air hunger, the diaphragm engages more effectively, and vagal tone along with healthy intra-abdominal pressure are supported, all of which can contribute to healthier digestion. With these foundations in place, common discomforts such as bloating, urgency, constipation or irregular appetite may ease.

Elsewhere, the changes unfold with quiet consistency. People often describe sleeping more deeply, and noticing that the mind, once caught in loops of urgency, discovers space for clearer thought. Emotions are less heightened and daily decisions feel less like cliffs to leap from and more like paths to walk. Some people also notice the return of libido or the lifting of persistent mental fog. The most meaningful change is the one that threads through all the others, as the nervous system begins to meet the world from a calmer baseline.

When the Gut Stops Predicting the Worst

When gut signals settle into coherence, the nervous system is no longer compelled to fall back on the same patterns it once repeated. In neuroscience, this capacity is called 'degeneracy' – a term that sounds negative, but simply describes the ability for the same internal signal to give rise to different outcomes, depending on context, memory and prediction. The flutter in the belly that once narrowed into fear can instead be felt as simple anticipation.

Clearer signals expand emotional, perceptual and behavioural range. You begin to inhabit states your system once could not hold. Reflex softens into fluidity, and behaviours that once seemed like fixed traits start to loosen – whether it is the need for approval, the compulsion for perfection, the habit of lateness or rigidity, or the inner voice that insists, 'This is just who I am.'

No. It is who you learned to be in order to bear what was once unbearable, creating a pattern that was repeated until it calcified into identity. Freedom feels different. It belongs to the whole of you. It has the capacity to be tender and maintain boundaries, and it moves with the present because the body has learned it can.

Chapter 15

Movement

How Breath Unlocks the Body's
Innate Rhythm and Resilience

Human beings have always turned to movement as a way of shifting states. Across cultures and centuries, people danced in circles to celebrate, swayed together to grieve, or walked long distances in silence to let the body metabolise what words could not. Movement was more than exercise or performance – it was part of the fabric of ritual and season, embedded in ceremony and song, and it worked because it changed the body itself.

When people moved, chemistry shifted. Muscles working produced more carbon dioxide, breathing adapted and oxygen was released more freely into the tissues. The nervous system was aroused to meet the demand and then softened into recovery as the pace settled. Attention followed this arc, drawn out of scattered thought and into step with the body itself. What we now explain through physiology, ancient traditions spoke of through breath and spirit, through prana in India, qi in China, pneuma in Ancient Greece; different words pointing to the same reality, that movement transformed the body and gave rise to new states of being.

This is why movement mattered in ritual. It gave people a way to process intense emotions; to mark transitions and rites of passage as meaningful and worthy of recognition; to restore connection and support within community; and to remember we are part of something larger than ourselves. Movement changes physiology, and physiology opens the door to possibilities that have not been available before. In the Breath Reset Plan, movement continues this role as the body's way of shifting state so it can meet the challenges of life and return to balance again.

The Body Remembers Rhythm

Some years ago, I travelled to Ghana; a place where the sea meets the land and deep poverty moves side by side with an irrepressible human spirit. We stayed in humble huts by the lake, along red dirt roads where makeshift stalls sold fresh nut butter, thick and roasted, alive with flavour, and poured that very morning into reused soda bottles.

I had signed up for an African drumming and dance immersion – two hours of dance each morning and two hours of drumming in the afternoon. For most, it was part of a structured study tour. I had taken one drumming lesson, then a full-body *yes* hurled me into something deeper. I had no agenda beyond joy. I did not know it would undo and remake my relationship with movement forever.

The Ghanaian men who taught us had little in the way of material possessions. They lived in simple cement huts where one thin mattress might be shared by all the siblings, and where old televisions, often stacked in odd abundance, seemed to outnumber the furniture. Meals were plain – mostly rice with tomato sauce from what I saw, washed down with water drawn from the well. However, what they lacked in objects was compensated by an abundance within their bodies: the rhythm of music and dance written into the grain of their muscle as though each fibre had been braided by movement, breath drawn clear through wide-set nostrils as they moved, and spines loose and sinuous, undulating like silk unspooling in slow motion. Even sorrow had a djembe beat. The Ghanaian men lived in rhythm with nature, and celebration was built into the day and night, with no separation between the sacred and the ordinary.

I had danced ballet as a child: refined; restrained. Always sucking my tummy in. This was something else entirely.

'You dance like you are doing sport,' they'd tease. 'Too high. Too tight.'

'Go low,' they'd laugh. 'Go low and break your back.' Not in pain but in openness, in ripening and undoing the tight fist of control.

My thighs burned. All those years of yoga, of elegant inversions and polished alignment, and I still could not move like they did. Their spines rippled as though ocean waves had taken root in the marrow of their bones.

After long days of work, they drummed again, for us and with us. We danced beside them as they lifted their instruments, sometimes blindfolded. I watched one of them play the gyil (a traditional Ghanaian xylophone) flipped upside-down, his hands flying across the keys between his legs like birds in murmuration.

These men's bodies spoke a mother tongue. You could see it in the children, too; the way rhythm lived in their feet, in the arc of their tiny backs and in the way they mirrored movement without instruction. It felt as though it had been encoded in the womb.

The little girls sat beside me, brushing my hair back from my face with quiet tenderness, while babies passed from arm to arm – even the smallest arms – and in that passing, the village held itself together. What struck me was the texture of safety, carried in touch and presence, and woven through the smallest gestures of daily life.

By the end of that month, my body had changed, if only slightly. I still moved like myself, but softer. I no longer danced to be perfect; I danced for joy and for belonging and for a connection to something more primal. Once again, I could feel that movement was sacred, a way of leaning into the collective pulse of being alive.

Movement as Integration

As the internal state reorganises, the way you move begins to show it. The spine finds new lines of support, distributing weight with greater efficiency and responsiveness. Breath couples with movement in ways that conserve energy, each gesture carried by a steadier exchange of air. Postural tone recalibrates and muscles that had been fixed in tension begin to release into motion. These changes are signs of greater energetic availability, because less is being spent on maintaining high tone and defensive postures.

You might think you are always moving, and you are, but there is a difference between movement shaped by habit and movement that arises from a recalibrated state. Habitual motion is narrow and repetitive, while integrated and embodied motion carries more variability, adjusting to the smallest fluctuations in the environment. It unfolds as a living dialogue between the body and the world.

In this dialogue, movement gives the system feedback on its own capacity, showing how much range it can access, how quickly it can adjust and how ready it is to maintain presence. Through this feedback, the body learns its possibilities and begins to recognise itself as a living process in motion.

The Breath-Responsive Core

Functional movement depends on the internal synchronisation of pressure, breath and timing. At the centre of this system is the core – not the visible 'six-pack', but the internal container supported by breath. The diaphragm forms its upper boundary, the pelvic floor is the 'floor of the core' and wrapped around the centre like a corset is the transversus abdominis, along with a network of deep stabilisers that respond to every shift in orientation and demand.

These tissues can be consciously accessed (and we will explore that shortly), but their role in movement is primarily reflexive. They are interoceptive and adaptive, always in dialogue with breath, load and internal cues. When breathing moves with depth and fluency, coordination is built into the timing, and support arises with the breath itself.

Together, these structures regulate intra-abdominal pressure – a dynamic, breath-responsive system that stabilises the spine, balances the pelvis and enables efficient, fluid movement. Pressure rises with the inhale and falls with the exhale, modulating with each breath. These rhythms organise posture from within and allow the body to stabilise without tension. The core is the architecture of functional freedom.

This system adapts moment to moment. When breathing becomes thoracic-dominant or disconnected from the deep core, coordination falters and other structures are forced to compensate. Sometimes this appears as a belly that pulls inwards with every inhale – a paradoxical pattern that shows the diaphragm and abdominal wall working against each other. Other times, it is the opposite – a soft and passive belly that offers little containment for the spine or organs. You might hold your breath to lift something heavy, which can create pressure in the moment, but if it is the only strategy available to you, it reflects a lack of deeper coordination.

Ideally, support arises from the rhythm of breath and core strength, not from rigid bracing, reliance on a Valsalva-style breath-hold, or over-recruitment of superficial muscles. A simple cue is to inhale before the lift to generate pressure and prepare, then exhale to initiate movement while maintaining support, allowing the breath to release with control. The breath sets the timing and the core responds.

When that coordination is lacking, the body finds workarounds. Shoulders tense, trapezius muscles climb up towards the ears, and the back takes on the load the core is not managing. Prolonged sitting without dynamic postural support places strain on passive structures such as ligaments and spinal joints. In this state, the back ends up doing the work of the core, but doing it inefficiently and under strain.

In dynamic movement such as lifting, walking uphill or shifting under load, the ribs may flare forwards. If drawing them back in feels exhausting or hard, it often suggests the diaphragm is not contributing effectively to stabilisation.

These are subtle shifts in how the body manages demand, but they accumulate. Over time, they influence how you move, how you stabilise and how much effort it takes to simply live in your body.

....

The Hidden Pattern: Extension, Asymmetry and the Right-Side Story

Human beings are naturally asymmetrical, and this is part of our design. However, when stress, repetitive habits and modern lifestyles reinforce these asymmetries, they evolve into rigid patterns that pull our posture, breath and movement out of balance.

One of the most common asymmetries is the extension-compression pattern, where the pelvis tips forward into an anterior tilt, the ribs lift and flare, and the lower back arches. The posture can appear upright and strong, but the stability is deceptive. This pattern is the body's unconscious armour against chronic stress and vigilance. And within this armour sits another nuance that most of us not only extend but we also spiral into asymmetry.

Understanding the Right-Side Bias

Have you noticed how the right hip flexor, especially the psoas, always seems tighter? Several forces converge here:

- **Internal asymmetry:** The liver sits on the right, nudging the diaphragm slightly upwards and altering breath mechanics from the start.
- **Daily habits:** You likely favour standing or shifting weight onto the right leg, pushing predominantly with the right foot, and unconsciously loading that side more (this applies regardless of whether someone's dominant side is their right or left).
- **Structural consequences:** This habitual bias shortens the right psoas, pulling the pelvis forwards and down on that side.

The result is a subtle but significant rotational imbalance. The right hip moves into deeper extension while the left side compensates in its own way. Try to breathe deeply in this twisted posture and the diaphragm cannot descend evenly. The 360-degree intra-abdominal pressure needed for true stability is compromised. Slowly but decisively, this imbalance fosters muscular tension, shallow breathing and even emotional rigidity; the body mirroring the posture of constant alertness.

The Impact on Breath and Posture

When the diaphragm and pelvic floor are misaligned, the internal pressure system inside loses coordination:

- The core draws in on itself rather than expanding with breath.

- The pelvic floor loses elasticity, caught between weakness and tension.
- The body expresses a sense of rigidity or instability, even when standing apparently straight.

Pulling the shoulders back or forcing the pelvis under by gripping the glutes alters the external shape but it does not restore the coordinated pressure dynamics between the diaphragm, abdominal wall and pelvic floor. Functional alignment is restored through reorganisation within, with breath leading posture. This internal sequencing allows the core container to share the work of support, creating stability that adapts with every movement.

Breath Reset

Balloon Breathing to Rebalance the Spiral

This standing Breath Reset complements the awareness gained from the Hidden Pattern: Extension, Asymmetry and the Right-Side Story breakout. It re-patterns breathing mechanics by strengthening the left side of the diaphragm, allowing pressure to distribute more evenly across the ribs and pelvis. Do not switch sides unless a practitioner has asked you to. Here is a step-by-step guide:

Step 1: Set your stance

Stand upright with your feet hip-width apart in a staggered stance. Both feet face straight ahead. Unlock your left knee and let more of your weight settle through the left (back) foot. Keep your pelvis facing forward.

Step 2: Position your arms

Hold a balloon in your left hand. Let your right arm relax by your side, then drift it slightly behind the shoulder line to open the right side of your rib cage. Keep your torso facing forward.

Step 3: Create the seal

Place the neck of the balloon gently between your lips and close them so no air can leak. Keep your jaw and cheeks relaxed, with the tongue resting high against the roof of the mouth just behind the front teeth.

Step 4: Inhale

Take a few quiet nasal breaths. Sense the left foot as your anchor, the weight through the heel and mid-foot, and the smooth expansion and contraction of the ribs as you breathe. Notice how the inhale finds more space through the right ribs and back, as the left side holds its shape.

Step 5: Exhale into the balloon

Blow out slowly and evenly into the balloon. Feel a gentle gathering through the left side as the ribs draw in and down. Keep the right side open to receive the next inhale. Let the jaw and shoulders stay relaxed, and keep the weight grounded through the left foot.

Step 6: Pause and feel

After the exhale, pause for a few seconds. Keep the balloon in your hand and find subtle activation along the left side. Allow the next breath to arrive through the nose while the left ribs stay low and the pelvis stays centred over the left foot.

Step 7: Inhale into restriction

With the balloon still in place, inhale slowly through your nose. Keep the left side steady and usher the breath into the right ribs and mid-back. Pinch the neck of the balloon if needed to prevent air from escaping.

Step 8: Continue the cycle

Repeat the inhale–exhale cycle a few times. With each breath, maintain left-side engagement. Allow the upper body to open and rotate naturally to the right as the ribs release.

Step 9: Rest and repeat

Remove the balloon, let the air out, rest briefly and repeat up to four sets. Do you notice any change in balance or ease throughout the body?

Bandhas as Breath-Led Integration

Traditionally, bandhas were used to enhance the capacity for breath suspension and retention. We now know that their effects reach further: they shape how pressure is managed in the body, influence chemoreceptors and affect how the nervous system responds to rising carbon dioxide.

Chemoreceptors located in both the central and peripheral nervous systems detect internal changes such as carbon dioxide levels and relay signals to the brain stem. The brain coordinates a response through the phrenic and vagus nerves. The phrenic nerve, originating in the neck, directs contraction of the diaphragm. When the diaphragm is stabilised or lifted, as in uddiyana bandha, phrenic input is reduced and the urge to breathe softens. The vagus nerve – 'the wandering nerve' that stretches from the brain stem to the abdomen – is deeply affected by internal pressure and the quality of breath.

When engaged with precision, the bandhas modulate this system beautifully. They reduce the drive to inhale, extend breath-hold times and create coherence in the internal state. Each bandha supports this from a different point of contact: the pelvic floor (mula bandha), diaphragm (uddiyana bandha) and neck muscles (jalandhara bandha). Together, they refine the body's internal environment. They reduce noise, increase clarity and coordinate the breath, spine and core as one integrated system.

Many people feel this long before they know what a bandha is. If you have ever shifted from audible, effortful breathing in yoga to something quieter and more contained, you have likely felt that internal lift – that inward-pulling focus; the moment practice becomes about how it feels rather than how it looks. What you were sensing was the body's natural capacity to stabilise itself through the very systems the bandhas describe.

For many practitioners, this shift is profound. It feels complete enough to rest there, because the mind has finally arrived inside the body. The bandhas orchestrate an internal symphony, each layer playing in time with the others to support the whole.

When engaged together, the three bandhas form a continuous kinetic chain, anchoring the base, lifting the centre and stabilising the top. Like the root, stem and bloom of a plant: mula bandha anchors, uddiyana bandha draws energy upwards through the vine and jalandhara bandha gathers and contains it at the crown. Together, the bandhas create continuity, growth with direction and structure with flow.

The result is a body that moves with less energetic 'leakage' and more precision. Breath distributes evenly, effort becomes efficient and clarity within the system supports not only the posture but presence.

The Muscles Behind the Bandhas

In many yoga spaces, the bandhas are presented as advanced, subtle energetic practices that are often elusive or reserved for experienced practitioners. Traditionally, they were passed down through direct transmission from teacher to student, emphasising their subtlety and depth. It makes sense, then, that these refined energetic elements have been softened or even omitted as yoga transitioned into modern, often group-based practices.

Even without full energetic mastery, though, you can still experience the bandhas' influence through the physical structures they engage: your diaphragm, pelvic floor and deep core muscles. Here we are differentiating between the energetic effect of the bandhas, as intended in yoga, and the activation of the physical muscles associated with them.

The muscles of the bandhas are already part of you – physical and energetic at once – and they become more accessible with consistent breath awareness and practice. Through simple, breath-led attention, the core system adapts, bridging the physical with the subtle and opening the way to internal stability, ease and integration.

To experience this yourself, refer back to the Uddiyana Bandha Breath Reset in chapter 13.

The Body, the Brain and the Felt Sense of Movement

Movement begins with perception – more specifically, with how the brain interprets signals from the body and how much background activity interferes with the message. The body generates signals, the brain assigns them meaning, and the translation is not always clean.

Perception is a collaboration between what the body sends and what the brain expects to find. The brain constructs perception through predictive modelling, blending incoming sensory signals with prior beliefs about what they mean.[1] These interpretations are influenced by memory, context, emotional bias and nervous system tone. When the signal-to-noise ratio drops and background activity rises, the brain loses confidence in external cues and turns to its own predictions. Many of these predictions are outdated, distorted or coloured by survival-based prior experiences, so orientation to what is present narrows, perception contracts and movement constricts as the body follows internal templates rather than the reality of current input.

This is why the work is not about posture or external form – as is so often emphasised in modern yoga and movement culture – but about refining how the nervous system interprets signals from the body. By mobilising the body while teaching the nervous system that sensation can be experienced as safe, these practices restore accuracy to prediction. With greater accuracy, the body regains agency because action arises in response to what is present rather than to the remnants of past experience.

Two brain regions are central to this regulation of signals and noise. The thalamus regulates how much sensory information is relayed onwards and filters and modulates the quality of input that reaches higher regions,[2] while the posterior insula integrates interoceptive signals with context and familiarity to generate a lived sense of the body.[3]

When internal volume is heightened through arousal, poor sleep or inflammation, background activity increases, the signal-to-noise ratio deteriorates, and the brain begins to misinterpret even neutral sensations as noxious input. This is why someone with PTSD or chronic anxiety can feel their own heartbeat and spiral, because the signal is buried in interference and the brain cannot discern whether the acceleration of the heart is a marker of excitement or an aversive cue.[4]

What Amplifies Internal Static?

Many common patterns in modern movement practices can amplify noise, especially if they are unbalanced or disconnected from embodied attention:

- **Chronically intense workouts** without adequate recovery, causing sustained stress and diminishing resilience.
- **Habitual tension or postural habits** that restrict breath, reduce parasympathetic influence and reinforce a persistent stress response.
- **Shallow, erratic or disconnected breathing** during movement, which impairs interoceptive accuracy and weakens nervous system regulation.
- **Persistently overriding signals of pain or exhaustion**, reinforcing dysregulation and amplifying static.

These familiar wellness habits are state disruptors – inputs that alter how the body's signals are interpreted. They condition the nervous system towards hyperarousal,[5] leaving perception less precise, reactivity heightened and the sense of embodiment diminished.[6] Intentionally engaging in challenging experiences such as Wim Hof Method breathing or cold exposure can either amplify or reduce internal static depending on context, mindful integration and appropriate recovery.[7]

What Increases a Clear Signal?

By contrast, when the system is downregulated and offered clear, familiar input, interference settles and sensations are easier to discern. This is the ground of embodied safety. Attentive awareness, social connection, high-quality sleep, gut health, and movement practised with presence, with breathwork woven through them all, create the conditions for the nervous system to trust what it is sensing.

Movement can be breath-led, intuitive and nourishing. Inputs with these qualities naturally restore clarity. Examples include yoga, ecstatic dance, Pilates, rhythmic walking or running practised with intention and presence. In fact, anything done with these qualities can become deeply regulating. You could even be horse riding with gentle, nasal breathing and embodied awareness, becoming such a remarkably connected and intuitive rider that your horse actually responds to your internal state.

Rewriting Your Relationship to Movement

Many people dislike exercise because, often without awareness, their system has a low tolerance for the sensations that accompany effort. When arousal runs high or adaptive reserve is reduced, ordinary markers of exertion such as breathlessness, pulse and muscular strain are amplified and over-interpreted, and the brain integrates them with prior experiences that lean towards avoidance.[8] That experience is organised by state. Other people lean towards relentless intensity because high excitability is the state their system can most reliably access, so adrenaline and urgency become the familiar entry points into movement.

Few people register themselves from the inside while they move. Unless training has cultivated interoceptive attention in a discipline such as dance, martial arts or yoga-inspired practices, movement is usually performed for output rather than inhabited as sensation.

Even with training, it is easy to reinforce what the body already does well rather than slowing enough to sense what is unfamiliar or missing. Humans have a remarkable capacity to magnify existing patterns rather than revise them. When movement feels awkward, overwhelming, inaccessible or emotionally charged, the issue is often less about muscle length or joint mobility than about how the brain predicts and interprets what the body is doing.

In a group class, it can seem as if everyone else is catching the sequence with ease while you are barely holding it together. In the gym, your sense of self can dissolve under the lights. Following a video, you may find a left limb moving when you had intended the right. Even in ordinary conversation, attention can suddenly fix on your hands, leaving you with no idea how to place them. These are the moments when perception slips and the brain attempts to resolve the mismatch between its prediction and the body's actual signals.

Let's set the concept of exercise aside for a moment and picture simple motion that is allowed to be honest.

Years ago, in Thailand, I was deep in study, living by schedules for breath and movement, and my closest friend Georgia had come with me, carving out her own rhythm with less structure. After a few days without hearing from her, I called and texted but there was no reply. An uneasy feeling arose, so I took my rented scooter and rode over to check on her. The hut was closed and the doors were locked. I called out, and there was silence. A knot tightened in me. I found a window I could climb through and let myself in. And there she was, in front of the mirror with headphones on, grooving away, hours into a private dance party. Dancing had always been her way of returning to herself, as well as her way of settling. She was not applying a structured technique; she was accessing the body's intrinsic capacity for spontaneous motion to train the breath and restore equilibrium without conscious effort. Research shows why this happens – rhythmic movement couples naturally with respiration through shared pattern generators, so each cycle of motion stabilises breathing without deliberate control.[9] The predictability of these rhythmic signals reduces interoceptive noise, allowing the brain to register them as safe and integrate them with less energetic, metabolic and emotional effort. In this way, unstructured dance can regulate chemistry, smooth motor output, and settle state as effectively as any formal practice, and often more intuitively.

What I came to understand is that movement like that restores the natural loop between breath and body. Every step, sway and spin modulated her respiratory rhythm without conscious effort. Motion organised breath, breath fed back into physiology, and coherence returned through the simple cadence of movement without instruction.

This is the piece so often missed when we separate movement from breath, or breath from the body. They are elements of one circuit. When motion is rhythmic and the person feels safe enough to sense it, respiration aligns, and when breathing finds a steady cadence, the body treats that timing as trustworthy information. You do not need to perform breathwork for breath to work; you simply need the conditions in which native rhythm can return, because rhythm is the body's primal language. That is what she discovered in those hours of dancing alone. It is what we all once knew, before the body was reduced to something to control or manage rather than somewhere to inhabit. When rhythm leads, the breath self-organises, the body trains the breath, and state shifts.

When perception clears, motor efficiency improves, and effort feels lighter because the signals are integrated with less neural and metabolic cost.[10] In lived experience, this is the difference between movement as a task to complete and movement as an experience to inhabit.

The Western world has trained us to chase output and visible form, and social media platforms reward us for display and approval. Yet long before this, we moved in celebration of being alive in a body that could sense and express itself. What we return to is movement that carries presence and finds its meaning as it emerges from inside the body and expresses outwards.

Case Study: Freediving Mastery and the Paradox of Panic

Keane was an elite freediver, able to remain underwater for several minutes at a time; a feat that demanded extraordinary tolerance for rising carbon dioxide levels and a nervous system trained to stay calm despite the progressive hypercapnic ventilatory responses that drive most people to the surface.[11] However, away from the ocean he was undone by a very different challenge. Whenever he felt hot and his heart rate climbed, he experienced waves of panic so strong they left him debilitated.

The contradiction was striking. Panic is often assumed to be a reaction to external events, yet it is most often a story unfolding inside the body. Heightened sensitivity to internal physiological sensations, particularly carbon dioxide fluctuations, alters breathing drive and can trigger breathlessness, dizziness and the kind of heightened arousal the nervous system interprets as anxiety.[12]

In the water, Keane found refuge. Surfing gave him natural temperature control, predictable breathing patterns and calming sensory input, all of which his nervous system trusted. On land, without the sensory anchors of water, his nervous system interpreted the same shifts as unsettling. Heat – whether from a sauna, a warm day or exertion – layered extra load on his system and consistently set off panic. The combined increase in heart rate, temperature and respiration proved overwhelming for Keane.

Freedivers are experts in cultivating hypercapnic tolerance – the physiological ability to comfortably withstand elevated carbon dioxide levels in the blood and lungs that would feel intolerable to most.[13] Yet those specialised adaptations do not automatically transfer into daily life. In his pursuit of underwater mastery, Keane had learned to override signals of air hunger, dulling the interoceptive pathways that would normally register them. Similar patterns have been observed in other high-level performers where the fine line between resilience and dissociation is easily crossed.

On land, without deliberate breath-holds, Keane slipped into subtle but chronic hyperventilation, breathing more air than metabolically required. This lowered his carbon dioxide and led to hypocapnia. The irony was stark. The same discipline that served him through long immersions made him vulnerable in everyday settings. Hypocapnia constricted cerebral blood vessels, leaving him dizzy, confused and breathless, while also fuelling sympathetic nervous arousal with a racing heart and a heightened sensitivity to internal cues.[14] The very mastery that silenced his urge to breathe below the surface left his nervous system misinterpreting ordinary sensations above it.

This underscores an essential yet frequently overlooked insight about breath training and state-dependent learning. Skills acquired in one physiological state, such as tolerating elevated carbon dioxide while underwater, do not automatically transfer into a different state, because the nervous system interprets signals through the filter of internal conditions.[15] Keane's system had come to read the ordinary fluctuations of mild hypocapnia in daily life as destabilising.

Keane's turning point came when we shifted from overriding to listening. We progressed slowly by following these steps:

- **Baseline regulation** involved restoring foundational breathing patterns through gentle nasal breathing and relaxed, permission-based exhales allowing the breath to release without force.
- **Interoceptive accuracy** was rebuilt gradually, restoring trust in subtle physiological signals such as heart rate, warmth and air hunger, and with it a renewed line of communication between body and mind.[16]
- **Graded exposure** followed, with mild physiological stressors such as heat or moderate exertion paired deliberately with breath

regulation, so Keane's nervous system could relearn how to interpret these sensations safely.[17]

- **Integrated training** wove this awareness into Keane's routine, progressively expanding his nervous system's capacity for everyday stress, not just performance extremes.

As Keane's window of tolerance widened, he reconnected his mind and body. His excellence in the water became transferrable to everyday resilience, and his story illustrated a principle at the heart of the Breath Reset Plan. Regulation returns when attention turns inwards, when the body's shifts are listened to with care, and when trust in its intrinsic intelligence is restored. For detailed guidance on navigating panic and anxiety, see the Restless and Reactive breath reset plan in chapter 18.

A Conversation Beyond Words: How Yoga Feels to Me Now

Over the years, I have cultivated an attuned and curious dialogue with my body – one built on listening, trust and fluidity. From this intimacy, guidance now rises from within, so I no longer depend on another's voice to guide my practice. I still delight in moving with favourite teachers and friends, absorbing their imagery and exploring fresh pathways into familiar shapes, and discovering inventive ways of entering and leaving a posture. These days, though, that is a joyful choice rather than a necessity.

Often, I step onto no mat at all. My fingers press into the fibres of a shaggy rug, my toes tack down, anchoring me to wooden floors, or sink into the shifting textures of sand. Practice unfolds through the conversation between body and environment, each surface inviting its own response. Movement adapts instinctively, just as breath does, and my body meets what is present – the salt wind across my skin or the tangible feeling of prana streaming along the inner lines of -my bones.

In stillness, energy takes on texture, gathering and dispersing as awareness moves. It shifts wherever attention lingers, from the space behind the eyes to the flow of the nostrils, as if breath and consciousness were joined threads woven through the same fabric. Yoga, for me, has become a dialogue with aliveness itself made immediate and fully embodied.

When practice closes, the release through muscle and fascia mirrors the clarity of my mind, and the afterglow carries a sense of integration and spaciousness. This arises not because every posture is effortless or soothing but because the act of tending to myself leaves behind a residue of order that organises me at the core.

The postures that bring joy have shifted with time. Where a handstand once brought exhilaration, I now find the same depth of satisfaction in the sustained opening of a lunge; my hips yielding in arcs of motion that deepen with breath. The form itself matters less than the effect, which is consistent. Movement serves as medicine. It metabolises emotion, digests experience through sensation and allows life to pass through without lodging in the body. For me, yoga is how I remain porous to the world while anchored in myself. It's also how I practise letting life move freely so I never have to hold on too tightly.

Breath Reset

Core Breathing

This practice integrates the principles discussed earlier. It demonstrates how breath coordinates with the diaphragm, deep abdominal muscles and pelvic floor to create internal support. Though the experience may feel unfamiliar, the body remembers and re-establishes its original pattern of support. With repetition, breath and muscle coordination are restored as reflex rather than a task that requires thought.

Core breathing is especially helpful for anyone with a weakened or disconnected core, whether through chronic stress, injury, pregnancy and birth, or years of over-recruitment or under-recruitment of the abdominal wall. For those seeking renewed connection to their centre, this practice offers a way back to natural integrated stability.

Because the effects are tactile and directly sensed, core breathing is often more approachable than subtle breathing alone. The feeling of active participation helps make breath training feel approachable and engaging.

Practice Overview

The breath sequence unfolds in three clear parts:

1. **Subtle breathing** (preparation and settling the breath)
2. **Abdominal-diaphragmatic breathing** (gentle, even lower-rib expansion)
3. **Pelvic floor activation** (functional engagement of deep core musculature)
4. **Coordinated core activation**.

Step 1: Subtle breathing

Lie comfortably on your back with your knees bent and feet flat. Support your head and neck with a thin folded blanket. Place one hand on your chest and the other on your lower ribs or upper abdomen.

Let the breath flow naturally through your nose. Gradually soften the volume until it becomes quieter and more effortless.

Continue easing the breath by relaxing into the feeling of taking in slightly less breath than normal. You will find a threshold where you experience a light, tolerable sense of air hunger. (See chapter 14 for the full subtle breathing practice.)

Step 2: Abdominal-diaphragmatic breathing

Soften your shoulders and invite the breath to move downwards into your lower ribs.

As you inhale, feel the lower ribs expand outwards, backwards into the floor, and subtly forwards. As you exhale, sense the ribs drawing inwards again towards the midline.

Step 3: Pelvic floor activation

Internal anatomy to keep in mind:

- **Diaphragm:** The primary breathing muscle beneath the ribs.
- **Transversus abdominis:** The deepest abdominal layer wrapping around the waist like a corset.
- **Pelvic floor:** The supportive base of the core, spanning from pubic bone to the coccyx and between the sitting bones. These muscles support the pelvic organs and assist in posture and stability.

Sit on a foam roller – or, if you do not have one, use a folded blanket, a rolled towel, or even the edge of a firm cushion. Rock forward and back between pubic bone and coccyx until you find your centre. Then rock side to side between your sitting bones and again, find neutral.

From this position, begin to lift internally. Imagine drawing the front of the pelvic floor (just behind the pubic bone) towards your back. Then gather inwards from the sitting bones towards the midline. Combine these actions and feel the entire pelvic floor lift together. Think of this lift occurring in three grades of intensity: light, moderate and full. Ensure that the area around the anus is included in the action. Keep the movement internal, without tilting or rocking the pelvis.

Step 4: Coordinated core activation

Rest one hand gently between your pubic bone and navel. As you exhale, lift the pelvic floor as described above, then imagine zipping up a pair of jeans from the pubic bone towards the navel, and continuing towards the lower ribs. Add a gentle hugging sensation around the waist, as if drawing a cord evenly. This activates the transverse abdominis, creating integrated support. Hold this coordination for 2–4 seconds at the bottom of the exhale before releasing with the next inhale. As you inhale, allow the support to release gradually from the top to bottom, ribs to navel and navel to pelvic floor.

Build from 5 minutes to 10 or 20 minutes, refining the smoothness of this coordination each time.

Levels of Engagement

Pelvic floor and core activation can vary in intensity depending on context:

- **Light engagement:** Everyday postural support.
- **Moderate engagement:** Suitable for yoga or moderate exercise.
- **Full engagement:** For direct core work such as planks. Keep the activation steady while allowing the lower ribs to expand with the breath, and avoid creating excess tension in the jaw, shoulders or chest.

If you have given birth, begin by re-establishing comfort at the lightest level. Practise relaxation and release of the pelvic floor as well – for example, with a massage ball between the inside of the sitting bone and tailbone, in supported squats, or by doing the happy baby pose. The goal is muscles that are both strong and supple, not tight and weak.

Reflections

Pause and notice after practising:

- *How does your internal support and alignment feel?*
- *Can you maintain subtle breathing while your core is engaged?*
- *Do you sense any change in internal stability or responsiveness, or a deeper ease in how your body holds itself?*

Walking Apnoeas: Something More Advanced

Once you have established the mechanics of healthy breathing through practices such as Balloon Breathing to Rebalance the Spiral (chapter 15) and Core Breathing (described above), you may feel ready to expand your capacity in a different dimension. The following practice, drawn originally from freediving drills and adapted into breath retraining by Patrick McKeown[18], introduces dynamic breath-holds known as 'walking apnoeas'. The aim is to gently increase tolerance to carbon dioxide while teaching the body to maintain cadence and composure during light movement. You are ready to start integrating walking apnoeas when you have:

- established a baseline level of nervous system safety during rest and gentle activity
- developed the capacity to settle into stillness without avoidance or aversion

- established a consistently broader window of tolerance, able to handle mild stress without tipping into anxiety, panic or overwhelm
- developed a clear awareness of breath sensations, with comfort exploring slight air hunger while moving.

Avoid this practice or seek professional guidance if you are experiencing:

- pregnancy, as breath-holds are not recommended
- severe cardiovascular disease, including recent heart attack, unstable angina or arrhythmias
- poorly controlled or unstable high blood pressure
- epilepsy or a history of seizures
- severe respiratory conditions such as uncontrolled asthma or advanced COPD
- recent surgery or serious medical conditions that have not been cleared by a medical provider
- anxiety or panic disorders worsened by breath-holds.

Important note: If breath-holds provoke anxiety, agitation or panic, stop. Return to your grounding and restorative practices before attempting again. Progress gradually, keeping breath-holds within 30–40 per cent or less of your maximum comfortable capacity. Resilience develops through patience and consistency, not intensity.

Breath Reset

Walking Apnoeas

Learning to tolerate mild air hunger while moving expands your resilience and conditions breathing efficiency under physical demand, broadening the range in which your system can remain organised as load increases.

Walking apnoeas harness state-dependent learning by pairing breath-holds with movement. In this way, the system learns that breathlessness during effort can be met without agitation, and in time the responses become more economical and refined within that moving state.

Step 1: Establish your maximum breathlessness test (MBT)

Begin by walking at a natural pace, breathing quietly through your nose. After a normal exhale, seal the nose fully with a light pinch and count your steps until you feel a definite strong urge to breathe, stopping before panic or distress arises. The number of steps you reach is your MBT. Release your nose, return to quiet nasal breathing and allow the breath to recover fully.

Step 2: Practise walking apnoeas

Once you know your MBT, practise breath-holds at around 30–40 per cent of that number. For example, if your MBT is 50 steps, practise breath-holds of about 15–20 steps. Continue walking at a natural, unhurried pace, breathing through your nose. After a normal exhale, close the nose fully with a light pinch and hold the breath as you walk for the chosen number of steps, then release and resume nasal breathing. Let the recovery breaths arrive without gasping or force. At first you may prefer to pause walking as the breath settles, though with practice you can continue moving between holds. Allow 30–60 seconds of quiet nasal breathing between rounds, and aim for five rounds in a standard session.

Part III
State Shifts

Chapter 16

The Reset Breath

Conscious Connected Breath in the Physiology of Stress

On competition days, before his hands even touch the wall, a climber's heart is already galloping. From a resting pulse near forty beats per minute it can surge fourfold, vaulting past one hundred and sixty before the first move, at times driving close to its maximum as the climb begins. The body enters full fight-or-flight before the fingertips have even searched for grip.

This climber is Alex, a competitor of exceptional conditioning. Early in his career, a series of falls became indelibly marked in Alex's nervous system. On training walls, he moved with fluid precision, but beneath competition lights, where every slip carried consequence, his body recalled something else entirely and with it came a physiological memory so swift it overtook the present.

Years of rigorous training, technical refinement and the counsel of sports psychology could not fully untether that hook. Alex's physiology reacted as though the fall had already begun so that each surge of sympathetic activation bound performance to what the body had learned to expect. Even in the prime of his fitness, the body bore an association between the wall and the fall with reflexes firing before movement had even started.

This is the paradox faced by many athletes and performers. The body can be conditioned to extraordinary levels of endurance and strength, but under pressure it may still respond as if an old imprint is unfolding again. The nervous system does not distinguish memory from immediacy. It reacts to the patterns it has come to expect, and until those cycles are rewritten, performance remains constrained by the legacy of earlier experiences.

The Power of Embodied Simulation

When perception and memory combine to recreate events through sensation rather than recollection, this experience is known as embodied simulation. At a wellness retreat, Alex wandered into a breathwork session with no plans or expectations, only curiosity. The group lay in rows as the room rested in half-light and the facilitator beat a handmade buffalo-hide drum in a lilting measure that guided the breath. As Alex followed the pulse, his breathing drew into long connected waves and each inhale poured into the next without pause.

After a while, Alex lost track of the beat, and time itself seemed to dissolve as the minutes slipped free of their measure. A presence came into view with startling clarity and he saw his younger self, the boy who once froze midway up a wall, speaking in a voice that felt immediate and real, 'You do not have to fear falling anymore.'

Alex's pulse accelerated and adrenaline coursed as the body moved through its familiar sequence. It was the same surge that seized him before competition, only this time he did not fear it. He kept breathing in the continuous circular cycle and allowed the sensations to rise.

Outwardly, Alex remained still. Inwardly, the climb replayed in vivid detail. He felt the slip, the rush of falling from a height, the body alive with the same intensity that had undone him in the past.

The difference was that he turned towards the sensations, staying close to what he was feeling.

In the moments that followed, Alex's nervous system met a paradox. The racing heart and surge of adrenaline were strong as ever, yet he felt able to stay with them. That pairing created a mismatch between expectation and experience, and in that moment the prediction itself began to update.

What Is Conscious Connected Breathing?

When people picture breathwork today, they often imagine one of two scenes. One is the fire-driven intensity of the Wim Hof Method and the other is the immersive, often emotionally cathartic journeys of conscious connected breathing. These have become two of the most recognisable gateways into modern breathwork, and both belong to the family of high-ventilation practices.

Breathwork is not a single method, but a spectrum of techniques – each designed to shift physiology, perception and state. Within that spectrum, conscious connected breathing stands out for its capacity to open powerful learning experiences. At its core, this practice is a continuous cycle of breath where the inhale flows straight into the exhale with no pause, no holding and no restraint, only the circular stream of air coming and going.

Sessions usually last between 20 and 40 minutes, though some extend for over an hour. This style of breathing deliberately evokes a state of mild to moderate arousal, which is where the learning window opens. In that space, the body mobilises energy through sympathetic activation and the heightened physiological state can bring forward material that has been held below awareness. Stress responses that were once interrupted or suppressed may be completed, and in their completion the system begins to revise how it interprets bodily signals of arousal.

How State-Dependent Learning Reshapes Your Nervous System

Conscious connected breathing guides the nervous system into heightened physiological and emotional states in order to create a mismatch between what the body anticipates and what actually unfolds.

The nervous system thrives on prediction. It links sensations such as a racing heart, fast breath or the unease of anxiety with behaviours like freezing, withdrawing or seeking quick relief. Repetition makes these pairings automatic, and the body reacts before conscious awareness has a chance to intervene.

Think about a phone ringing. If every incoming call for months on end brought stressful news or difficult conversations, the nervous system would learn to link the act of answering with tension. In time, the sound of the ringtone alone could set that sequence in motion so that the body reacted as though the bad news had already arrived. When later calls brought warm conversations and reassuring news, the body still followed the old groove. With each positive call, the nervous system can register a mismatch because the level of stress it prepared for does not unfold as expected, and gradually small shifts accumulate. This recalibration, however, is slow in everyday life. In conscious connected breathing, the same principle is intensified because the learning window is deliberately opened and prediction errors become unmistakable.

When you breathe continuously and without pause, sensations and emotions arise that the body would normally interpret as signals of overwhelm or something that needs to be interrupted. In this setting, you maintain the continuity of the breath and allow whatever arises to be felt without interruption or escape.

Because this behaviour contradicts the prediction, the nervous system registers a clear mismatch and a direct moment of learning. When this contradiction is encountered repeatedly in an environment where the person feels safe, the internal model begins to shift. The original signals lose their authority because they no longer lead to the expected outcome. With continued exposure, the sensations remain strong but they can be met with a new understanding as the nervous system learns they do not reliably indicate a negative outcome.

Real integration occurs after the practice ends and daily life begins. Each time familiar sensations emerge (such as anxiety during a confrontation or discomfort when setting a boundary) and you consciously choose a new response (such as maintaining steady breathing, staying engaged, and speaking clearly), you strengthen the updated model. Gradually, the sensations arrive with less force and have less hold over you, reinforcing the nervous system's recognition that they are not instructions to react but states that can be experienced differently.

Research Spotlight: Science and Conscious Connected Breathing

Recent studies provide evidence that conscious connected breathing can evoke profound emotional and neurological shifts, comparable in measurable ways to states sometimes associated with psychedelics.

In a 2024 exploratory study, Canello and colleagues examined the impact of conscious connected breathing on emotional processing, altered states of consciousness and autonomic regulation, using heart rate variability as their primary physiological marker.[1] Participants consistently reported vivid 'non-ordinary' states of consciousness characterised by altered perceptions of time, reduced self-consciousness, heightened bodily sensations such as tingling, warmth or energetic currents, and powerful emotional release.

The most substantial improvements in heart rate variability followed sessions in which participants engaged deeply with complex or challenging emotions. This suggests that emotional depth and authenticity, rather than pleasantness alone, may be essential for lasting nervous system adaptation.

Complementing this physiological evidence, EEG research led by Camille Bahi revealed brainwave changes during conscious connected breathing that were strikingly similar to those seen with the use of psilocybin.[2] Delta and theta activity (frequencies often linked to deep meditation or sleep) decreased, while gamma activity increased – a frequency associated with emotional integration, heightened awareness and states of insight. Participants also reported striking subjective experiences, including moments of ego dissolution and interconnectedness, traditionally regarded as hallmarks of psychedelic states.

Physiologically, Canello's team observed that heart rate variability decreased during the active breathing phase, reflecting temporary sympathetic mobilisation, but rebounded above baseline after sessions, indicating enhanced parasympathetic recovery and greater autonomic resilience. Crucially, it was the depth of emotional exploration, not transient fluctuations of heart rate variability, that most strongly predicted these beneficial outcomes.

Both studies remain preliminary and limited by small samples, yet they offer intriguing initial evidence of breathwork's measurable emotional and neurological effects. Further research is needed to clarify whether these changes arise primarily from emotional release, stress-response activation and recovery, shifts in self-perception and ego boundaries, or other mechanisms not yet defined. Nonetheless, these findings suggest that conscious connected breathing holds potential to facilitate meaningful emotional and physiological changes, especially when guided responsibly by skilled facilitators.

The Shift

In the weeks following the breathwork workshop, Alex discovered something quietly astonishing. At his next competition, standing at the foot of the wall with the crowd watching, his heart rate was lower and his breathing was effortless and smooth. He no longer had to consciously try to slow it down – the calm was already there.

Reaching for the first hold, the usual markers of nerves had diffused. Visualisation had always helped in part, yet this felt different. This was effortless, woven into his nervous system and unfolding as something automatic rather than imposed.

Alex vividly remembered one particularly intimidating move – a reach above an overhang that had always loomed over him like a shadow waiting to fall. This time, the adrenaline surge did not scatter him – it sharpened his focus. His fingers closed on the hold with precision and his muscles responded instinctively.

Alex's body had rewritten its relationship with the internal concoction of stress and adrenaline. What once registered as anxiety in this context now translated into clarity and readiness. And best of all, it was not temporary. This lower heart rate and effortless breathing became his new baseline; something he carried into every climb.

Breath Reset

The 3-Minute Anchor

Change is registered most deeply when the body feels it. Three minutes of uninterrupted breathing, continuous and circular, are enough to disturb the familiar balance and alter the dialogue between brain and body. In that short span, chemistry tilts into imbalance, arousal stirs, perception reorients and the body rehearses a different way of being. Three minutes may seem slight, yet it is long enough for the breath to open the window of neuroplasticity so that new patterns can take root.

Safety note: This practice is not recommended during pregnancy or for anyone with epilepsy, cardiovascular conditions, unmanaged mental health disorders or a history of seizures. If you have medical concerns, consult your healthcare provider before beginning any form of breathwork.

Step 1: Choose your intention (sankalpa)

As in yoga nidra (described in chapter 9), choose a short, powerful statement – something your body is ready to remember. Keep it simple and in the present tense. For example:

- 'I am steady.'
- 'I belong here.'
- 'I am safe to feel this.'
- 'I am abundant.'
- 'Every day, in every way, I feel better and better. Yes.'
- 'I am held.'

Step 2: Breathe for 3 minutes

Inhale through the nose with intention and let the exhale empty through the nose, inviting the breath to pour out effortlessly. Create a continuous, circular rhythm with no pause or holding.

You may feel the urge to rest at the bottom of the exhale, yet you return to the inhale immediately, for that is the essence of the practice. Allow the breath to remain fluid and rhythmic and let it carry a little more energy than your everyday breathing without tipping into force.

Within minutes, carbon dioxide drops and a temporary state of respiratory alkalosis sets in. This subtle change in blood chemistry signals to your brain and body that something unfamiliar is occurring. It is within this shift that the nervous system becomes more receptive to learning.

Step 3: Anchor the phrase

Let your phrase move with your breath as though it is being woven into the state your body is entering. Usher it in on the inhale and let it deepen on the exhale. Feel the words expand with the breath in, and sink in on the breath out. You are allowing your body to receive the association; this is how encoding takes place.

Step 4: Close and integrate

After 3 minutes, return to gentle nasal breathing. Do not extend beyond this time without guidance or supervision. Inhale softly through the nose and exhale gently through the nose.

Rest in stillness while your blood gases recalibrate and your system settles. Shift into cadence breathing to restore balance. Inhale for 3 seconds and exhale for 6 seconds (3:6). If that feels too short, move to 4 seconds and 8 seconds (4:8). Find the cadence that feels comfortable.

That is all. In 3 minutes, you have created the conditions for synaptic change and planted a seed for something new to bloom.

Chapter 17

....

State Shift or State Escape?

Breathwork, Neuroplasticity and the Fragile Terrain of Altered States

When you breathe intentionally in continuous circular rhythms that move faster than your everyday breath, the chemistry inside you begins to shift. Carbon dioxide falls and the blood becomes more alkaline. This shift alters cortical excitability and may reduce activity in the prefrontal regions linked with planning, reasoning and self-monitoring, as suggested in preliminary EEG work on conscious connected breathing.[1] Broader imaging shows that even spontaneous breathing helps train cortical and limbic networks. When ventilation increases and chemistry shifts, these same breath–brain couplings may strengthen, with reduced prefrontal oversight and more vivid limbic and sensory activity. This could help explain the emotional intensity and imagery many people encounter in breathwork.[2]

In this state, the boundary between conscious and subconscious grows porous and the mind becomes particularly receptive to impressions and associations. Neurologically, this state bears resemblance to hypnagogia and to the liminal depth of yoga nidra, both of which unfold in the transitional terrain between waking and sleep.[3] Breathwork practices that elevate ventilation are typically energising rather than drowsy, but the qualities of permeability and suggestibility are shared.

Research supports this openness. Neuroscientist Charan Ranganath emphasises that memory is fluid rather than fixed, and that information introduced in receptive states can be incorporated into existing networks to alter how reality is later perceived.[4] Memory researchers such as Elizabeth Loftus have shown how readily impressions and suggestions can weave themselves into recollection, reframing experience in ways that feel wholly real.[5]

It is this receptive plasticity that lends breathwork both its power and its delicacy. Whatever is spoken, implied or sensed in the room can embed with unusual depth. The line between therapeutic effect and suggestibility is extraordinarily fine.

To guide breathwork is to hold responsibility for creating conditions in which perception and memory may be influenced. Practitioners must be conscious of the weight of their words and presence, and participants must choose their guides and settings with care. In such receptive states, breathwork reaches beyond the moment itself and opens a window where lived experience may be imprinted as lasting change within the nervous system.

When Suggestibility and False Memories Surface

This profound openness during breathwork comes with risks. Scientific research shows that during states of heightened suggestibility, people become vulnerable to forming false memories. One of the most famous demonstrations of this phenomenon is the 'Lost in the Mall' experiment, where participants were asked to recall four childhood events provided by a family member. Three of the events were real and one was fabricated. The fabricated story was about being lost in a shopping mall as a child. Through repeated interviews and subtle cues, about a quarter of participants came to 'remember' the false event with vivid detail and high confidence.[6]

A single suggestion during this vulnerable window does not need to sound dramatic to carry weight. A facilitator might frame an experience as a 'release', speak of a 'blockage' and interpret a surge of emotion as trauma leaving the body. Even when well-intentioned, such framings can alter how a participant remembers and narrates what occurred. Sometimes, it reinforces a story they had not originally held.

Alex's story, introduced earlier, illustrates this point. Through conscious connected breathing he was able to move through fear as an experience that was not simply an emotional breakthrough but a neurological rewriting. His experience is a reminder that the potential to rewrite carries with it the need for clarity, integrity and responsibility.

Suggestion does not only come from facilitators. Group dynamics can be just as influential. When one participant interprets their experience as a release, a blockage clearing or trauma surfacing, others in the circle may adopt that same framing. What began as raw sensation can be reorganised into a shared narrative, and over time the story may feel more certain than the original experience itself.

The Many Doors of Breathwork

Breathwork has been taken into remarkably diverse settings. In large personal development seminars, high-energy breathing practices are used alongside music and movement to foster the possibility of breakthroughs in emotion or beliefs. In psychospiritual retreats and transformational workshops, modalities such as holotropic or rebirthing breathwork are used to evoke altered states and prompt deep emotional enquiry.

In performance coaching, athletes, artists and business leaders turn to breathing patterns to transform anxiety into focused presence and peak performance. In clinical practice, certain techniques are integrated into trauma therapy as a means of processing unresolved emotional material. Within wellness retreats, breathwork is often presented as a practice for regulation, insight and connection, while in yogic traditions pranayama is cultivated as a discipline for steadying the mind and preparing for meditation.

The range of settings is wide, yet what unites them is the search for a state shift. To see why breathwork can serve such different aims, we need to move beyond context and into the body where its mechanisms unfold.

The High-Ventilation Route

In chapter 10, we traced the physiological cascade of high ventilation as a form of hormetic stress. Here we return to the same terrain but with a different lens, looking at how these shifts in chemistry and circulation open the door to altered states of consciousness.

Within the altered chemistry of high ventilation, another process emerges, one that changes how the brain fuels itself. As oxygen delivery drops, neurons draw more heavily on lactate – the same substance that sustains muscle during anaerobic effort. Lactate provides energy and it may also stimulates the release of brain-derived neurotrophic factor (BDNF) – a molecule central to neuroplasticity.[7] The presence of BDNF increases the likelihood that new synaptic connections will form and stabilise, priming the nervous system for adaptation.

This is why high-ventilation breathwork can feel unusually potent. The nervous system is not only aroused but also primed to learn, so whatever impressions accompany the breath have a greater chance of embedding. In a supportive environment, this openness can create lasting transformation, but when the window is carelessly held, the same plasticity can reinforce fear, confusion or dissociation.

What rises in these states, whether tears or waves of grief or fragments of memory, is not conjured from nowhere. The nervous system is interpreting internal signals through patterns it has learned before. Breathlessness and the rush of light-headedness, or the disorienting sense of being out of control are read against past experience and the brain fills in meaning from the closest match. Neuroscientists describe this as 'perceptual inference' and it is the continuous prediction of what sensations signify. In conditions of heightened plasticity, those predictions are amplified and old associations can feel immediate and convincing.

High-ventilation breathing can drift from a tool for recalibration into a cycle of reliance. If the system learns to associate regulation only with the altered state of the practice, then relief becomes state-dependent and does not generalise into daily life.[8] In this pattern, the practice reinforces a coping state rather than expanding capacity. Some people notice this when they feel unsettled once the effect fades, while others take the euphoria with the session as evidence of integration. However, when the nervous system is conditioned to rely on repeated induction of the state in order to feel balanced, it is practising dependence rather than adaptation.

Resets or Escapes

Breathwork influences physiology in many ways, but one of the clearest distinctions is whether it functions as a reset or an escape.

A 'reset' is the deliberate use of breath to shift into a new physiological state while awareness remains present. With practice, these shifts can accumulate to recalibrate the baseline. In this form, the practice engages the system in learning, and the nervous system can reorganise around the new pattern. Such moments hold the potential for re-patterning and recalibration because the state is integrated into conscious experience.

An 'escape' is when the breath is used primarily as a coping mechanism and a way to blunt or discharge arousal without awareness or engagement, so the underlying patterns remain untouched. The body may feel lighter or clearer – even euphoric – but the change is transient because the system has not learned anything new. What seemed like a breakthrough is often temporary relief, and when a person becomes dependent on the practice to feel a particular way, the shift does not expand capacity – it reinforces dependence.

There is nothing unusual in using the breath for short-term relief – everyone does at times. However, transformation arises when practice creates capacity that carries beyond the session so regulation is no longer bound to the technique itself but becomes part of everyday life.

What About Out-of-Body Experiences?

In high-ventilation breathwork, it is not unusual to feel sensations that stretch beyond everyday perception, including a sense of leaving the body, surges of emotion, a feeling of profound openness or altered states of consciousness. These experiences often reflect shifts in chemistry, circulation and neural excitability during high-ventilation states, although similar sensations can also surface in other contexts where the brain's integration of body signals is disrupted.

Such experiences can contribute to a constructive reset when the return from them is accompanied by coherence. If, instead, the return brings disorientation or a lingering sense that another session is needed just to feel balanced, the episode is more likely to represent escape. In this case, the breath has provided relief, but the nervous system has learned to depend on the practice to recreate a state rather than expanding its capacity to regulate across daily life.

Out-of-body or disembodied states are not exclusive to breathwork, and they can also emerge in other circumstances where multisensory integration is disrupted, including sleep transitions, vestibular disturbance, certain meditation practices and psychedelic or drug-induced states. These experiences reflect the brain reorganising its map of the body in response to changing internal conditions.

Breath Reset Reflection

After Your Next Session

Take 5 minutes to consider these prompts:

- *What did I notice in my body during the session?* (For example, tension, release, numbness, movement.)
- *Did I have enough capacity to stay with what was arising? If not, what helped me remain present, or what pulled me away?*
- *Was there something that felt settled or integrated?* (For example, a memory, a release, a new awareness, a change in perspective.)
- *How do I feel in my body now, after the session?* (For example, grounded, spaced out, energised, disconnected.)
- *What is different, if anything, in the way I show up today?* (This is the small hinge on which larger change can turn.)

Your reflections are a way of noticing whether the practice is expanding capacity or fostering dependence. The work is not only in entering these states but in how you return.

State Dependency

State dependency often shows up not only in breathwork communities but also in the wider wellness culture. A common morning routine might include breathwork, cold immersion, caffeine and high-intensity training, each stacked to create a rush of sympathetic energy that can feel like vitality itself. The effect can be exhilarating, but if the day cannot begin without this sequence, then the system has become dependent on stimulation rather than maintaining its physiological baseline.

These practices stimulate the release of catecholamines, producing a transient sense of clarity and power. However, that energy is borrowed from the body's reserves and sustained reliance bears a cost.[9] The more enduring path is not built by pushing a depleted system harder, but by restoring it through adequate sleep and proper recovery, which provide the foundations for homeostatic regulation and for immune, metabolic and cognitive health.[10]

Chapter 18

Integration

Coming Home to Yourself

I could not hurry this book. Breath by breath and page by page it revealed its own tempo, teaching me that the pace you keep becomes the life you inhabit. For so long, I drove myself by deadlines and demands, pushing past what my body asked for. Here, I let the work take longer than expected and found a truer ground beneath me. Just as breath expands and contracts, life also asks for moments of acceleration and for moments of pause, and it is through listening that we learn to hold these polarities in balance. In the end, the feeling I am left with is that breath composes the passages of time and the boundaries that contain them more faithfully than any clock.

Integration is Not Perfection

There is a misconception that integration is an end state bearing semblance to a neatly tied bow at the close of transformation. In truth, it is the skill of returning, again and again, to centre even when life inevitably knocks you away from it.

I tested this recently. The final deadline for this book was close and boxes filled our new living room after moving house. Every reasonable voice urged me to stay home, unpack and finish. Instead, our little family boarded a plane for Western Australia. It felt inconvenient, indulgent, even irresponsible, yet it also felt like integrity. Integration was choosing life and connection and presence over productivity and perfection.

Those ten days were neither productive nor perfectly regulated. They were profoundly alive. Meals lingered and conversations unfolded slowly. My daughter roamed free, her laughter carrying across open spaces. A friend said quietly, 'It is good to slow down with you.' The words struck me because for most of my life I have not been slow by any measure. To be seen in that moment as someone who could soften the pace felt like the clearest reminder of the impact of this work.

I still get triggered and reactive, and I doubt that will ever end. Each time I come apart, breath does not fix me – it only waits until I am willing to look at myself truthfully and find my way back.

Your Breath Reset Plan

It is time to bring everything you have learned into one place. What follows are three nervous system profiles, each offering a pathway towards deeper self-understanding, breath retraining and lasting change. Begin with the state that most closely mirrors your present experience and allow yourself to explore from there, noticing what unfolds as you experiment. You are not only a nervous system but a whole human being, and the way you meet these practices will change with the seasons of life and the circumstances that surround you.

Restless and Reactive (Chronically Activated, Overstimulated)

Emotionally, this state carries impatience and irritability because the brain perceives time as contracted, interpreting even neutral situations as urgent. The alarm system stays switched on, creating a feedback loop of restlessness and reactivity. This state can arise in many ways, from the subtle effects of poor sleep to periods of ongoing stress. It may also follow more acute experiences such as loss, fear, panic or sleep-disordered breathing. Common breath patterns include:

- vertical, shallow breathing in the upper chest
- frequent sighing or yawning
- breath-holding during concentration, often preceded by unconscious bursts of hard and fast breathing
- mouth breathing under stress or during sleep, especially in REM phases
- night-time breathing instability, including flow-limited or mild forms of sleep-disordered breathing (such as UARS or REM-related apnoea), instability from high loop gain or frequent arousals.

Overthinking and Stuck (Conflicted Nervous System)

This state is marked by loops of rumination, chronic indecision and internal conflict. You may feel restless on the inside yet immobilised on the outside, caught between numbness and anxiety, detachment and reactivity, often all at once. Sleep is long but unrefreshing, with late-night coping strategies that add to fatigue. Many people in this state feel drained, foggy and confused, struggling to access clarity or intuition. This state often arises during periods of unresolved grief, prolonged states of uncertainty or entrenched self-criticism, when thoughts and emotions circle without resolution. Common breath patterns include:

- shallow, almost imperceptible breathing with minimal chest or abdominal movement (rigid, over-controlled)

- unconscious breath-holding, especially during indecision or mental conflict
- irregular breath timing with uneven pauses or catch-up breaths
- occasional mouth breathing during distraction or internal absorption (secondary, but common enough to be recognisable).

Emotionally Withdrawn (Shut Down, Burnt Out)

This state is marked by numbness, detachment and exhaustion. Energy is low, concentration is dulled and motivation feels out of reach. Social connection often becomes difficult, and even restorative sleep seems elusive, with long hours in bed that do not bring rest. It can follow chronic stress, long-term grief or loss, caregiver fatigue or emotional depletion from prolonged overwhelm. Common breath patterns include:

- shallow or restricted breathing with limited diaphragmatic movement, reflecting fatigue and collapse
- irregular breathing with pauses, sighs or erratic timing, signalling disrupted autonomic regulation
- reduced responsiveness to breathwork with difficulty adjusting breath due to exhaustion or emotional detachment (secondary, but often recognisable).

Important Safety Notes

The breath practices introduced in the Breath Reset Plans are generally safe and supportive for most people. Some techniques, however, have stronger physiological effects and may not be appropriate in all circumstances. These include practices involving intentional breath-holding (apnoeas), extended retentions or suspensions such as uddiyana bandha, deliberate over-breathing even for short periods, rhythmic connected breathing (circular breathing), dynamic pranayama such as kapalabhati, and subtle under-breathing practices that intentionally evoke air hunger. Avoid these practices if you:

- are pregnant
- have epilepsy or a history of seizures
- have cardiovascular disease or uncontrolled hypertension
- are living with unmanaged or severe mental health conditions (including severe anxiety, panic disorders, PTSD or dissociative disorders)
- are recovering from recent surgery or experiencing severe respiratory illness or other acute medical conditions.

Some practices are designed to evoke mild discomfort or a manageable sense of challenge, such as air hunger practices, to safely build nervous system resilience. If discomfort becomes excessive, or if anxiety, dizziness or strong unease arise, pause immediately and allow your breathing to return to normal. If you have medical concerns or health conditions, consult a qualified healthcare professional before beginning any breathwork practice.

The Restless and Reactive
Breath Reset Plan

....

This plan is for a system caught in constant activation, where stimulation outweighs recovery and breath mirrors that imbalance. The practices build capacity to move more fluidly between mobilisation and rest while strengthening awareness of how breathing habits modulate regulation.

Progress into subtle breathing, core breathing or walking apnoeas only when you can remain calmly present with mild air hunger. Let your body set the pace. The clearest sign of readiness is the ability to stay relaxed and composed, even as sensation intensifies.

Weeks 1–2:
Rest, Simplify and Cultivate

Intention: Simplify evenings, introduce breath awareness and establish breathing checks as the foundation for later stages.

Simplify Your Evenings (Daily)

Identify your main evening stressor (whether it is dinner preparation, decision fatigue, digital overload or late-night workouts) and take one step to reduce friction. Establish a wind-down routine that happens an hour or two before bed, with actions such as dimming lights, limiting screens, stretching, reading, listening to music or using a soothing scent. (See Breath Reset: The Pre-Sleep Protocol from chapter 12.)

Breath Awareness (3–5 Minutes, Nightly)

Observe the breath without trying to change it. Ask yourself, 'Can I allow the exhale to pour out effortlessly, as if letting go?' (See Understanding Breath: A Gentle Wave from the Bottom Up from chapter 1.)

Functional Breathing Checks (Brief Pauses During Transitions, Daily)
Choose two daily transitions, such as the afternoon slump or arriving home. Pause for 1–2 minutes and notice whether the breath is nasal, quiet, low and expansive. Check that the shoulders are relaxed and the mouth is closed. (See section The Foundation of Healthy Breathing from chapter 1.)

Weekly Bedtime Adjustment
Experiment with moving bedtime 30 minutes earlier while maintaining a consistent wake time that aligns with morning light. Track changes in your morning energy, mood and sleep quality in a simple diary, noting caffeine or alcohol intake, evening screen time and exercise timing. (See Breath Reset: The Patterns Beneath the Numbers from chapter 11.)

Integrated Education
Attending to the breath without immediately altering it rebuilds trust in the body's intelligence and loosens the impulse to control every detail of experience. Chronic activation fuels the reflex to over-manage. Allowing the breath to unfurl naturally initiates a restoration of balance between effort and ease, and between active participation and release, tending to the patterns that keep the system on constant alert.

> ### Reflection
> Ask yourself: *What new ease do I notice as I simplify my evenings and soften the exhale?*

Note: At first, the breath may feel as though it catches at the end of the exhale. This is normal. With practice and with parasympathetic tone increasing, the exhale will extend more easily and the pause after exhalation will naturally re-establish itself.

Weeks 3–4:
Regulate, Track and Reduce Daily Arousal

Intention: Introduce cadence breathing to downregulate the nervous system; begin tracking emotional triggers and recognise how these triggers influence your regulation through the lens of the window of tolerance. Continue all foundational practices from weeks 1–2.

Evening Cadence Breathing (5 Minutes Pre-Bed, Daily)
Practise cadence breathing beginning with a 3-second inhale, 6-second exhale, and progressing comfortably towards a 4-second inhale and an 8-second exhale. You may include brahmari, the humming bee breath. (See Breath Reset: The Edge-State Breath Reset from chapter 11.)

Window of Tolerance Tracking (Daily)
At the end of each day, reflect on the following in a notebook:

- *What nudged me out of my window of tolerance today?*
- *Did anything help to bring me back?*

(See Breath Reset: The Window of Tolerance Diary from chapter 7.)

Daytime Arousal Management
Where possible, move high-intensity exercise to earlier in the day. Consider replacing one or two sessions with yoga or nasal breathing walks in nature. If this is not possible, maintain the exercise but follow it with 5–10 minutes of intentional downregulation such as a body scan, breath awareness or cadence breathing. This conditions the nervous system to expect recovery after stimulation. Optionally, practise the Gastric Reset or Diaphragm Release from chapter 13 once or twice per week, ideally in the morning, to support diaphragm mobility, breathing efficiency and relaxation.

Reduce Reliance on Stimulation

Notice the stimulants and distractions you lean on and gradually reduce them. This may include caffeine after midday, sugary foods, compulsive checking of emails or rapid task switching.

> **Reflection**
> Ask yourself: *How are cadence breathing, emotional tracking and small lifestyle changes influencing my energy and emotional stability?*

Weeks 5–6:
Deepen Breath Regulation and Mind–Body Connection

Intention: Expand your capacity to stay with mild air hunger and strengthen the integration of body and mind. Continue daily practices from previous weeks.

Extended Evening Cadence Breathing (8–12 Minutes, 3–5 Times Weekly)

Increase the duration of this practice when you can maintain a smooth air volume and focused attention without agitation.

Introduce Subtle or Core Breathing (Optional, 5–10 Minutes, Nightly)

Once cadence breathing feels established, begin occasional sessions of subtle breathing or core breathing. Subtle breathing reduces air volume to create mild air hunger, training awareness of small shifts in breathing and improving your ability to stay present with the sensation of wanting more air. Core breathing extends this by engaging the deep core muscles in synchrony with the breath, adding a more tangible felt sense and biomechanical support to the same process. (See Breath Reset: Subtle Breathing from chapter 14, and Breath Reset: Core Breathing from chapter 15.)

Yoga Nidra or Non-Sleep Deep Rest (10–20 Minutes, 3 Times Weekly, Midday or Pre-Sleep)

Include regular sessions of yoga nidra or non-sleep deep rest to strengthen interoceptive awareness, regulate arousal and improve recognition of subtle bodily cues such as tension, agitation or unease that might otherwise remain outside awareness. (See Breath Reset: Yoga Nidra from chapter 8.)

Integrated Education

In yoga nidra, the slowing of breath slightly increases carbon dioxide in the blood. At first, the brain may read this rise as stress and create the impulse to sigh, move or breathe more quickly to relieve the sensation. These reactions lower carbon dioxide and bring temporary ease, but they also interrupt the chance for the nervous system to learn that stillness can be tolerated. When restlessness arises, remind yourself that this is part of the process. With repetition, the system adapts and stillness begins to register less as unease and more as a state of quiet restoration.

> **Reflection**
> Ask yourself: *Am I becoming more at ease with subtle breathing and mild air hunger? Do I sense greater fluidity in how I move between activation and rest as I practise yoga nidra or non-sleep deep rest?*

Weeks 7–8:
Integrate Practices, Expand Capacity and Build Agency

Intention: Strengthen resilience, widen the window of tolerance and cultivate emotional clarity. Emotional clarity deepens as the nervous system becomes more regulated and interoceptive awareness increases. When the system is calmer, vagal signalling to the brain is clearer, allowing greater emotional insight and adaptability. Continue the established practices from earlier weeks.

Full-Duration Evening Cadence or Subtle Breathing (15 Minutes, Nightly)

Increase evening sessions to 15 minutes, using cadence breathing (beginning with a 3-second inhale and a 6-second exhale [3:6], and extending towards a 4-second inhale and an 8-second exhale [4:8], or longer) or progressing into subtle or core breathing. Enthusiasm to practise is the most important driver.

Walking Apnoeas (Gentle 5-Round Protocol, 3 Times Weekly)

Practise short breath-holds while walking, aiming for around 30 per cent of your comfortable maximum breath-hold, increasing gradually without strain (see Breath Reset: Walking Apnoeas from chapter 15). Alternatively, practise uddiyana bandha (abdominal suction with breath retention) first thing in the morning on an empty stomach (see Breath Reset: Uddiyana Bandha from chapter 13) to build tolerance to air hunger, strengthen diaphragm and abdominal tone and support stress resilience.

Heart Coherence Breathing (Throughout the Day or After Stressful Events)

Practise balanced nasal breathing of 5 seconds in and 5 seconds out. This pattern is associated with improvements in heart rate variability, steadier emotional tone and stable autonomic regulation. Keep the breath soft, nasal and unforced. Avoid taking larger breaths than needed. (See Understanding Breath: Heart Coherence Breathing from chapter 3.)

Yoga Nidra (20 Minutes, Midday Preferred, 3–5 Times Weekly)

Extend yoga nidra sessions to 20 minutes, ideally shifting them to midday. This helps the nervous system develop flexibility, moving with more ease between peak activation and deep rest.

Reflection

Ask yourself:

- *Do I notice my breath-hold capacity increasing through walking apnoeas or through dynamic practices that evoke air hunger?*
- *Am I approaching these practices with connection to internal sensations rather than disconnecting or pushing through?*
- *Do I feel less rushed, clearer in thought or more emotionally stable and better able to navigate the stresses and demands of daily life?*

A Note of Encouragement

This progression makes use of the brain's neuroplasticity – that is, its ability to reorganise and form new predictive pathways. You begin with practices that reset the breathing baseline and then gradually introduce stronger physiological challenges. Each step teaches the system to accurately distinguish between genuine threats and tolerable discomfort.

Trust the intelligence of your body as your capacity expands. This reset is not a finish line but the foundation of a lifelong skill in navigating your internal landscape with agency and confidence. Progress is not linear, so honour your personal timeline, revisit phases when needed and trust the cumulative value of consistency.

The Overthinking and Stuck
Breath Reset Plan

This plan addresses a nervous system caught between activation and immobilisation, where energy surges but action stalls and the mind becomes trapped in loops of rumination and indecision. Through deliberate movement, breath retraining and interoceptive training, you will refine how the brain interprets internal signals. Over time, this reduces confusion and supports clearer perception of emotions and sensations and renewed agency.

Weeks 1–2:
Mobilise Energy and Establish Connection

Intention: Establish consistent daily routines that mobilise physical energy, interrupt patterns of mental stagnation and reconnect with bodily sensations.

Morning Circadian Reset (Daily)
Wake at the same time each morning and seek direct morning sunlight for 5–10 minutes within 30 minutes of waking.

Morning Pages (Daily)
Write three full pages of stream-of-consciousness journalling to mentally declutter.

Movement Practice (30+ Minutes, Daily)
Engage in movement that prioritises thoracic and diaphragm mobility such as spinal undulations, diaphragm release, dynamic yoga or somatic shaking, breathing nasally throughout. Optionally, engage in more vigorous activities such as running, dancing or martial arts if you feel drawn to them.

Mobilisation practices disrupt the inertia of freeze states, jump-starting your nervous responsiveness and generating momentum.

Brief Body Scan (5 Minutes, Post-Movement, Daily)
After movement, lie on your back with palms facing upwards and arms relaxed slightly away from your body. Slowly rotate presence through your body from head to toes, tuning into the full spectrum of sensations from obvious to subtle, allowing them to shift or dissolve without effort.

Evening Routine (Nightly)
Identify your primary coping strategy such as screens or social media and limit it to short, defined intervals of 15–30 minutes. Replace excess use with presence-based practices such as yin yoga, intuitive somatic movement, guided relaxation or body scans, or an evening wind-down routine. (See Breath Reset: The Pre-Sleep Protocol from chapter 12.)

> **Reflection**
> Ask yourself: *Am I noticing changes in my energy levels as I establish these routines? How are my mood and sleep responding to these initial shifts?*

Weeks 3–4:
Restore Functional Breathing and Track Triggers

Intention: Retrain breathing patterns to stabilise the physiological baseline and begin identifying triggers that contribute to cycles of overthinking, indecision and emotional confusion. Continue all practices from weeks 1–2.

Functional Breathing (5 Minutes, 5 Times Weekly)
Sit comfortably with your lips sealed and tongue resting on the roof of the mouth. Breathe nasally, quietly and without effort, allowing the lower ribs to expand laterally, travelling outwards and into the back of your body. Keep the shoulders supple and attention focused inwards. (See The Foundation of Healthy Breathing from chapter 1.)

Somatic Release (2–3 Minutes, as Needed, Daily)
After moments of stress or when feeling immobilised, shake, bounce or move freely to loosen the body and restore responsiveness.

Yoga Nidra or Non-Sleep Deep Rest (10–15 Minutes, 3 Times Weekly)
Practise yoga nidra or non-sleep deep rest in an environment that feels supportive, using supports such as blankets, scent or chosen company that help the body settle. Choose a time of day that fits naturally with your routine, as consistency is what anchors the habit.

Window of Tolerance Tracking (Daily)
Every day, reflect on the following in your notebook:

- *What nudged me out of my window today?*
- *What sensations did I notice when I felt stuck, uncertain or activated?*
- *Did anything specific help to bring me back into balance?*

(See Breath Reset: The Window of Tolerance Diary from chapter 7.)

Additional Lifestyle Adjustments
Minimise caffeine intake after midday and reduce alcohol where relevant. Aim for consistent hydration, as dehydration amplifies stress signalling. Eat balanced meals at the same time each day to stabilise blood sugar. Reduce physiological triggers of anxiety and indecision.

> **Reflection**
>
> Ask yourself:
>
> - *Am I experiencing fewer spirals of overthinking?*
> - *Do bodily sensations feel clearer and easier for me to interpret?*
> - *Are any specific triggers or patterns becoming more evident?*

Weeks 5–6:
Deepen Interoceptive Clarity and Expand Regulation

Intention: Improve the nervous system's accuracy in reading internal cues. Mild air hunger becomes a training tool, showing the system that not all discomfort signals danger. Continue all foundational practices from weeks 1–4.

Sama Vritti Breathing (5–10 Minutes, 5 Times Weekly)

Practise seated or lying down after movement or as part of your evening wind-down. Inhale, pause, exhale and pause in equal counts. Begin at a count of 4:4:4:4 and adjust if needed. The breath should remain effortless and quiet throughout.

Subtle Breathing (5 Minutes, 3 Times Weekly)

Practise subtle breathing with curiosity and openness towards mild air hunger. Remind yourself: *I have enough air. These sensations can be felt.* (See Breath Reset: Subtle Breathing from chapter 14.)

Extended Yoga Nidra or Non-Sleep Deep Rest (20+ Minutes, Midday or After Movement, 3 Times Weekly)

Extend sessions gradually, shifting them towards midday or early afternoon, or immediately following movement. If restlessness arises, treat it as useful feedback rather than a reason to stop.

Body-Breath Check-In and Contemplation (15 Minutes, Weekly)
Recall a recent experience of stuckness or overwhelm. Spend 1–2 minutes feeling the sensations it evoked, then practise 10–12 minutes of cadence breathing (3:6 or 4:8). In your journal, consider these reflections:

- *Before cadence breathing, I noticed ...*
- *After breathing, I noticed ...*
- *Insights about body–emotion connections include ...*

Play, Creativity and Social Engagement (Weekly and Fortnightly)
Schedule meaningful social contact weekly and creative or playful activities such as art-making, dance or music at least fortnightly

> ### Reflection
> Ask yourself:
> - *Am I more willing to remain with sensations like subtle air hunger?*
> - *Are these sensations clearer and less confusing?*
> - *Do I feel greater agency and clarity in response to stressors?*

Weeks 7–8:
Expand Interoceptive Exposure and Breath Reset Integration

Intention: Refine the nervous system's precision in interpreting internal signals so adaptability becomes second nature. Continue all foundational practices from weeks 1–6.

Walking Apnoeas (3–5 Rounds, 3–5 Times Weekly)
Practise short breath-holds during relaxed walking, aiming for around 30 per cent of your maximum breath-hold capacity. Alternatively, extend subtle breathing sessions towards 20 minutes. (See Breath Reset: Walking Apnoeas from chapter 15.)

3-Minute Anchor (3–5 Times Weekly)

Practise circular breathing paired with embodied affirmations that resonate physiologically rather than cognitively. (See Breath Reset: The 3-Minute Anchor from chapter 16.) Examples include:

- 'I can allow these sensations.'
- 'I feel supported.'
- 'I am here.'

> **Reflection**
>
> Ask yourself: *Am I becoming more at ease with sensations that previously felt intolerable? Do emotional states feel clearer and more distinguishable?*

A Note of Encouragement

Your dedication has shifted the way your nervous system interprets internal signals. Where confusion once fuelled indecision and rumination, you have cultivated clarity, agency and a stronger connection between body and mind, and this is worthy of self-acknowledgement. This reset is not a finish line but the foundation of ongoing trust in your own perception and the choices that flow from it.

The Emotionally Withdrawn
Breath Reset Plan

The emotionally withdrawn state reflects a system that has moved into shutdown, marked by depletion, low capacity to recover and greater susceptibility to illness. The immediate priority is to re-establish restorative processes. In the early weeks, the practices focus on improving sleep quality and reducing stimulation, as well as creating the conditions for the nervous system to begin rebuilding.

Weeks 1–2:
Sleep Regulation and Emotional Balance

Intention: In nervous system shutdown or burnout, the body typically requires extended rest and increased sleep for weeks or months to replenish energy reserves and restore emotional capacity. Incrementally increasing rest each week supports slow recalibration.

Sleep Tracking and Sleep Routine Adjustments (Daily)

Each evening, record your bedtime, waking time, total sleep duration, any awakenings and your subjective sense of sleep quality. (See Breath Reset: The Patterns Beneath the Numbers from chapter 11.)

As you track, notice connections between daily habits, mood and sleep quality. For example, did an event at work or home unsettle you? Did you eat late, choose less nourishing foods, drink alcohol or spend time watching TV or scrolling before bed?

Trust your instincts and identify one or two realistic changes to reduce friction. If dinner preparation is a source of stress, for example, simplify by meal-prepping on weekends, cooking lighter meals or preparing earlier in the day so that evenings feel more spacious and conducive to winding down.

Managing Arousal (Daily)

Notice the habits and interactions that heighten arousal or push you out of your window of tolerance. These may include emotionally charged exchanges or late vigorous exercise. Where exercise is the factor, trial nasal-only walks, earlier or lighter sessions, shorter duration with less exertion and more restorative forms of movement. If reducing your activity level stirs guilt or worry, trial halving the intensity and observe your body's response. If no improvement follows, your system likely needs deeper rest. Use The Window of Tolerance Diary to reflect on what contributed, including people, specific tasks or environments and whether anything helped to restore capacity. (See Breath Reset: The Window of Tolerance Diary from chapter 7.)

Evening Routine (Nightly)

Limit coping strategies such as screens or scrolling to defined intervals of 15–30 minutes. One by one, replace them with presence-based practices such as yin yoga, intuitive somatic movement, guided relaxation or body scans or your breath reset evening wind-down routine. (See Breath Reset: The Pre-Sleep Protocol from chapter 12.)

Reflection

Ask yourself: *Am I noticing small improvements in sleep or subtle emotional steadiness? Do I feel more settled?*

If not, this is normal and your system may need more repetition and time.

Weeks 3–4:
Functional Breathing and Increased Rest

Intention: Support ongoing recovery by consolidating functional breathing patterns and sustaining extended rest.

Functional Breathing (5 Minutes, Ongoing, Daily)

Practise nasal breathing that is light, quiet and unforced, with 360-degree expansion around the lower ribs. Allow the diaphragm and rib cage to move freely and pair the practice with daily cues so it embeds more easily – for example, pause and take three relaxed breaths whenever you pick up your phone. (See The Foundation of Healthy Breathing from chapter 1.)

Extended Rest and Sleep (As Necessary, Daily)

Continue to prioritise more time for rest and longer sleep than you would typically give yourself. Recovery from depletion unfolds slowly, and accepting that weeks or even months of extended rest may be necessary is often the turning point for genuine repair. Focus on earlier bedtimes and consistent waking times, and integrate short breaks at least every 90 minutes to align with the ultradian rhythm. Use these pauses to step back from stimulation or concentrated effort to let your mind wander and your body soften. Practise yoga nidra or non-sleep deep rest 3–5 times a week for 20 minutes or more. This initiates deeply restorative brainwave states that recalibrate stress pathways. (See Breath Reset: Yoga Nidra from chapter 8.)

Recovery from the red zone of burnout cannot be rushed. Taking a step back in this stage replenishes your energy reserves and safeguards against further depletion or the likelihood of illness.

> ### Reflection
> Ask yourself: *Do I feel patient enough to accept the extended timeframe my body needs to replenish?*
>
> If the honest answer is no, this reaction is common, especially for those accustomed to constant productivity. Consider the following:
> - *What specifically makes rest feel difficult or uncomfortable right now?*
> - *Am I linking rest or slower progress to negative beliefs about myself?*
> - *Can I view rest as a purposeful investment in my recovery?*

Consider seeking additional support. Share these reflections with someone you trust, a family member, a colleague or a professional who can encourage patience and self-compassion. Remind yourself regularly, *Two steps back will bring me back.* Resting deeply now is not losing ground; it is intentionally gathering strength and will ultimately propel you forwards into renewed energy.

Weeks 5–6:
Build Capacity and Resilience

Intention: Continue practices from weeks 1–4. Once signs of nervous system stability are consistent, you are ready for this next phase. Readiness is reflected in steadier sleep with fewer awakenings, a clearer sense of waking refreshed, an increase in baseline energy, a more regulated emotional tone with reduced reactivity, nasal breathing that feels effortless during practice and, for those tracking, improvements in heart rate variability.

When these markers appear with some consistency, begin with cadence breathing. When this feels sustainable and easeful, progress into subtle air hunger.

Cadence Breathing (5 Minutes, Ongoing, Daily)

Practise a comfortable, effortless breathing rhythm of 3:6, 4:6 or 4:8. The idea is to find a cadence that brings you to around six breaths per minute. Research shows that benefits come from slowing the overall breathing rate rather than holding exact ratios.[1] Comfort matters most, and if you force the exhale or push the timing, the practice can tip into over-breathing. (See Breath Reset: The Edge-State Breath Reset from chapter 11.)

Subtle Breathing (5 Minutes at First, 3–5 Times Weekly)

Once cadence breathing is established, begin to introduce subtle breathing. Keep the practice free from muscular effort. It is about relaxing into less, not forcing or controlling the breathing muscles into less. (See Breath Reset: Subtle Breathing from chapter 14.)

Integrated Education: Air Hunger and Fear Processing

Mild air hunger modestly raises carbon dioxide, activating chemo-receptors in the medulla that communicate with brain regions involved in fear and appraisal, including the amygdala. In states of burnout or emotional withdrawal, even this slight elevation may trigger alarm or withdrawal behaviours, reinforcing predictions that something is wrong. However, repeated gentle exposure helps the system relearn that these sensations are tolerable. The brain can then predict them as safe, which reduces anxiety and strengthens the accuracy with which internal signals are interpreted.

Reflection

Ask yourself: *Do I feel comfortable and consistent with cadence breathing? Am I noticing more tolerance for mild air hunger?*

Weeks 7–8:
Playful Exploration and Emotional Reintegration

Intention: This phase invites exploration of play, creativity and connection in ways that expand energy and emotional engagement without overwhelming the recovering system. For some, these may be familiar states being reclaimed, and for others, they may feel entirely new. Readiness is shown by steadier energy levels, more consistent emotional balance, comfort in earlier breathing practices, greater tolerance for mild stimulation and sleep that feels more restorative across several weeks. Plateaus and setbacks are a natural part of the recovery process.

Integrated Breathing and Movement (5–10 Minutes, Daily)

Pair functional breathing with relaxed movement that feels spontaneous and enjoyable. The purpose here is to restore comfort in connecting with your body, in sensing and feeling, and in moving in ways that elicit reverence while using the breath as a guide to turn inwards. Music can support this process immensely, helping expression emerge more naturally. If you feel awkward or uncomfortable, notice it as part of the process of loosening patterns of holding and rigidity.

Modified 3-Minute Anchor (3–5 Times Weekly)

Practise circular breathing and pair it with embodied reminders, such as, 'I am listening deeply to what I feel', 'My body is my home' or 'I am pouring presence into every fibre and tissue'.

Exploration of Play (Short Sessions, Weekly)

Engage in low-pressure playful or creative activities with no goal or defined outcome attached, such as barefoot nature walks, ceramics, freestyle writing or mirror dancing.

> **Reflection**
>
> Ask yourself:
> - *Am I noticing shifts towards greater connection?*
> - *Does my energy feel more available?*
> - *Does it feel easier to reconnect with creativity or playfulness in my day?*

A Note of Encouragement

When the body has been in withdrawal, neural circuits that govern arousal and motivation often move into prolonged low activity. Recovery depends on more than willpower, as you are untangling neuroplastic changes in the brain alongside autonomic networks that have prioritised output at the expense of repair. Even when your progress feels imperceptible, know that the cumulative effects of energy restoration are reorganising the design behind the scenes and preparing the ground for your life force to pour through.

Acknowledgements

Before you read these acknowledgements, forgive me. This may be the driest and least poetic part of the whole offering. It's no reflection of the people I am about to name. Perhaps some seasoned book pros finish buoyant at the end of the line, but despite my enduring commitment to preserving sleep and sanity, I am crawling to this final page like someone who has just run an ultramarathon with ten stitches and a cramping calf. This book came into being because of the people who encouraged me to begin and cheered me on along the way, who listened to me when I moaned and complained, and who supported me from start to finish.

To Ally Nolan, who first told me to write and without whose ongoing encouragement this book would not exist. To Kelly Doust, for believing in the project and taking it up. To David Golding, who walked into a field of tangled weeds and helped me pluck the thorns one by one. David's structural edit shaped the architecture of these chapters. To Gabriella Sterio, whose first copyedit refined the sentences and grammar and whose tiny notes and smiley faces of joyful positivity in the margins made a difference in the trenches. To Sam van Zweden, the copyeditor, and Kirstie Innes-Will, the proofreader who took the manuscript through its final stages, thank you for taking it across the line. And to the wider team at Affirm, whose tireless work I may not see day to day but without whom this book could not have found its way into the world, my gratitude runs deep.

I have spent many years immersed in yoga and movement, guided by internationally respected mentors including, most notably, Noelle Connolly, Meghan Currie and Gwyn Williams. Their influence continues to mould my connection to my body, which is, after all, the centre of this book. I thank the countless hours I have spent in the laboratory of my own body, day after day.

To my mother, Jane Elliston, the most wonderful mother and grandmother, thank you for your endless support and especially for helping with extra writing time by taking Lhotse Blue on breakfast dates and doing extra pickups. Thanks to my father, Peter Elliston, for being the best dad a girl could have, with constant love and support. To my partner, Josh Fergus, for being the inspirer of creative juice, the rock of the family, a loving partner and the best father every day to our girl, playing music that fills our house with life and creating rituals that keep magic alive within the routine of parenting. To baby Blue, the brightest little spark and my reason for breathing at all, I love you. Without these foundations nothing built on top could stand.

To my Advanced Breath Instructor students, clients and community over the last decade and more, your practice, presence and the bonds we have created are interwoven through every page. And to the readers who take these practices into your own lives, and the teachers and practitioners who will pass them on, you are the living continuation of the work that began here.

References

Chapter 1: The First Breath Reset

1   Hamasaki, H. (2020). Effects of diaphragmatic breathing on health: A narrative review. *Medicines, 7*(10), Article 65.

2   Cleveland Clinic. (2022, May 12). Hypoxia. *Health Library.* https://my.clevelandclinic. org/health/diseases/23063-hypoxia

3   Boulding, R., Stacey, R., Niven, R., & Fowler, S. J. (2016). Dysfunctional breathing: A review of the literature and proposal for classification. *European Respiratory Review, 25*(141), 287–294.

Boyle, K. L., Olinick, J., & Lewis, C. (2010). The value of blowing up a balloon. *North American Journal of Sports Physical Therapy, 5*(3), 179–188.

Vidotto, L. S., de Carvalho, C. R. F., Harvey, A., & Jones, M. (2019). Dysfunctional breathing: What do we know? *Jornal Brasileiro de Pneumologia, 45*(1), Article e20170347.

4   Bradley, H., & Esformes, J. D. (2014). Breathing pattern disorders and functional movement. *International Journal of Sports Physical Therapy, 9*(1), 28–39.

Depiazzi, J., & Everard, M. L. (2016). Dysfunctional breathing and reaching one's physiological limit as causes of exercise-induced dyspnoea. *Breathe, 12*(2), 120–129.

Hamasaki, H. (2020).

5   Vlemincx, E., Severs, L. J., & Ramirez, J. M. (2022). The psychophysiology of the sigh: II: The sigh from the psychological perspective. *Biological Psychology, 173*, 1–8.

6   Banushi, B., Brendle, M., Ragnhildstveit, A., Murphy, T., Moore, C., Egberts, J., & Robison, R. (2023). Breathwork interventions for adults with clinically diagnosed anxiety disorders: A scoping review. *Brain Sciences, 13*(2), 256.

Bradley, H., & Esformes, J. D. (2014).

Roussel, N., Nijs, J., Truijen, S., Vervecken, L., Mottram, S., & Stassijns, G. (2009). Altered breathing patterns during lumbopelvic motor control tests in chronic low back pain: A case–control study. *European Spine Journal, 18*(7), 1066–1073.

Vidotto, L. S., de Carvalho, C. R. F., Harvey, A., & Jones, M. (2019).

7   Behan, M., & Wenninger, J. M. (2008). Sex steroidal hormones and respiratory control. *Respiratory Physiology & Neurobiology, 164*(1–2), 213–221.

8   Harvard Health Publishing. (2016, March 10). Learning diaphragmatic breathing. *Harvard Health Publishing.* https://www.health.harvard.edu/lung-health-and-disease/learning-diaphragmatic-breathing

9   Benner, A., Patel, A. K., Singh, K., & Dua, A. (2023). Physiology, Bohr effect. *StatPearls.* Retrieved October 18, 2025, from https://www.ncbi.nlm.nih.gov/books/NBK526028

10   Benner, A., Patel, A. K., Singh, K., & Dua, A. (2023).
     Patel, S., Jose, A., & Mohiuddin, S. S. (2023). Physiology, oxygen transport and carbon dioxide dissociation curve. *StatPearls.* Retrieved October 18, 2025, from https://www.ncbi.nlm.nih.gov/books/NBK539815

11   Benner, A., Patel, A. K., Singh, K., & Dua, A. (2023).
     Patel, S., Jose, A., & Mohiuddin, S. S. (2023).

12   Kraler, M. (2022). *Yoga breath: The reinvention of prāṇa and prāṇāyāma in early modern yoga* [Doctoral dissertation, University of Vienna]. https://utheses.univie.ac.at/detail/63089

13   Paulus, M. P. (2013). The breathing conundrum – interoceptive sensitivity and anxiety. *Depression and Anxiety, 30,* 315–320.

Chapter 2: Small Steps

1   Govindasamy, K., Kaur, D., Elayaraja, M., Sethi, D., Kalidas, S., Karmakar, D., & Orhan, B. E. (2024). Immediate effect of uddiyana bandha on heart rate variability in patients with hypertension: A randomised controlled study. *Annals of Neurosciences.*

2   Kyriakoulis, P., Kyrios, M., Nardi, A. E., Freire, R. C., & Schier, M. (2021). The implications of the diving response in reducing panic symptoms. *Frontiers in Psychiatry, 12,* Article 784884.
     Meuret, A. E., Wilhelm, F. H., Ritz, T., & Roth, W. T. (2008). Feedback of end-tidal pCO_2 as a therapeutic approach for panic disorder. *Journal of Psychiatric Research, 42*(7), 560–568.

3   Ashhad, S., Kam, K., Del Negro, C. A., & Feldman, J. L. (2022). Breathing rhythm and pattern and their influence on emotion. *Annual Review of Neuroscience, 45,* 223–247.
     Vidotto, L. S., de Carvalho, C. R. F., Harvey, A., & Jones, M. (2019). Dysfunctional breathing: What do we know? *Jornal Brasileiro de Pneumologia, 45*(1), Article 20170347.

4   Australian Government Department of Health and Aged Care. (2024). *Natural therapies review 2024 – Buteyko evidence evaluation.* Australian Government Department of Health and Aged Care. https://www.health.gov.au/resources/publications/natural-therapies-review-2024-buteyko-evidence-evaluation
     Banushi, B., Brendle, M., Ragnhildstveit, A., Murphy, T., Moore, C., Egberts, J. & Robison, R. (2023). Breathwork interventions for adults with clinically diagnosed anxiety disorders: A scoping review. *Brain Sciences, 13*(2), Article 256.
     Barker, N. J., Jones, M., O'Connell, N. E., & Everard, M. L. (2013). Breathing exercises for dysfunctional breathing/hyperventilation syndrome in children. *Cochrane Database of Systematic Reviews, 2013*(12), Article CD010376.

5   Ma, X., Yue, Z.-Q., Gong, Z.-Q., Zhang, H., Duan, N.-Y., Shi, Y.-T., Wei, G.-X., & Li, Y.-F. (2017). The effect of diaphragmatic breathing on attention, negative affect and stress in healthy adults. *Frontiers in Psychology, 8*, Article 874.

6   Jerath, R., & Beveridge, C. (2020). Respiratory rhythm, autonomic modulation, and the spectrum of emotions: The future of emotion recognition and modulation. *Frontiers in Psychology, 11*, Article 1980.

7   Vidotto, L. S., de Carvalho, C. R. F., Harvey, A., & Jones, M. (2019).

8   Levine, P. A. & Frederick, A. (1997). *Waking the tiger: Healing trauma.* North Atlantic Books.

9   Ma, X., Yue, Z.-Q., Gong, Z.-Q., Zhang, H., Duan, N.-Y., Shi, Y.-T., Wei, G.-X., & Li, Y.-F. (2017).
     Toussaint, L., Nguyen, Q. A., Roettger, C., Dixon, K., Offenbächer, M., Kohls, N., & Hirsch, J. (2021). Effectiveness of progressive muscle relaxation, deep breathing, and guided imagery in promoting psychological and physiological states of relaxation. *Evidence-Based Complementary and Alternative Medicine, 2021*, Article 5924040.

Chapter 3: Breath and the Biology of Stress

1   Bravo, C., HernándezGarcía, D., TrinidadFernández, M., Badia, G., Solé, S., & Serrano, J. (2024). Movement awareness therapies in eating disorders: A systematic review and metaanalysis. *Nursing & Health Sciences, 26*(4), Article e13181.

2   McEwen, B. S. (2000). Allostasis and allostatic load: Implications for neuropsychopharmacology. *Neuropsychopharmacology, 22*(2), 108–124.

3   McEwen, B. S. (2000).

4   Young, H. A., & Benton, D. (2018). Heartrate variability: A biomarker to study the influence of nutrition on physiological and psychological health? *Behavioural Pharmacology, 29*(2 and 3), 140–151.

5   Szulczewski, M. T. (2019). An antihyperventilation instruction decreases the drop in endtidal CO_2 and symptoms of hyperventilation during breathing at 0.1 Hz. *Applied Psychophysiology and Biofeedback, 44*(3), 247–256.
     Marchant, J., Khazan, I., & Cressman, M. (2025). Comparing the effects of square, 4-7-8, and six-breaths-per-minute breathing conditions on heart rate variability, CO_2 levels and mood. *Applied Psychophysiology and Biofeedback, 50*(2), 261–276.

6   Marchant, J., Khazan, I., & Cressman, M. (2025).

7   Cole, S. W. (2019). The conserved transcriptional response to adversity. *Current Opinion in Behavioral Sciences, 28*, 31–37.

8   Ravi, M., Miller, A. H., & Michopoulos, V. (2021). The immunology of stress and the impact of inflammation on the brain and behavior. *BJPsych Advances, 27*(S3), 158–165.

9   Cole, S. W. (2019).
     Ravi, M., Miller, A. H., & Michopoulos, V. (2021).

10   Beese, S., Postma, J., & Graves, J. M. (2022). Allostatic load measurement: A systematic review of reviews, database inventory, and considerations for neighborhood research. *International Journal of Environmental Research and Public Health, 19*(24), Article 17006.

Brosschot, J. F., Verkuil, B., & Thayer, J. F. (2018). The generalized unsafety theory of stress: Unsafe environments and conditions, and the default stress response. *International Journal of Environmental Research and Public Health*, 15(3), 464.

11 Masaoka, Y., & Homma, I. (2000). The source generator of respiratoryrelated anxiety potential in the human brain. *Neuroscience Letters*, 283(1), 21–24.

Masaoka, Y., Koiwa, N., & Homma, I. (2005). Inspiratory phaselocked alpha oscillation in human olfaction: Source generators estimated by a dipole tracing method. *Journal of Physiology*, 566(3), 979–997.

12 Masaoka, Y., Koiwa, N., & Homma, I. (2005).

13 Masaoka, Y., Koiwa, N., & Homma, I. (2005).

14 Zelano, C., Jiang, H., Zhou, G., Arora, N., Schuele, S., Rosenow, J., & Gottfried, J. A. (2016). Nasal respiration entrains human limbic oscillations and modulates cognitive function. *Journal of Neuroscience*, 36(49), 12448–12467.

15 Masaoka, Y., Koiwa, N., & Homma, I. (2005).
Zelano, C., Jiang, H., Zhou, G., Arora, N., Schuele, S., Rosenow, J., & Gottfried, J. A. (2016).

16 Armour, J. A. (2008). Potential clinical relevance of the 'little brain' on the mammalian heart. *Experimental Physiology, 93*(2), 165–176.

17 Garfinkel, S. N., Minati, L., Gray, M. A., Seth, A. K., Dolan, R. J., & Critchley, H. D. (2014). Fear from the heart: Sensitivity to fear stimuli depends on individual heartbeats. *Journal of Neuroscience, 34*(19), 6573–6582.

18 Lehrer, P. M., & Gevirtz, R. (2014). Heart rate variability biofeedback: How and why does it work? *Frontiers in Psychology, 5*, 756.

19 McCraty, R., & Shaffer, F. (2015). Heart rate variability: New perspectives on physiological mechanisms, assessment of self-regulatory capacity, and health risk. *Global Advances in Health and Medicine, 4*(1), 46–61.

20 Iorgulescu, G. (2009). Saliva between normal and pathological: Important factors in determining systemic and oral health. *Journal of Medicine and Life, 2*(3), 303–307.

21 Vidotto, L. S., de Carvalho, C. R. F., Harvey, A., & Jones, M. (2019). Dysfunctional breathing: What do we know? *Jornal Brasileiro de Pneumologia, 45*(1), Article e20170347.
Evans, R. W. (2024, September 3). Hyperventilation syndrome. *MedLink Neurology*. https://www.medlink.com/articles/hyperventilation-syndrome

22 Levine, P. A. & Frederick, A. (1997).

Chapter 4: The Four Dimensions of Breath

1 McKeown, P. (2015). *The oxygen advantage*. HarperCollins.
McKeown, P. (2021). *The breathing cure: Develop habits for a healthier, happier and longer life*. Humanix Books.

2 Dudai, Y. (2002). *Memory from A to Z: Keywords, concepts, and beyond*. Oxford University Press.
Eich, J. E. (1980). The cue-dependent nature of state-dependent retrieval. *Memory & Cognition, 8*(2), 157–173.

3 Brinkman, J. E., Toro, F., & Sharma, S. (2023). Physiology, respiratory drive. *StatPearls*. Retrieved October 18, 2025, from https://www.ncbi.nlm.nih.gov/books/NBK482414

4   Brinkman, J. E., Toro, F., & Sharma, S. (2023).

5   Paulus, M. P. (2013). The breathing conundrum – interoceptive sensitivity and anxiety. *Depression and Anxiety, 30*(4), 315–320.

6   Schottelkotte, K. M., & Crone, S. A. (2022). Forebrain control of breathing: Anatomy and potential functions. *Frontiers in Neurology, 13*, Article 1041887.

7   Burki, N. K., & Lee, L. Y. (2010). Mechanisms of dyspnea. *Chest, 138*(5), 1196–1201.

8   Marlow, L. L., Faull, O. K., Finnegan, S. L., & Pattinson, K. T. S. (2019). Breathlessness and the brain: The role of expectation. *Current Opinion in Supportive and Palliative Care, 13*(3), 200–210.

9   Nakai, H., Tsujimoto, K., Fuchigami, T., Ohmatsu, S., Osumi, M., Nakano, H., Fukui, M., & Morioka, S. (2015). Effect of anticipation triggered by a prior dyspnea experience on brain activity. *Journal of Physical Therapy Science, 27*(3), 635–639.

10 Maric, V., Ramanathan, D., & Mishra, J. (2020). Respiratory regulation and interactions with neurocognitive circuitry. *Neuroscience & Biobehavioral Reviews, 112*, 95–106.
    Paulus, M. P. (2013).

11 Banzett, R. B., Lansing, R. W., & Binks, A. P. (2021). Air hunger: A primal sensation and a primary element of dyspnea. *Comprehensive Physiology, 11*(2), 1449–1483.

12 Brinkman, J. E., Toro, F., & Sharma, S. (2023).

13 Gardner, W. N. (1996). The pathophysiology of hyperventilation disorders. *Chest, 109*(2), 516–534.

14 McEwen, B. S. (1998). Stress, adaptation, and disease: Allostasis and allostatic load. *Annals of the New York Academy of Sciences, 840*(1), 33–44.

15 Gardner, W. N. (1996).

16 Nelson, D. L., & Cox, M. M. (2017). *Lehninger principles of biochemistry* (7th ed.). W. H. Freeman.

17 Punjabi, N. M. (2008). The epidemiology of adult obstructive sleep apnoea. *Proceedings of the American Thoracic Society, 5*(2), 136–143.

18 McEwen, B. S. (1998).

19 Vidotto, L. S., Carvalho, C. R. F., Harvey, A., & Jones, M. (2019). Dysfunctional breathing: What do we know? *Jornal Brasileiro de Pneumologia, 45*(1), Article e20170347.
    Vierra, J., Boonla, O., & Prasertsri, P. (2022). Effects of sleep deprivation and 4-7-8 breathing control on heart rate variability, blood pressure, blood glucose, and endothelial function in healthy young adults. *Physiological Reports, 10*(13), Article e15389.

20 Balban, M. Y., Neri, E., Kogon, M. M., Weed, L., Nouriani, B., Jo, B., Holl, G., Zeitzer, J. M., Spiegel, D., & Huberman, A. D. (2023). Brief structured respiration practices enhance mood and reduce physiological arousal. *Cell reports. Medicine, 4*(1), 100895.

Chapter 5: The Past Is in Your Breath

1   Panksepp, J. (1998). *Affective neuroscience: The foundations of human and animal emotions*. Oxford University Press.

2   Homma, I., & Masaoka, Y. (2008). Breathing rhythms and emotions. *Experimental Physiology, 93*(9), 1011–1021.

LeDoux, J. E. (1996). *The emotional brain: The mysterious underpinnings of emotional life.* Simon & Schuster.

Panksepp, J. (1998).

3 Leech, K., Stapleton, P., & Patching, A. (2024). A roadmap to understanding interoceptive awareness and post-traumatic stress disorder. *Frontiers in Psychiatry, 15,* Article 1190597.

4 Porges, S. W. (2011). *The polyvagal theory: Neurophysiological foundations of emotions, attachment, communication, and self-regulation.* W. W. Norton.

van der Kolk, B. A. (2014). *The body keeps the score: Brain, mind, and body in the healing of trauma.* Viking.

5 Schore, A. N. (2003). *Affect dysregulation and disorders of the self.* W. W. Norton.

6 Hopper, J. W., Frewen, P. A., van der Kolk, B. A., & Lanius, R. A. (2007). Neural correlates of reexperiencing, avoidance, and dissociation in PTSD: Symptom dimensions and emotion dysregulation in responses to script-driven trauma imagery. *Journal of Traumatic Stress, 20*(5), 713–725.

7 van der Kolk, B. A. (2014).

8 Lanius, R. A., Bluhm, R., & Frewen, P. A. (2011). How understanding the neurobiology of complex post-traumatic stress disorder can inform clinical practice: A social cognitive and affective neuroscience approach. *Acta Psychiatrica Scandinavica, 124*(5), 331–348.

Chapter 7: Awareness

1 Leech, K., Stapleton, P., & Patching, A. (2024). A roadmap to understanding interoceptive awareness and post-traumatic stress disorder. *Frontiers in Psychiatry, 15,* Article 1190597.

2 van der Kolk, B. A., Stone, L., West, J., Rhodes, A., Emerson, D., Suvak, M., Spinazzola, J. (2014). Yoga as an adjunctive treatment for posttraumatic stress disorder: A randomized controlled trial. *Journal of Clinical Psychiatry, 75*(6), e559–e565.

3 Siegel, D. J. (2012). *The developing mind: How relationships and the brain interact to shape who we are* (2nd ed.). Guilford Press.

Chapter 8: Connection to Safety

1 Datta, K., Bhutambare, A., Mamatha, V. L., Narawa, Y., Srinath, R., & Kanitkar, M. (2023). Improved sleep, cognitive processing and enhanced learning and memory task accuracy with yoga nidra practice in novices. *PLoS ONE, 18*(12), Article e0294678.

Moszeik, E. N., von Oertzen, T., & Renner, K.-H. (2022). Effectiveness of a short yoga nidra meditation on stress, sleep, and well-being in a large and diverse sample. *Current Psychology, 41,* 5272–5286.

2 Boukhris, O., Suppiah, H., Halson, S., Russell, S., Clarke, A., Geneau, M. C., Stutter, L., & Driller, M. (2024). The acute effects of nonsleep deep rest on perceptual responses, physical, and cognitive performance in physically active participants. *Applied Psychology: Health and Well-Being, 16*(4), 1967–1987.

Huberman Lab. (2025, January). *What are the benefits of non-sleep deep rest (NSDR)? Ask Huberman Lab.* https://www.hubermanlab.com

3   Satyananda Saraswati, S. (1976). *Yoga nidra*. Bihar School of Yoga.

4   Pandi-Perumal, S. R., Spence, D. W., Srivastava, N., Kanchibhotla, D., Kumar, K., Sharma, G. S., Gupta, R., & Batmanabane, G. (2022). The origin and clinical relevance of yoga nidra. *Sleep Vigilance, 6*(1), 61–84.

5   Datta, K., Mallick, H. N., Tripathi, M., Ahuja, N., & Deepak, K. K. (2022). Electrophysiological evidence of local sleep during yoga nidra practice. *Frontiers in Neurology, 13*, Article 910794.

6   Datta, K., Bhutambare, A., Mamatha, V. L., Narawa, Y., Srinath, R., & Kanitkar, M. (2023).

7   Gambhirananda, S. (1958/2007). *Mandukya Upanishad with Gaudapada Karika*. Advaita Ashrama.
    Olivelle, P. (1998). *The early Upanishads: Annotated text and translation*. Oxford University Press.

Chapter 9: Connection to Context

1   Engel, G. L. (1977). The need for a new medical model: A challenge for biomedicine. *Science, 196*(4286), 129–136.
    Engel, G. L. (1980). The clinical application of the biopsychosocial model. *The American Journal of Psychiatry, 137*(5), 535–544.

2   Almahayni, O., & Hammond, L. (2024). Does the Wim Hof Method have a beneficial impact on physiological and psychological outcomes in healthy and non-healthy participants? A systematic review. *PLOS One, 19*(3), Article e0286933.

3   Citherlet, T., Crettaz von Roten, F., Kayser, B., & Guex, K. (2021). Acute effects of the Wim Hof breathing method on repeated sprint ability: A pilot study. *Frontiers in Sports and Active Living, 3*, Article 700757.

4   Ainslie, P. N., & Duffin, J. (2009). Integration of cerebrovascular CO_2 reactivity and chemoreflex control of breathing: Mechanisms of regulation, measurement, and interpretation. *American Journal of Physiology – Regulatory, Integrative and Comparative Physiology, 296*, R1473–R1495.

5   Kox, M., van Eijk, L. T., Zwaag, J., van den Wildenberg, J., Sweep, F. C., van der Hoeven, J. G., & Pickkers, P. (2014). Voluntary activation of the sympathetic nervous system and attenuation of the innate immune response in humans. *Proceedings of the National Academy of Sciences, 111*(20), 7379–7384.

6   Boulding, R., Stacey, R., Niven, R., & Fowler, S. J. (2016). Dysfunctional breathing: A review of the literature and proposal for classification. *NPJ Primary Care Respiratory Medicine, 26*, 16014.

7   Kox, M., van Eijk, L. T., Zwaag, J., van den Wildenberg, J., Sweep, F. C., van der Hoeven, J. G., & Pickkers, P. (2014).

8   Roy, B., Diez Roux, A. V., Seeman, T., Ranjit, N., Shea, S., & Cushman, M. (2010). Association of optimism and pessimism with inflammation and hemostasis in the Multi-Ethnic Study of Atherosclerosis (MESA). *Psychosomatic Medicine, 72*(2), 134–140.

9   Colloca, L., & Barsky, A. J. (2020). Placebo and nocebo effects. *The New England Journal of Medicine, 382*(6), 554–561.

10 Kox, M., van Eijk, L. T., Zwaag, J., van den Wildenberg, J., Sweep, F. C., van der Hoeven, J. G., & Pickkers, P. (2014).

11 Muzik, O., Reilly, K. T., & Diwadkar, V. A. (2018). Brain over body: A study on the willful regulation of autonomic function during cold exposure. *NeuroImage*, *172*, 632–641.

12 Muzik, O., Reilly, K. T., & Diwadkar, V. A. (2018).

13 Harricharan, S., Rabellino, D., Frewen, P. A., Densmore, M., Théberge, J., McKinnon, M. C., Schore, A. N., & Lanius, R. A. (2016). fMRI functional connectivity of the periaqueductal gray in PTSD and its dissociative subtype. *Brain and Behavior*, *6*(12), Article e00579.

Chapter 10: Connection to Real Life

1 Friston, K. (2010). The free-energy principle: A unified brain theory? *Nature Reviews Neuroscience*, *11*(2), 127–138.

2 Raichle, M. E. (2015). The brain's default mode network. *Annual Review of Neuroscience*, *38*, 433–447.

3 Lee, K., Noda, Y., Nakano, Y., Ogawa, S., Kinoshita, Y., Funayama, T., & Furukawa, T. A. (2006). Interoceptive hypersensitivity and interoceptive exposure in patients with panic disorder: Specificity and effectiveness. *BMC Psychiatry*, *6*, Article 32.

4 Owens, A. P., Allen, M., Ondobaka, S., & Friston, K. J. (2018). Interoceptive inference: From computational neuroscience to clinic. *Neuroscience & Biobehavioral Reviews*, *90*, 174–183.

Seth, A. K., & Friston, K. J. (2016). Active interoceptive inference and the emotional brain. *Philosophical Transactions of the Royal Society B: Biological Sciences*, *371*(1708), Article 20160007.

5 Dempsey, J. A., Veasey, S. C., Morgan, B. J., & O'Donnell, C. P. (2010). Pathophysiology of sleep apnea. *Physiological Reviews*, *90*(1), 47–112.

Seth, A. K., & Friston, K. J. (2016).

6 Nivethitha, L., Mooventhan, A., Manjunath, N. K., Bathala, L., & Sharma, V. K. (2017). Cerebrovascular hemodynamics during pranayama techniques. *Journal of Neurosciences in Rural Practice*, *8*(1), 60–63.

7 Fincham, G. W., Kartar, A., Uthaug, M. V., Anderson, B., Hall, L., Nagai, Y., Critchley, H., & Colasanti, A. (2023). High-ventilation breathwork practices: An overview of their effects, mechanisms, and considerations for clinical applications. *Neuroscience & Biobehavioral Reviews*, *155*, Article 105453.

8 Boyadzhieva, A., & Kayhan, E. (2021). Keeping the breath in mind: Respiration, neural oscillations, and the free energy principle. *Frontiers in Neuroscience*, *15*, Article 647579.

9 Gorman, J. M., Kent, J. M., Sullivan, G. M., & Coplan, J. D. (2001). Hyperventilation challenge test in panic disorder and depression with panic attacks. *Psychiatry Research*, *103*(1), 87–97.

10 Fincham, G. W., Kartar, A., Uthaug, M. V., Anderson, B., Hall, L., Nagai, Y., Critchley, H., & Colasanti, A. (2023).

11 Fincham, G. W., Kartar, A., Uthaug, M. V., Anderson, B., Hall, L., Nagai, Y., Critchley, H., & Colasanti, A. (2023).

12 Fincham, G. W., Kartar, A., Uthaug, M. V., Anderson, B., Hall, L., Nagai, Y., Critchley, H., & Colasanti, A. (2023).

13 Malhotra, V., Javed, D., Wakode, S., Bharshankar, R., Soni, N., & Porter, P. K. (2022). Study of immediate neurological and autonomic changes during Kapalabhati pranayama in yoga practitioners. *Journal of Family Medicine and Primary Care, 11*(2), 720–727.

Chapter 11: Sleep

1 Trinder, J., Kleiman, J., Carrington, M., Smith, S., Breen, S., Tan, N., & Kim, Y. (2001). Autonomic activity during human sleep as a function of time and sleep stage. *Journal of Sleep Research, 10*(4), 253–264.

2 Van Cauter, E., Leproult, R., & Plat, L. (2000). Age-related changes in slow wave sleep and REM sleep and relationship with growth hormone and cortisol levels in healthy men. *JAMA, 284*(7), 861–868.

3 Xie, L., Kang, H., Xu, Q., Chen, M. J., Liao, Y., Thiyagarajan, M., O'Donnell, J., Christensen, D. J., Nicholson, C., Iliff, J. J., Takano, T., Deane, R., & Nedergaard, M. (2013). Sleep drives metabolite clearance from the adult brain. *Science, 342*(6156), 373–377.

4 Irwin, M. R. (2019). Sleep and inflammation: Partners in sickness and in health. *Nature Reviews Immunology, 19*(11), 702–715.

5 Goldstein, A. N., & Walker, M. P. (2014). The role of sleep in emotional brain function. *Annual Review of Clinical Psychology, 10*, 679–708.

6 Trinder, J., Kleiman, J., Carrington, M., Smith, S., Breen, S., Tan, N., & Kim, Y. (2001).

7 Dempsey, J. A., Veasey, S. C., Morgan, B. J., & O'Donnell, C. P. (2010). Pathophysiology of sleep apnoea. *Physiological Reviews, 90*(1), 47–112.

8 Riemann, D., Spiegelhalder, K., Feige, B., Voderholzer, U., Berger, M., Perlis, M., & Nissen, C. (2010). The hyperarousal model of insomnia: A review of the concept and its evidence. *Sleep Medicine Reviews, 14*(1), 19–31.

9 van der Helm, E., & Walker, M. P. (2011). Overnight therapy? The role of sleep in emotional brain processing. *Psychological Bulletin, 137*(6), 910–933.

10 Dempsey, J. A., Veasey, S. C., Morgan, B. J., & O'Donnell, C. P. (2010).

11 van der Helm, E., & Walker, M. P. (2011).

12 Eckert, D. J., & Malhotra, A. (2008). Pathophysiology of adult obstructive sleep apnoea. *Proceedings of the American Thoracic Society, 5*(2), 144–153.

13 Malhotra, A., & White, D. P. (2002). Obstructive sleep apnoea. *Lancet, 360*(9328), 237–245.

14 Eckert, D. J., White, D. P., Jordan, A. S., Malhotra, A., & Wellman, A. (2013). Defining phenotypic causes of obstructive sleep apnea: Identification of novel therapeutic targets. *American Journal of Respiratory and Critical Care Medicine, 188*(8), 996–1004.

Wellman, A., Eckert, D. J., Jordan, A. S., Edwards, B. A., Passaglia, C. L., Jackson, A. C., Gautam, S., Owens, R. L., Malhotra, A., & White, D. P. (2013). A method for measuring and modeling the physiological traits causing obstructive sleep apnea. *Journal of Applied Physiology, 114*(6), 911–922.

15 McKeown, P. (2021).

16 Valipour, A., Lothaller, H., Rauscher, H., Zwick, H., & Burghuber, O. C. (2007). Gender-related differences in symptoms of patients with suspected breathing disorders in sleep: A clinical population study using the Sleep Disorders Questionnaire. *Sleep*, *30*(3), 312–319.

17 Edwards, B. A., Eckert, D. J., McSharry, D. G., Sands, S. A., Desai, A., Kehlmann, G., Bakker, J. P., Genta, P. R., Owens, R. L., White, D. P., Wellman, A., & Malhotra, A. (2014). Clinical predictors of the respiratory arousal threshold in patients with obstructive sleep apnea. *American Journal of Respiratory and Critical Care Medicine*, *190*(11), 1293–1300.

18 Baker, F. C., & Lee, K. A. (2018). Menstrual cycle effects on sleep. *Sleep Medicine Clinics*, *13*(3), 283–294.

19 Antonaglia, C., Citton, G. M., Siciliano, M., Salton, F., Ruaro, B., Salton, M., & Confalonieri, M. (2025). Obstructive sleep apnea syndrome in women: Gender in sleep respiratory medicine is a first step towards personalized medicine. *Sleep and Breathing*, *29*, Article 250.

20 Russo, M. A., Santarelli, D. M., & O'Rourke, D. (2017). The physiological effects of slow breathing in the healthy human. *Breathe*, *13*(4), 298–309.

 Zaccaro, A., Piarulli, A., Laurino, M., Garbella, E., Menicucci, D., Neri, B., & Gemignani, A. (2018). How breath-control can change your life: A systematic review on psychophysiological correlates of slow breathing. *Frontiers in Human Neuroscience*, *12*, 353.

Interlude: Sleep and the Limits of Breathwork

1 Russo, M. A., Santarelli, D. M., & O'Rourke, D. (2017). The physiological effects of slow breathing in the healthy human. *Breathe*, *13*(4), 298–309.

2 Jordan, A. S., McSharry, D. G., & Malhotra, A. (2014). Adult obstructive sleep apnoea. *The Lancet*, *383*(9918), 736–747.

 Pathak, R. K., Middeldorp, M. E., Lau, D. H., Mehta, A. B., Mahajan, R., Twomey, D., Alasady, M., Hanley, L., Antic, N. A., McEvoy, D., Kalman, J. M., Abhayaratna, W. P., & Sanders, S. (2015). Aggressive risk factor reduction study for atrial fibrillation and implications for the outcome of ablation: The ARREST-AF cohort study. *Journal of the American College of Cardiology*, *64*(21), 2222–2231.

3 Chung, F., Abdullah, H. R., & Liao, P. (2009). STOP-Bang questionnaire: A practical approach to screen for obstructive sleep apnea. *Anesthesiology*, *108*(5), 812–821.

4 Eckert, D. J., & Malhotra, A. (2008). Pathophysiology of adult obstructive sleep apnea. *Proceedings of the American Thoracic Society*, *5*(2), 144–153.

 Wellman, A., Eckert, D. J., Jordan, A. S., Edwards, B. A., Passaglia, C. L., Jackson, A. C., Gautam, S., Owens, R. L., Malhotra, A., & White, D. P. (2013). A method for measuring and modeling the physiological traits causing obstructive sleep apnea. *Journal of Applied Physiology*, *114*(6), 911–922.

Chapter 12: Sleep and Stillness

1 Besedovsky, L., Lange, T., & Born, J. (2011). Sleep and immune function. *Pflügers Archiv – European Journal of Physiology*, *463*(1), 121–137.

References

2   Xie, L., Kang, H., Xu, Q., Chen, M. J., Liao, Y., Thiyagarajan, M., O'Donnell, J., Christensen, D. J., Nicholson, C., Iliff, J. J., Takano, T., Deane, R., & Nedergaard, M. (2013). Sleep drives metabolite clearance from the adult brain. *Science, 342*(6156), 373–377.

3   Scullin, M. K., & Gao, C. (2018). Dynamic contributions of slow wave sleep and REM sleep to cognitive longevity. *Current Sleep Medicine Reports, 4*(4), 284–293.

4   Vandekerckhove, M., & Wang, Y. (2018). Emotion, emotion regulation and sleep: An intimate relationship. *AIMS Neuroscience, 5*(1), 1–17.

5   Haynes, E. R., Dong, J., & Abbott, S. B. G. (2019). Neural circuitry underlying waking up to hypercapnia. *Frontiers in Neuroscience, 13*, 401.

6   Madan, V., & Jha, S. K. (2012). A moderate increase of physiological CO_2 in a critical range during stable NREM sleep episode: A potential gateway to REM sleep. *Frontiers in Neurology, 3*, 19.

7   Diekelmann, S., & Born, J. (2010). The memory function of sleep. *Nature Reviews Neuroscience, 11*(2), 114–126.

     Walker, M. P., & van der Helm, E. (2009). Overnight therapy? The role of sleep in emotional brain processing. *Psychological Bulletin, 135*(5), 731–748.

8   Abbott, S. B. G., & Souza, G. M. P. R. (2021). Chemoreceptor mechanisms regulating CO_2-induced arousal from sleep. *The Journal of Physiology, 599*(10).

     Smith, H. R., Leibold, N. K., Rappoport, D. A., Ginapp, C. M., Purnell, B. S., Bode, N. M., Alberico, S. L., Kim, Y. C., Audero, E., Gross, C. T., Buchanan, G. F. (2018). Dorsal raphe serotonin neurons mediate CO_2-induced arousal from sleep. *Journal of Neuroscience, 38*(8), 1915–1925.

9   Bernardi, L., Gabutti, A., Porta, C., & Spicuzza, L. (2001). Slow breathing reduces chemoreflex response to hypoxia and hypercapnia, and increases baroreflex sensitivity. *Journal of Hypertension, 19*(12), 2221–2229.

     Beutler, E., Beltrami, F. G., Boutellier, U., & Spengler, C. M. (2016). Effect of regular yoga practice on respiratory regulation and exercise performance. *PLoS ONE, 11*(4), Article e0153159.

     Spicuzza, L., Gabutti, A., Porta, C., Montano, N., & Bernardi, L. (2000). Yoga and chemoreflex response to hypoxia and hypercapnia. *The Lancet, 356*(9240), 1495–1496.

10   Gardner, W. N. (1996). The pathophysiology of hyperventilation disorders. *Chest, 109*(2), 516–534.

     Lum, L. C. (1975). Hyperventilation: The tip and the iceberg. *Journal of Psychosomatic Research, 19*(5–6), 375–383.

11   Griez, E., de Loof, C., Pols, H., Zandbergen, J., & Lousberg, H. (1990). Specific sensitivity of patients with panic attacks to carbon dioxide inhalation. *Psychiatry Research, 31*(2), 193–199.

12   Carskadon, M. A., & Dement, W. C. (2011). Normal human sleep: An overview. In M. H. Kryger, T. Roth, & W. C. Dement (Eds.), *Principles and practice of sleep medicine* (5th ed., pp. 16–26). Elsevier Saunders.

13   Weitzman, E. D., Zimmerman, J. C., Czeisler, C. A., & Ronda, J. M. (1983). Cortisol secretion is inhibited during sleep in normal man. *The Journal of Clinical Endocrinology & Metabolism, 56*(2), 352–358.

14 Jordan, A. S., McSharry, D. G., & Malhotra, A. (2014). Adult obstructive sleep apnoea. *The Lancet, 383*(9918), 736–747.

15 Krause, A. J., Simon, E. B., Mander, B. A., Greer, S. M., Saletin, J. M., Goldstein-Piekarski, A. N., & Walker, M. P. (2017). The sleep-deprived human brain. *Nature Reviews Neuroscience, 18*(7), 404–418.

16 Soroka, T., Ravia, A., Snitz, K., Honigstein, D., Weissbrod, A., Gorodisky, L., Weiss, T., Perl, O., & Sobel, N. (2025). Humans have nasal respiratory fingerprints. *Current Biology, 35*(13), 3011–3021.

17 Bonnet, M. H., & Arand, D. L. (2003). Clinical effects of sleep fragmentation versus sleep deprivation. *Sleep Medicine Reviews, 7*(4), 297–310.

18 Stalder, T., Kirschbaum, C., Kudielka, B. M., Adam, E. K., Pruessner, J. C., Wüst, S., Dockray, S., Smyth, N., Evans, P., Hellhammer, D. H., Miller, R., Wetherell, M. A., Lupien, S. J., & Clow, A. (2016). Assessment of the cortisol awakening response: Expert consensus guidelines. *Psychoneuroendocrinology, 63*, 414–432.

19 Stepanski, E. J. (2002). The effect of sleep fragmentation on daytime function. *Sleep, 25*(3), 268–276.

20 Spiegel, K., Tasali, E., Penev, P., & Van Cauter, E. (2004). Sleep curtailment in healthy young men is associated with decreased leptin levels, elevated ghrelin levels, and increased hunger and appetite. *Annals of Internal Medicine, 141*(11), 846–850.

21 Khalsa, S. S., Adolphs, R., Cameron, O. G., Critchley, H. D., Davenport, P. W., Feinstein, J. S., Feusner, J. D., Garfinkel, S. N., Lane, R. D., Mehling, W. E., Meuret, A. E., Nemeroff, C. B., Oppenheimer, S., Petzschner, F. H., Pollatos, O., Rhudy, J. L., Schramm, L. P., Simmons, W. K., Stein, M. B., ... Paulus, M. P. (2018). Interoception and mental health: A roadmap. *Biological Psychiatry: Cognitive Neuroscience and Neuroimaging, 3*(6), 501–513.

22 van der Helm, E., Yao, J., Dutt, S., Rao, V., Saletin, J. M., & Walker, M. P. (2011). REM sleep depotentiates amygdala activity to previous emotional experiences. *Current Biology, 21*(23), 2029–2035.

23 Rasch, B., & Born, J. (2013). About sleep's role in memory. *Physiological Reviews, 93*(2), 681–766.
   Siclari, F., & Tononi, G. (2017). Local aspects of sleep and wakefulness. *Current Opinion in Neurobiology, 44*, 222–227.

24 Besedovsky, L., Lange, T., & Born, J. (2011).
   Rasch, B., & Born, J. (2013).

25 Barrett, L. F., & Simmons, W. K. (2015). Interoceptive predictions in the brain. *Nature Reviews Neuroscience, 16*(7), 419–429.

Chapter 13: The Gut

1 Yatsunenko, T., Rey, F. E., Manary, M. J., Trehan, I., Dominguez-Bello, M. G., Contreras, M., Magris, M., Hidalgo, G., Baldassano, R. N., Anokhin, A. P., Heath, A. C., Warner, B., Reeder, J., Kuczynski, J., Caporaso, G., Lozupone, C. A., Lauber, C., Clemente, J. C., Knights, D., ...Gordon, J. I. (2012). Human gut microbiome viewed across age and geography. *Nature, 486*(7402), 222–227.

References

2 Smits, S. A., Leach, J., Sonnenburg, E. D., Gonzalez, C. G., Lichtman, J. S., Reid, G., Knight, R., Manjurano, A., Changalucha, J., Elias, J. E., Dominguez-Bello, M. G., & Sonnenburg, J. L. (2017). Seasonal cycling in the gut microbiome of the Hadza hunter-gatherers of Tanzania. *Science, 357*(6353), 802–806.

3 Bonaz, B., Bazin, T., & Pellissier, S. (2018). The vagus nerve at the interface of the microbiota–gut–brain axis. *Frontiers in Neuroscience, 12,* Article 49.

4 Del Toro-Barbosa, M., Hurtado-Romero, A., Garcia-Amezquita, L. E., & García-Cayuela, T. (2020). Psychobiotics: Mechanisms of action, evaluation methods and effectiveness in applications with food products. *Nutrients, 12*(12), Article 3896.

5 Bonaz, B., Bazin, T., & Pellissier, S. (2018).

6 Dinan, T. G., Stanton, C., & Cryan, J. F. (2013). Psychobiotics: A novel class of psychotropic. *Biological Psychiatry, 74*(10), 720–726.

7 Terry, N., & Margolis, K. G. (2017). Serotonergic mechanisms regulating the GI tract: Experimental evidence and therapeutic relevance. *Handbook of Experimental Pharmacology, 239,* 319–342.

8 Patterson, E., Tan, H. T. T., Groeger, D., Andrews, M., Buckley, M., Murphy, E. F., & Groeger, J. A. (2024). Bifidobacterium longum 1714 improves sleep quality and aspects of well-being in healthy adults: A randomized, double-blind, placebo-controlled clinical trial. *Scientific Reports, 14,* 3725.
Pinto-Sanchez, M. I., Hall, G. B., Ghajar, K., Nardelli, A., Bolino, C., Lau, J. T., Martin, F. P., Cominetti, O., Welsh, C., Rieder, A., Traynor, J., Gregory, C., de Palma, G., Pigrau, M., Ford, A. C., Macro, J., Berger, B., Bergonzelli, G., Surette, M. G., ... Bercik, P. (2017). Probiotic Bifidobacterium longum NCC3001 reduces depression scores and alters brain activity: A pilot study in patients with irritable bowel syndrome. *Gastroenterology, 153*(2), 448–459.

9 Bonaz, B., Bazin, T., & Pellissier, S. (2018).

10 Carabotti, M., Scirocco, A., Maselli, M. A., & Severi, C. (2015). The gut–brain axis: Interactions between enteric microbiota, central and enteric nervous systems. *Annals of Gastroenterology, 28*(2), 203–209.
Guyton, A. C., & Hall, J. E. (2020). *Guyton and Hall Textbook of Medical Physiology* (14th ed.). Elsevier.

11 Panksepp, J. (1998).

12 Barrett, L. F. (2017). *How emotions are made: The secret life of the brain.* Houghton Mifflin Harcourt.
Craig, A. D. (2002). How do you feel? Interoception: The sense of the physiological condition of the body. *Nature Reviews Neuroscience, 3*(8), 655–666.

13 Mayer, E. A. (2011). Gut feelings: The emerging biology of gut–brain communication. *Nature Reviews Neuroscience, 12*(8), 453–466.

14 Craig, A. D. (2002).

15 Vanuytsel, T., van Wanrooy, S., Vanheel, H., Vanormelingen, C., Verschueren, S., Houben, E., Rasoel, S. S., Toth, J., Holvoet, L., Farre, R., van Oudenhove, L., Boeckxstaens, G., Verbeke, K., & Tack, J. (2014). Psychological stress and corticotropin-releasing hormone increase intestinal permeability in humans by a mast cell-dependent mechanism. *Gut, 63*(8), 1293–1299.

16   Schneider, M., & Schwerdtfeger, A. (2020). Autonomic dysfunction in posttraumatic stress disorder indexed by heart rate variability: A meta-analysis. *Psychological Medicine*, 50(12), 1937–1948.

17   Dinan, T. G., Stanton, C., & Cryan, J. F. (2013).
Cryan, J. F., O'Riordan, K. J., Cowan, C. S. M., Sandhu, K. V., Bastiaanssen, T. F. S., Boehme, M., Codagnone, M. G., Cussotto, S., Fulling, C., Golubeva, A. V., Guzzetta, K. E., Jaggar, M., Long-Smith, C. M., Lyte, J. M., Martin, J. A., Molinero-Perez, A., Moloney, G., Morelli, E., Morillas, E., … Dinan, T. G. (2019). The microbiota-gut-brain axis: From microbiome to host physiology. *Physiological Reviews*, 99(4), 1877–2013.

18   Ng, Q. X., Soh, A. Y. S., Loke, W., Venkatanarayanan, N., Lim, D. Y., & Yeo, W. S. (2019). Systematic review with meta-analysis: The association between post-traumatic stress disorder and irritable bowel syndrome. *Journal of Gastroenterology and Hepatology*, 34(1), 68–73.

19   Muktibodhananda, S. (2002). *Hatha Yoga Pradipika* (Swami Satyananda Saraswati, Trans.). Bihar School of Yoga.

20   Khalsa, S. S., & Lapidus, R. C. (2016). Can interoception improve the pragmatic search for biomarkers in psychiatry? *Frontiers in Psychiatry*, 7, Article 121.

21   Noble, D. J., & Hochman, S. (2019). Hypothesis: Pulmonary afferent activity patterns during breath holding contribute to vagal–autonomic balance. *Frontiers in Physiology*, 10, Article 1196.

22   Muktibodhananda, S. (2002).

Chapter 14: The Gut and Breaking the Bias of Survival

1   Selye, H. (1950). *The stress of life*. McGraw-Hill.

2   Mayer, E. A. (2016). *The mind-gut connection: How the hidden conversation within our bodies impacts our mood, our choices, and our overall health*. Harper Wave.

3   Barrett, L. F. (2017).

4   Lehrer, P. M., & Gevirtz, R. (2014). Heart rate variability biofeedback: How and why does it work? *Frontiers in Psychology*, 5, Article 756.

5   Morrow, R. L., Garland, E. J., Wright, J. M., Maclure, M., Taylor, S., & Dormuth, C. R. (2012). Influence of relative age on diagnosis and treatment of attention-deficit/hyperactivity disorder in children. *Canadian Medical Association Journal*, 184(7), 755–762.

6   Kazdin, A. E. (2009). Understanding how and why psychotherapy leads to change. *Psychotherapy Research*, 19(4–5), 418–428.

7   Adler, A. (1927). The practice and theory of individual psychology. London, UK: Routledge.

8   Kazdin, A. E. (2009).

9   Rothbart, M. K. (2011). *Becoming who we are: Temperament and personality in development*. Guilford Press.

10   McEwen, B. S. (1998). Stress, adaptation, and disease: Allostasis and allostatic load. *Annals of the New York Academy of Sciences*, 840(1), 33–44.

11   Panksepp, J. (1998).

12 Barrett, L. F. (2017).

13 Mayer, E. A. (2011). Gut feelings: The emerging biology of gut–brain communication. *Nature Reviews Neuroscience, 12*(8), 453–466.

14 Quigley, E. M. M. (2017). Microbiota–brain–gut axis and neurodegenerative diseases. *Current Neurology and Neuroscience Reports, 17*(12), Article 94.

15 Lundberg, J. O., & Weitzberg, E. (1999). Nasal nitric oxide in man. *Thorax, 54*(10), 947–952. West, J. B. (2012). *Respiratory Physiology: The Essentials* (9th ed., pp. 57–59). Wolters Kluwer/Lippincott Williams & Wilkins.

16 Bowler, S. D., Green, A., & Mitchell, C. A. (1998). Buteyko breathing techniques in asthma: A blinded randomised controlled trial. *Medical Journal of Australia, 169*(11–12), 575–578.
    Cooper, S., Oborne, J., Newton, S., Harrison, V., Thompson Coon, J., Lewis, S., Tattersfield, A. (2003). Effect of two breathing exercises (Buteyko and pranayama) in asthma: A randomised controlled trial. *Thorax, 58*(8), 674–679.

Chapter 15: Movement

1 Barrett, L. F., & Simmons, W. K. (2015). Interoceptive predictions in the brain. *Nature Reviews Neuroscience, 16*(7), 419–429.

2 Sherman, S. M. (2007). The thalamus is more than just a relay. *Current Opinion in Neurobiology, 17*(4), 417–422.

3 Craig, A. D. (2009). How do you feel—now? The anterior insula and human awareness. *Nature Reviews Neuroscience, 10*(1), 59–70.

4 Paulus, M. P., & Stein, M. B. (2010). Interoception in anxiety and depression. *Brain Structure and Function, 214*(5–6), 451–463.

5 Porges, S. W. (2009). The polyvagal theory: New insights into adaptive reactions of the autonomic nervous system. *Cleveland Clinic Journal of Medicine, 76*(4), S86–S90.

6 Paulus, M. P., & Stein, M. B. (2010).

7 Mattson, M. P. (2008). Hormesis defined. *Ageing Research Reviews, 7*(1), 1–7.

8 Marcora, S. M. (2009). Perception of effort during exercise is independent of afferent feedback from skeletal muscles, heart, and lungs. *Journal of Applied Physiology, 106*(6), 2060–2062.

9 Stickford, A. S. L., & Stickford, J. L. (2014). Ventilation and locomotion in humans: Mechanisms, implications, and perturbations to the coupling of these two rhythms. *Springer Science Reviews, 2*(2–3), 95–122.

10 Wolpert, D. M., & Flanagan, J. R. (2001). Motor prediction. *Current Biology, 11*(18), PR729–R732.

11 Lindholm, P., & Lundgren, C. E. G. (2009). The physiology and pathophysiology of human breath-hold diving. *Journal of Applied Physiology, 106*(1), 284–292.

12 Klein, D. F. (1993). False suffocation alarms, spontaneous panics, and related conditions. *Archives of General Psychiatry, 50*(4), 306–317.

13 Lindholm, P., & Lundgren, C. E. G. (2009).

14 Gardner, W. N. (1996). The pathophysiology of hyperventilation disorders. *Chest, 109*(2), 516–534.

Lum, L. C. (1975). Hyperventilation: The tip and the iceberg. *Journal of Psychosomatic Research*, *19*(5–6), 375–383.

15 Critchley, H. D., & Garfinkel, S. N. (2017). Interoception and emotion. *Current Opinion in Psychology*, *17*, 7–14.

16 Mehling, W. E., Price, C., Daubenmier, J. J., Acree, M., Bartmess, E., & Stewart, A. (2012). The Multidimensional Assessment of Interoceptive Awareness (MAIA). *PLoS ONE*, *7*(11), Article e48230.

17 Craske, M. G., Treanor, M., Conway, C. C., Zbozinek, T., & Vervliet, B. (2014). Maximizing exposure therapy: An inhibitory learning approach. *Behaviour Research and Therapy*, *58*, 10–23.

18 McKeown, P. (2016). *The oxygen advantage: Simple, scientifically proven breathing techniques to help you become healthier, slimmer, faster, and fitter.* Harper Collins.

Chapter 16: The Reset Breath

1 Canello, T., Tlaie, A., Chalise, K., Scholvinck, M. L., Pia, L., Havenith, M. N. (2024, November 20). *Non-ordinary states of consciousness evoked by breathwork correlate with improved heart-rate variability.* Research Square.

2 Bahi, C., Irrmischer, M., Franken, K., Fejer, G., Schlenker, A., Deijen, J. B., & Engelbregt, H. (2024). Effects of conscious connected breathing on cortical brain activity, mood and state of consciousness in healthy adults. *Current Psychology*, *43*(12), 10578–10589.

Chapter 17: State Shift or State Escape?

1 Bahi, C., Irrmischer, M., Franken, K., Fejer, G., Schlenker, A., Deijen, J. B., & Engelbregt, H. (2024). Effects of conscious connected breathing on cortical brain activity, mood and state of consciousness in healthy adults. *Current Psychology*, *43*(12), 10578–10589.

2 Evans, K. C., Dougherty, D. D., Schmid, A. M., Scannell, E., McCallister, A., Benson, H., Dusek, J. A., & Lazar, S. W. (2009). Modulation of spontaneous breathing via limbic/paralimbic–bulbar circuitry: An event-related fMRI study. *NeuroImage*, *47*(3), 961–971.
Kluger, D. S., & Gross, J. (2021). Respiration modulates oscillatory neural network activity at rest. *PLoS Biology*, *19*(11), Article e3001457.

3 Saraswati, S. (2009). *Yoga nidra.* Yoga Publications Trust.
Schacter, D. L. (1976). The hypnagogic state: A critical review of the literature. *Psychological Bulletin*, *83*(3), 452–481.

4 Ranganath, C., & Ritchey, M. (2012). Two cortical systems for memory-guided behaviour. *Nature Reviews Neuroscience*, *13*(10), 713–726.

5 Loftus, E. F. (2005). Planting misinformation in the human mind: A 30-year investigation of the malleability of memory. *Learning & Memory*, *12*(4), 361–366.

6 Hyman, I. E., Husband, T. H., & Billings, F. J. (1995). False memories of childhood experiences. *Applied Cognitive Psychology*, *9*(3), 181–197.
Loftus, E. F. (2005). Planting misinformation in the human mind: A 30-year investigation of the malleability of memory. *Learning & Memory*, *12*(4), 361–366.

7 El Hayek, L., Khalifeh, M., Zibara, V., Abi Assaad, R., Emmanuel, N., Karnib, N.,

El-Ghandour, R., Nasrallah, P., Bilen, M., Ibrahim, P., Younes, J., Haidar, E. A., Barmo, N., Jabre, V., Stephan, J. S., & Sleiman, S. F. (2019). Lactate mediates the effects of exercise on learning and memory through SIRT1-dependent activation of hippocampal brain-derived neurotrophic factor (BDNF). *Journal of Neuroscience*, *39*(13), 2369–2382.

Suzuki, A., Stern, S. A., Bozdagi, O., Huntley, G. W., Walker, R. H., Magistretti, P. J., & Alberini, C. M. (2011). Astrocyte–neuron lactate transport is required for long-term memory formation. *Cell*, *144*(5), 810–823.

8   Bouton, M. E. (2002). Context, ambiguity, and unlearning: Sources of relapse after behavioral extinction. *Biological Psychiatry*, *52*(10), 976–986.

9   McEwen, B. S. (1998). Protective and damaging effects of stress mediators. *New England Journal of Medicine*, *338*(3), 171–179.

Sapolsky, R. M. (2004). *Why zebras don't get ulcers: The acclaimed guide to stress, stress-related diseases, and coping* (3rd ed.). Holt Paperbacks.

10   Irwin, M. R. (2015). Why sleep is important for health: A psychoneuroimmunology perspective. *Annual Review of Psychology*, *66*, 143–172.

Walker, M. (2017). *Why we sleep: Unlocking the power of sleep and dreams*. Scribner.

Chapter 18: Integration

1   Lehrer, P. M., Vaschillo, E., & Vaschillo, B. (2000). Resonant frequency biofeedback training to increase cardiac variability: Rationale and manual for training. *Applied Psychophysiology and Biofeedback*, *25*(3), 177–191.